Preaching that Shows

Preaching that Shows

Revealing Relevance

Margaret Cooling

scm press

© Margaret Cooling 2022
Published in 2022 by SCM Press
Editorial office
3rd Floor, Invicta House,
108–114 Golden Lane,
London EC1Y 0TG, UK

www.scmpress.co.uk

SCM Press is an imprint of Hymns Ancient & Modern Ltd
(a registered charity)

Hymns Ancient & Modern® is a registered trademark of
Hymns Ancient & Modern Ltd
13A Hellesdon Park Road, Norwich,
Norfolk NR6 5DR, UK

Scripture quotations are from the New Revised Standard Version Bible:
Anglicized Edition, copyright © 1989, 1995 National Council of the
Churches of Christ in the United States of America. Used by permission.
All rights reserved worldwide.

British Library Cataloguing in Publication data
A catalogue record for this book is available
from the British Library

978-0-334-06184-7

Typeset by Regent Typesetting
Printed and bound by
CPI Group (UK) Ltd

Contents

Acknowledgements

I want to express my thanks to the Revd Professor David Wilkinson and the Revd Dr Kate Bruce for five years of support and guidance. I am indebted to the Revd Stephen Bowen and Mike Simmonds who read every page of this book and offered valuable comments and advice. Thanks are also due to the Revd Dr Stephen Wright, whose work on the Spurgeon's MTh in Preaching was a stimulus for this book, and to the Revd David Day, whose preaching freed me to preach in a revelatory style. Lastly, I am grateful for the patience and support of the congregation of St Mark, Cheltenham, as I experimented with different forms of preaching.

This book has a supporting website:
www.preachingthatshows.com.

Illustrations

Introduction

I have been preaching in my local churches for over thirty years and much has changed during that time. I am a lay preacher and I take my place on the church's preaching rota. Over the years I have attended various preaching courses as part of developing my preaching. One course I attended was run by the College of Preachers. I was nervous. I was aware that my manner of preaching was different from that of many preachers and I was fearful of being told my preaching style was wrong. Although my sermons are deeply embedded in the text, I tend not to quote verses or work through a biblical passage. Part of the course involved preaching in front of a small group and getting a response from a lecturer in preaching. I looked at the sermon I had prepared and the more I looked at it the more I felt my confidence draining away. Fortunately, before I had to deliver my sermon, I heard David Day preach; he was then Principal of St John's College, Durham. I was stunned. He took us deep within the biblical narrative in a way that was both relevant and challenging. My confidence moved up a notch. David Day had an unusual preaching style – maybe it was all right to be different.

The time came when I had to preach in front of a small group and I discovered the lecturer for my group was Dr Stephen Wright from Spurgeon's College, London. I need not have worried; they do not come more encouraging than Stephen Wright. That day sparked an interest in narrative preaching and, when I was able to, I enrolled in the Masters Course in preaching at Spurgeon's followed by a PhD in homiletics at St John's, Durham.

My initial degree was in theology and my working life has been spent communicating Christianity in an educational context, particularly through the creative arts. My studies in theology, my work in the creative arts, preaching and a lifetime's thinking came together in this book. The subject is how to show a biblical text when preaching rather than telling people about it. I have embedded this within a new revelatory approach but the guidance on showing can be used in any style of sermon.

The revelatory approach detailed in this book has relevance threaded throughout, as it is a deeply earthed and embodied form. Relevance is the pot of gold at the end of the sermon rainbow. It is that nod of recognition from the congregation: 'This concerns me.' 'Yes, that is what life is like.' 'That's how I think and feel.' 'This changes what I do.' Relevance is also the aspect of preaching that gets preachers sweating. Typically, as a preacher, you look up the reading for the following Sunday early in the week. That gives you the rest of the week to ponder, pray and seek the guidance of the Holy Spirit. With a groan you realize the reading for next week is the story of the Unjust Steward (Luke 16.1–13). How on earth do you show the relevance of that parable to working in an office or factory on Monday, looking after toddlers and the isolated lives of some of the elderly members of the congregation? How does it relate to twenty-first-century life? As one preacher commented, 'When desperate reach for Julian of Norwich':

All shall be well,
and all shall be well,
and all manner of things shall be well.

This is a practical book that describes an approach to preaching in which the relevance of texts is revealed rather than applied. Ways of using language and art are explored to aid preachers in showing a biblical narrative in a sermon. This practical approach stands on biblical foundations and four key theological themes: creation; being made in the image of God; incarnation; and revelation. Practice is underpinned by an understanding of how biblical texts are interpreted, how people come to know through sermons, and how the imagination can function in preaching.

Using this book

This book contains various ways to show in a sermon, and throughout there are exercises to try and questions to respond to. Reading the whole book without doing the exercises gives an overall understanding of the approach. Once that is done, preachers can choose sections to try, questions to respond to and exercises to work through. I refer to the work of various scholars throughout this book; some are named in the text, the work of others is detailed in the notes at the end of the chapters. The notes act as further reading for those who wish to delve deeper. Please note that many of the sermon extracts are laid out like poetry; this just happens to be my style and is not an integral part of the approach of this book.

I

Show and Plot

Showing

'Show and tell' is a refrain that many people remember from childhood. It involves children showing a favourite toy or object and telling the rest of the class about it. For many children this is their first attempt at public speaking. Some people look back on this experience with fond memories, others hated having to 'show and tell'. In preaching there is a different refrain: people training to preach are often told to 'show *not* tell'. The advice is to show a situation, event or character for the congregation to 'see' rather than tell them about it. This is easier said than done. How do you show a biblical narrative? There is advice concerning showing across the preaching literature; this book gathers some of that together as part of a new showing style and adds some new perspectives on showing. Through the course of this book practical and detailed ways of showing are explored, though the word 'show' is not always used. Showing is indicated by the words:

| Display | Present | Exhibit | Lay bare |
| Manifest | Reveal | Expose | Slice of life |

These words all indicate what the preacher does to show a biblical situation to a congregation. The other side of the coin is how a showing style is received; this is indicated by words that describe people imaginatively seeing what the preacher shows. A showing style from the congregation's perspective is indicated by the word 'see' but it is also signalled by the words:

| Perceive | Glimpse | Recognize | Notice | Observe |
| Identify | Watch | Witness | Look at | View |

Plots

We now move on to the second half of the title of this chapter – plot. If a mantra is needed it is 'show and plot'. You may be wondering what plots have to do with preaching. People have all sorts of associations with the word 'plot' (conspiracy, garden plot, story plot) but not many of them include the words 'showing' or 'sermon'. In literature and drama, a plot is what shapes the way a story is told. There are many different types of plots; two of the main forms are the resolution plot and the revelatory plot. Consider the following scenario.

> It's late in the evening, you are tired, it has been a long day. Now you just want to relax in front of the television. You flick through what is on offer and opt for a thriller. The scene opens with the kidnap of a woman and a demand for money which must be paid within twenty-four hours. The husband and the police do everything they can to trace where she is and who might have taken her. The tension mounts as the deadline gets closer. The leads go in different directions but finally, very close to the deadline, there is a breakthrough and the woman is rescued.

You have just experienced the resolution plot. This type of plot resolves a situation, in this case a kidnap. It is a plot style that majors on action and event. The resolution plot is not the only way of telling a story; there is a different style of plot that you have probably already encountered. Consider the following scenario.

> You've got the popcorn and a drink. You take your seat and the cinema lights dim. For the next two hours you can escape into a story. You were given a cinema card as a Christmas present, so you go every week to get your money's worth. The films you watch vary: some are thrillers, some are 'whodunnits', others are romantic comedies with impossibly good-looking actors who just confirm your feelings about your own less than perfect body. Today's film is different, and it leaves you feeling intrigued. The acting was brilliant, but the story could be summed up in a sentence. It did not have a lot of action or a neat and tidy ending. No murderer was arrested in the final scene, no action man saved the world from aliens, there was no happy ever after, but it got you thinking. You come away feeling you understood the characters and the situation they faced – it gave you an insight into life. The ends may not have been tied but it did end with possibilities, with hope.

You have just encountered the revelatory plot. This type of plot puts the emphasis on character and insight, it tends to be reflective and it may end with possibilities rather than having all the ends tied. This type of plot presents or shows what is often termed 'a slice of life'. Films such as *Castaway* (2000) have a revelatory plot. Most of the film is a man stranded on a desert island talking to a football for company. Not a lot happens but viewers watch the main character change. The character who is driven by the clock at the beginning of the film is very different at the end. All the ends are not tied but the final shots give a hint of possibilities for the future, and we come away having understood something about life. The revelatory plot is a showing or revealing way of telling a story.

This book is about using some of the characteristics of the revelatory plot in preaching to help congregations engage with the characters and insights in biblical narratives. It is an approach with relevance at its heart. It does not make the text relevant; it helps preachers reveal the relevance that is already there. This is a style of preaching that is deeply immersed in Scripture, earthed in the realities of life, and is invitational. It shows rather than tells; it presents biblical narratives to the congregation so that they can see a situation and engage with the people and insights it contains. The rest of this book is an unfurling of ways in which the revelatory plot can shape sermons and create a style of preaching that relates to the whole person, affirms ordinary faith, and encourages ongoing reflection and participation by the congregation.

The resolution plot

Before exploring the revelatory plot, it is necessary to say more about the resolution plot, which is the plot style most people are familiar with, and it is the one some preachers already use to shape sermons. This plot form has much to sell it, but it also has some weaknesses that the revelatory plot addresses. We encounter resolution plots every day in dramas, films and novels. It is most clearly seen in the detective novel, the thriller and the romantic comedy.

- There is a dead body in the library, the detective encounters clues going in many directions, it all gets a bit complicated, then there is a breakthrough, a key clue is found that eventually resolves in the arrest of the murderer.
- A threatening message is received but it is unclear whether it is real or a hoax. The ambiguities increase; first it seems genuine then other evidence points to it being a hoax. Finally, something brings clarity and the situation is resolved.

- Boy meets girl but there is a problem, the families hate each other. Difficulties abound until a key incident that allows the conflict to be resolved and they finally get together.

All the examples share a similar shape, illustrated in Figure 1.

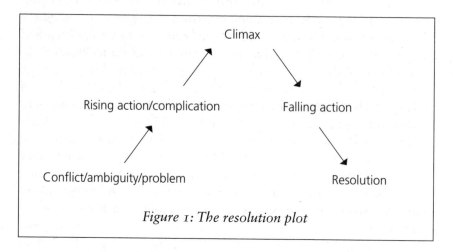

Figure 1: The resolution plot

The resolution plot emphasizes action and event, it moves from conflict, problem or ambiguity through rising action (complication) to a climax, then the action descends to resolution.

Question

Consider a film or TV drama you saw recently, or a novel you read that had this resolution shape. Did it clarify an ambiguity or resolve a problem or conflict? Think back to how the situation was resolved – what led to the resolution?

Eugene Lowry and the resolution plot

In 1980 Eugene Lowry took the resolution plot and adapted it for preaching. He created a form of narrative preaching that used the resolution plot as a structure for sermons.[1] That does not mean the sermon has to be a story, it is about using the stages of the resolution plot to shape a sermon, as in the example that follows. Over the years Lowry refined this and he sees sermons developing along the lines of a resolution plot with four stages, shown in Figure 2. I have illustrated how this might shape a sermon on Moses' address to the Israelites in Deuteronomy 30 (in italics).

1 The sermon starts with a **conflict, problem** or **ambiguity**, which upsets the equilibrium and provides the forward movement and suspense. This initial concern signals that there is an issue to be resolved, a difficulty to be overcome or an ambiguity to be clarified.
The people stand before Moses on the brink of entering the Promised Land, but Moses is not going to be there to lead them. Will they be faithful to God?

2 The preacher explores the complexities of the issue through the **complication** stage.
Moses has led them for forty years; he is the only leader they have known, and in that time their faithfulness has been tested and they have not always stayed true. The preacher considers the people's dependency on Moses and our dependencies; s/he explores reasons why the people did not always stay faithful and what tempts us to be unfaithful to God.

3 A **climax** is reached (Lowry calls it the **sudden shift**) providing the key to the resolution.
Moses presents the people with a choice framing it as a way of life and a way of death.

4 The **resolution** is reached (Lowry terms this the **unfolding**).[2]
'Now choose': The call of Israel to commit and God's call for us to commit.

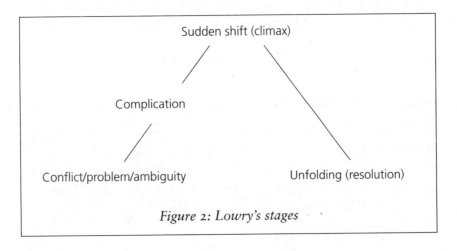

Figure 2: Lowry's stages

Lowry's scheme is no simplistic problem-solving format; he makes sure the realities and complexities of the issue are explored at the complication stage. Lowry's work introduced an approach to preaching that honoured narrative, a major genre of the Bible, gave sermons shape and movement and gave a structure within which preachers could exercise creativity.

The resolution plot in summary

Resolution plots have many variants, but their chief characteristics are:

- An emphasis on action and event.
- A dynamic forward movement and pace.
- Often a linear movement through time.
- Strong tension and suspense.
- Closure and completeness.

This type of plot dates to the ancient Greeks. It was Aristotle who saw action and event as taking the lead role, with character and thought (insight) coming in second and third place, though how a person behaves reveals something of their character.[3] The need to resolve the problem creates a strong forward movement and this supplies the tension and pace giving a narrative its 'what happens next' suspense. This is what creates 'page turners' that sell millions of copies. One of the hallmarks of the resolution plot is its emphasis on time, often expressed in a forward linear movement. Flashbacks and other time devices may be used but the movement is still onwards towards resolution. The resolution plot tends to have a sense of closure and completeness that can be very satisfying, it fulfils expectations that the narrative creates. It is that moment when you get to the end of a thriller and you can breathe a sigh of relief, the threat was averted, lives were saved but it was a close call.

Where do we encounter the resolution plot?

The resolution plot is all around us. We encounter it in novels, films and television dramas. We see it in comics; it is a style that worked for Wonder Woman and Desperate Dan. Many traditional tales have a resolution shape, beginning with a problem: Red Riding Hood is threatened by a wolf; the prince is in frog form, and the princess needs rescuing. The obstacles mount until a climax is reached and the wolf is defeated, the frog is returned to a prince and the princess is rescued. Resolution is reached. The resolution plot is even encountered in adverts that use mini narratives to sell products.

The windows are dirty (problem), the usual products are tried but they still leave smears (complication), a point of despair is reached then a helpful neighbour suggests new wonder product (climax) and smear-free windows are achieved (resolution).

The resolution plot is also present in certain forms of art.

Continuous art

The Bayeux Tapestry is a 70-metre-long embroidery where the scenes are continuous, one after the other, without frames to separate the different scenes. The tapestry takes viewers through William of Normandy's invasion of Britain in 1066, from the landing to the ferocity of the battle and finally to his victory that resolves the conflict. The complete tapestry can be viewed online.[4]

Sequential art

Sequential art is a visual story told in separate scenes, each scene framed or separated in some way (a little like a comic). In the Middle Ages scenes from the life of Jesus were often painted this way. The Scrovegni chapel is an example of a life of Jesus told sequentially.[5] William Hogarth told resolution stories through paintings where the plot developed across a series of separate scenes, each in a frame. *The Rake's Progress* is told in a series of paintings.[6] We see the young man gambling away his fortune, being arrested for debt and finally ending his life in the Bedlam asylum. The complete sequence can be seen online.

What's the problem?

If the resolution plot is the most common style of plot and is very successful in all genres, including preaching, what is the problem? Why is a new style of plot needed? There is not a problem with the resolution plot unless it is the only type of plot used. The texts on which we preach are many and varied and one plot style does not do justice to them all. There are also a few areas where there are issues with the resolution plot, concerning closure, movement, mystery and ordinary life

Closure

Novels based on the resolution plot often tie up any loose ends. A particularly clear instance of it is Anthony Trollope's ending of *The Warden*.

'Our tale is now done and it only remains to us to collect the scattered threads of our little story and to tie them into a seemly knot.'[7] Eugene Lowry stresses closure, he talks of people needing closure and not being content until they get it.[8] There are biblical subjects where resolution and closure are appropriate. However, complete closure does not always happen, even with the resolution plot. Narratives are seldom final, they generate other narratives; we see this in the endless film sequels, prequels and spinoffs. The trouble is, in life not everything resolves and too much stress on resolution can feel unrealistic. Alison Wilkinson comments, 'Faith is lived knee-deep in the mess of this world, when we don't see a happy ending, with everything resolved.'[9] The Christian life can be presented as too straightforward from the pulpit if sermons end in resolution too often. This can lead to disillusion when Christians seek to practise their faith in the complexities of the world where everything is not resolved.

Movement

Despite its advantages, the resolution plot can be rigid, with everything moving onwards towards resolution. This is not always a problem, but the preacher needs to ask if the hearer is given time and room for a range of responses and reflection or if the onward nature is sometimes too directive.

Mystery

Not every ambiguity can be resolved. At times we have to live with not knowing or partial knowing – St Paul called this seeing through a glass darkly (1 Cor. 13.12 AV). Mysteries are part of life; they can be explored but do not have to be solved. Exploring and solving are different. Lowry's approach emphasizes exploring complexity; he speaks positively about living with mystery and he shuns simplistic endings.[10] Nevertheless, a sermon structure that always resolves creates a tension concerning the relationship between mystery, ambiguity and resolution.

Ordinary life

Our lives are often likened to a story beginning with birth and resolving in death. Stephen Crites emphasized this narrative quality of life.[11] Ordinary life, however, is not always *experienced* as a resolution narrative. Sometimes life feels chaotic and does not seem to be telling a recognizable story about us with any sense of direction. For some people, life is more like a soap opera where the different episodes don't seem to be going in any particular direction. Galen Strawson challenged the idea of life as a narrative, seeing it as more like a series of episodes.[12] Even when our lives are understood as a narrative, life is not tidy and plotted like a novel. Authors carefully select material, often removing any distracting detail as they move towards a conclusion. Unfortunately, in real life things happen within a mass of detail. Richard Lischer admits that the shape of the resolution plot does not necessarily mirror real life.[13]

The postmodern world we live in tends to reject big stories, like Christianity, which make sense of life and give it direction; this may have contributed to the loss of the sense of life as a narrative. Postmodernism is a twentieth-century philosophical movement that tends to be sceptical about universal truths, certainties and ideologies, whether they be political, economic or religious. Postmodernism rejects beliefs that seek to interpret life as a whole and give absolute answers. It favours individual understanding and experience; it can also be suspicious of reason.

There may be truth in both views: life as narrative and life as a series of episodes. Sometimes life feels like a series of events with no overall direction, at other times we can look back and see a pattern that is telling a story of our lives, though it may not be as straightforward as the resolution plot. The resolution plot majors on action and event. Our lives can be mundane: get up, work, sleep, repeat. We don't always solve a problem or conflict or clarify an ambiguity. A group of writers called 'Modernists' (c.1890–1950) thought that the traditional resolution plot was not true to life – life was much more uneventful but meaning can be found within ordinary lives. The Modernists broke with the traditional resolution plot and wrote more open-ended works. Virginia Woolf, James Joyce and Katherine Mansfield are just a few of the members of this group. Some Modernist novels present a slice of life rather than focus on action.

Question

How do you see life? Does it feel like a narrative that is telling a story about you or is it more like lots of episodes that don't seem to be heading in any particular direction?

Is the resolution plot in the Bible?

Resolution plots are found in the Bible, and they are in the majority. David resolves the gigantic problem that is Goliath (1 Sam. 17), Nineveh's situation is resolved by repentance (Jonah 3) and Daniel's circumstances are resolved by being saved from the lions (Dan. 6). In the New Testament resolutions come in various ways. Jesus resolved situations by healing the sick and bringing life out of death (Mark 5.21–43), by feeding the hungry (Mark 6.31–44) and stilling storms (Mark 4.35–41), resolving the burdens of the past and sin (Luke 19.1–10; John 4). In Jesus' own life there are a series of resolutions concerning his identity (Mark 8.27–30) that are ultimately resolved in the resurrection and ascension (Luke 23.44–49; Luke 24; Acts 1.6–11). Across the Bible there is an overarching resolution narrative of creation, fall, redemption and recreation.

Question

Think of two Bible stories that have the shape of a resolution plot, one from the Old Testament and one from the New Testament. Do they start with a problem, a conflict or an ambiguity? How are they resolved?

The revelatory plot

The resolution plot is not the only type of plot. The revelatory plot is offered as an alternative to the resolution plot, not a replacement; it is an option where the resolution plot may not be appropriate. The two plot styles are like sisters who share some characteristics yet are distinct; the revelatory plot is the shy, quiet and less well-known sister who is rather overshadowed by her extravert sibling – the resolution plot. Although the resolution plot is the majority plot style in most genres, a significant minority of narratives are shaped by the revelatory plot that focuses on revealing character and insight. Much of what is said about the revelatory plot could also be said of the resolution plot to some degree. Revelatory plots are not completely without resolution and resolution plots do not ignore character and insight. Resolution plots can present complex characters, but the revelatory plot's lack of a push towards resolution and the primacy of character and insight make it easier to spend time on character and insight.

The revelatory plot in summary

The revelatory plot is about coming to know a person, an issue or a situation in depth. It is driven by character and insight (thought/theme) and the insights come through specific things: people, situations, ordinary life. It is an approach that is deeply grounded in the world reflected in the biblical text. Unlike the resolution plot there are no stages to go through and it cannot be reduced to a diagram. The revelatory plot is a constellation of characteristics which includes:

- Character and insight taking the lead with insights often coming through the physical life reflected in the text.
- A slice of life that shows/lays bare a situation, character, issue or insight.
- Reduced closure and suspense, more open-ended.
- A creative use of time, movement and language.
- A slower reflective pace with room for mystery.

The first three characteristics are central; after that the other characteristics tend to follow naturally or can be incorporated as appropriate.

Where do we encounter the revelatory plot?

Dramas or novels that centre on a character, or an insight into an issue or situation, are often based on the revelatory plot. The film *Forrest Gump* (1994) majors on character; it is not all about the ending. Works based on the revelatory plot can have some resolution but there is reduced closure, they can end with possibilities; it is a matter of emphasis. Many contemporary novels are about insight into issues and are open-ended and revelatory in nature. A well-known example is Margaret Atwood's *The Handmaid's Tale*, which may leave the reader wondering what happened to Offred but over the course of the novel issues such as freedom, sexism and control are explored.[14] Some comics have moved to a more revelatory style, an example of this is the Japanese Manga series *Baby and Me*, which explores everyday life rather than having dramatic action and strong resolution/closure.[15] Some adverts also embrace a more open-ended style. Every year in the UK the John Lewis department store creates an innovative Christmas advert. These short video adverts tell a story but not always a resolution one. One advert (2018) worked backwards through Elton John's life until we see a young boy being given a piano as a Christmas present. The audience is not told that buying presents can be significant, they are left to think about the message. (The adverts are available online.)

The revelatory plot is also encountered in art that tells a story in a single scene or an image in a single frame, something that will be explored in detail in Chapter 4. The artist holds up a slice of life from a narrative, showing and laying bare a situation for the viewer to reflect on. Rembrandt's *The Return of the Prodigal Son* reveals much about the biblical story but its purpose is not to resolve; it is about deep insights and its insights come through the presentation of life in the depicted scene. Meaning is expressed through composition, gesture and other elements of art such as line and colour.[16]

Art by its nature emphasizes character and insight more than action and art shows because it does not have a voice to tell. Art can create a slow, reflective pace and a degree of ambiguity and openness. Artists are creative with time and movement; they often combine times by placing a past biblical event in a contemporary scene, showing the relevance of the past to the present. This deliberate anachronism (putting things out of their correct time) leads to the feeling that there is a religious link between time past and time present, signalling the relevance of biblical narrative. Artists are creative with 'language' but theirs is the language of visual symbols and metaphors. Paintings of the Angel Gabriel coming to Mary often have lilies in them to indicate Mary's purity, there may be red for suffering or cross shapes formed by beams or other aspects of the scene to indicate what will happen to her child. Chapters 4 and 5 develop how art can help the preacher create sermons in a revelatory style and how artworks can help in preparation and in gaining insight into a text.

Question

Where have you encountered the revelatory plot? What was your reaction to this form of narration?

Revelatory plots and the Bible

Jean-Louis Ska noticed that sometimes Bible stories go into slow motion, the action slows and the focus changes. It feels as if the action and events are there to reveal the presence of God or illustrate a truth about God. In the story of David and Goliath the preparations and David's speech are given more time and detail than the battle that resolves the issue (1 Sam. 17). Jonah is another instance: the first half of the story is a resolution plot ending with the people of Nineveh repenting, but the story does not end there. The story goes on to expose Jonah's inner turmoil and nothing is resolved but we do learn a lot about Jonah as a person and the issue of grace and judgement (Jonah 1—4).[17] Time slows in John's Gospel in chapters 13–17; there is none of the urgency of Mark's Gospel. Many of Jesus' parables are open-ended, leaving the reader with things to think through. The parable of the workers in the vineyard (Matt. 20.1–16) is an example of this. Plots do not have to be resolution or revelatory, they can be mixed. The two plot styles are not opposites, they can be imagined as different points along a spectrum. Some plots sit in the middle having characteristics of both.

Resolution plots ------------ Mixed plots ------------ Revelatory plots

Bible stories are seldom tightly closed because there is a looking forward to the Messiah in the Old Testament and Jesus' return in the New Testament. The future hope endows other stories with a lack of complete closure. Some Bible stories end with possibilities or questions.[18] Jonah ends with a question.

> Then the LORD said, 'You are concerned about the bush, for which you did not labour and which you did not grow; it came into being in a night and perished in a night. And should I not be concerned about Nineveh, that great city, in which there are more than a hundred and twenty thousand people who do not know their right hand from their left, and also many animals?' (Jonah 4.10–11)

Sidney Greidanus observes that some biblical narratives are only partly resolved, or the resolution is postponed. God's promise to Abraham of being a great nation is only potentially fulfilled with the birth of Isaac; God's promise of land does not begin to be fulfilled until Abraham purchases a field in which to bury Sarah (Gen. 23).[19] Mark's short ending finishes with the women fleeing in fear (Mark 16.8) and the book of Acts ends with Paul under house arrest (Acts 28.16, 30–31). These open endings may seem strange to us but leaving a narrative with a more open ending was a practice used in the ancient world to encourage reflection on the part of the reader/hearer.[20]

Conclusion

This chapter has looked at two plot styles that can be used for shaping sermons. The revelatory plot is not a replacement for the resolution plot, it is an alternative for occasions when the resolution plot may not be suitable for the text and the context. The revelatory plot gives the preacher a narrative form of preaching with an emphasis on character and insight presented in a showing style.

Notes

1 Eugene L. Lowry, 2001, *The Homiletical Plot*, London: Westminster John Knox, p. 26.

2 Eugene L. Lowry, 1997, *The Sermon*, Nashville: Abingdon Press, pp. 60–89.

3 Aristotle, 'Poetics' vi, tr. S. H. Butcher, *The Gutenberg Project*, https://www.gutenberg.org/files/1974/1974-h/1974-h.htm#link2H_4_0009, accessed 14.11.2021.

4 Anon., *The Bayeux Tapestry* (embroidered linen, 1077; Bayeux Museum, Bayeux).

5 Giotto, *The Life of Jesus* (fresco, c.1305; the Scrovegni Chapel, Padua).

6 William Hogarth, *A Rake's Progress* (oil on canvas, 1734; Sir John Soane's Museum, London).

7 Anthony Trollope, 1984, *The Warden*, London: Penguin, p. 198.

8 Eugene L. Lowry, 1985, *Doing Time in the Pulpit*, Nashville: Abingdon Press, pp. 56–8.

9 Alison Wilkinson, 2016, 'Judges 19:16–30', in Kate Bruce and Jamie Harrison (eds), *Wrestling with the Word: Preaching on Tricky Texts*, London: SPCK, 2016, pp. 71–4 (p. 73).

10 Lowry, *Homiletical Plot*, pp. 39–52.

11 Stephen Crites, 'The Narrative Quality of Experience', *Journal of the American Academy of Religion*, 39/3 (1971), 291–311. www.jstor.org/stable/1461066, accessed 14.11.2021 (p. 291).

12 Galen Strawson, 'Against Narrativity', *Ratio*, 17/4 (2004), 428–52. doi.org/10.1111/j.1467-9329.2004.00264.x (p. 430).

13 Richard Lischer, 'The Limits of Story', *Interpretation*, 38/1 (1984), 26–38 (p. 30). https://doi.org/10.1177%2F002096438403800104.

14 Margaret Atwood, 2017, *The Handmaid's Tale*, London: Vintage.

15 Marimo Ragawa, 1992–1997, *Baby and Me*, 18 vols, San Francisco: VIZ Media.

16 Rembrandt, *The Return of the Prodigal* (oil on canvas, c.1668/9; Hermitage Museum, St Petersburg).

17 Jean-Louis Ska, 1990, *Our Fathers Have Told Us*, Rome: Editrice Pontifico Instutio Biblico, pp. 18–19.

18 Walter J. Ong, 'Maranatha: Death and Life in the Text of the Book', *Journal of the American Academy of Religion*, 45/4 (1977), 419–49 (pp. 439–40). www.jstor.org/stable/1463750, accessed 14.11.2021.

19 Sidney Greidanus, 'Detecting Plot Lines: The Key to Preaching the Genesis Narratives', *Calvin Theological Journal*, 43 (2008), 64–77 (pp. 65–6, 69–71).

20 William S. Kurtz, 'The Open-ended Nature of Luke and Acts as Inviting Canonical Actualisation', *Neotestamentica*, 31/2 (1997), 289–308 (pp. 292–3). www.jstor.org/stable/43048325, accessed 14.11.2021.

2

A Constellation of Characteristics

Although most people will have experienced the revelatory plot, the idea of using it in preaching is something few preachers will be familiar with. This chapter goes over its characteristics in detail and shows how each of those characteristics may be expressed in sermons. Although character and insight jointly take the lead in revelatory sermons, I have separated them for reasons of clarity. Throughout this book I use the term 'revelatory sermons' as shorthand for 'sermons in a revelatory plot style'. The term 'revelatory sermon' is not a comment on a sermon's status in terms of theological revelation.

Character

The focus of the revelatory plot is on character. In preaching this means that biblical characters are presented as genuine people, not just individuals who fulfil certain roles or are used to make spiritual or moral points. Points can be made concerning biblical characters but they should never be reduced to mere pegs to hang points on. Jesus portrays realistic characters in many of his parables: a desperate woman looking for lost money and wayward sons returning home (Luke 15.8–32). James Breech describes this as looking at the reality of people rather than looking through them.[1] If time is taken to present a character authentically, relevance is introduced from the beginning because there is the potential for the congregation to register the reality of a character and their situation and possibly identify with them.

Information concerning characters is sometimes limited in the Bible; much is left unsaid (Meir Sternberg describes biblical characterization as 'underground'[2]). Despite this, characters can be known by their thoughts, words and actions or what other people or the author says about them. We are told of Sarah's inner thoughts and feelings concerning the promise of a child (Gen. 18.12); Joseph's emotions are apparent when he meets his brothers (Gen. 42.24) and Mark tells us that Jesus felt pity (or anger) at seeing what disease could do to a person (Mark 1.40–41). By focusing on the experience of the characters in biblical narratives we see how they related to God, and we can learn from them. This exposes people and situations in which we may see ourselves or others.

An example of a character whose details are largely underground is Joseph, who is described in Matthew 1.19 as 'a righteous man', which is often rendered as a just man and faithful to the law. Joseph's character must be deduced mostly from his actions. In Matthew 1.18–24 we are told of a dream where an angel reassures Joseph of Mary's faithfulness. In the text, Joseph's character is shown by his obedience to the angel and later in taking Mary and Jesus to Egypt to protect Jesus from Herod (Matt. 2.13–15). That protective role would have carried on as it was made clear to Joseph that the baby was of the Holy Spirit and the long-awaited Saviour. Marrying Mary when she was already pregnant endangered Joseph's reputation in a culture where reputation was extremely important. It was a brave thing to do. This shows the depth of Joseph's character. Joseph had a reputation for being a just and righteous man; he had a lot to lose.

The dream dissolved, and Joseph was left with a decision.
For him there was no humble, 'be it unto me';
a practical man, he just obeyed and married Mary,
cutting through law to find grace.

Joseph shouldered the role of adopted father,
protected Mary, as he would her son.
Whatever life held for this child
Joseph knew he had to shield him,
care for him, provide.
The time may come when he would be unable to protect Jesus
but until then, that was his job.
It was not a starring role in God's drama of salvation
but it was a vital one.
Joseph had the grace to play a supporting role to Mary in a world
where men were the stars.

Mary had shown a faith worthy of Abraham
and had been prepared to stand under the shadow of shame.
Joseph matched her faith,
chose to stand beside her,
whatever the personal cost.[3]

> **Exercise**
>
> Read John 5.1–15. What can you tell about the man's character from this passage using only what is in the text? Try to put aside what you may assume or have read or heard. What is it in the text that informs you of his character? What words, sounds, actions, sights, etc. led to your conclusions?

Insight (thought/theme)

In revelatory writing ordinary things and mundane situations sometimes give an insight into life. Insight can be a slow process or come in sudden moments. James Joyce referred to these moments as 'epiphanies'; this is a moment when ordinary objects, actions, words, sounds, smells, textures, tastes or sights can suddenly take on significance and become a means of revelation. In James Joyce's short story 'A Little Cloud' it is the sound of a baby's cry that awakens the central character to his trapped situation within an unhappy marriage.[4] This is what happens in life, sometimes ordinary things take on greater meaning and bring insight:

- A gesture may give us an insight into a relationship.
- Body language may give an insight into how someone is feeling.
- A sound may alert us to the significance of a moment.
- An object may take on meaning for us.

Paul Scott Wilson notes how small, concrete details can capture what is significant about a person.[5] Sometimes sensed and specific details in biblical stories can carry a weight of meaning and significance. An example of this is Hannah's depression: an insight into her emotional state comes through a plate of untouched food (1 Sam. 1.7). An insight into David's choices comes through a piece of cloth cut from a cloak (1 Sam. 24). Insights are sensed in some way. Biblical narratives rarely utter truths in abstract form; seldom do biblical writers state, 'this story is about …' The insight is often implied and discovering it involves careful reading and prayer. We gain insights into biblical truths in narrative through specific people in particular situations. For example, nowhere in the parable of the prodigal son is the word 'forgiveness' mentioned. How does the son know he is forgiven? How do we come to know that this story is about forgiveness? We know it is about forgiveness by:

- seeing the father run,
- the touch of an embrace,
- the feel of a cloak around his shoulders,
- the sense of metal as a ring is pushed onto his finger,
- the sensation of sandals on his feet,
- the taste of the fatted calf.

From these sensations and actions, we deduce forgiveness. If we start a sermon from the general term 'forgiveness', we start at the wrong end; it's like reading the last page of a book when you start a novel.

Exercise

Read Luke 19.1–10. To begin with read the text from the position of the crowd, bearing in mind only what they would have experienced and what they saw and knew. (Ignore what you know as the reader of the whole story.) Repeat this for Zacchaeus. Having done this exercise, name one insight this text has given you and what sensed details led to that insight.

This aspect of the revelatory plot acknowledges how we learn. Usually, we come to know a general concept, such as faithfulness, through specific acts of faithfulness. Our understanding of forgiveness is not only acquired by the explicit teaching passages of the Bible, but by the narratives: the prodigal son, the crucifixion, the death of Stephen, the woman taken in adultery and Joseph's forgiveness of his brothers who sold him as a slave. Each story deepens the concept. Understanding is built up in layers.

Although in a revelatory approach insight often comes through the ordinary, this does not deny that insights come through miracles, divine intervention or more direct encounters with God. The revelatory plot does not ignore these direct encounters, but it recognizes that insights can also come through physical existence and ordinary life. God can speak through the mundane. For most Christians, most of the time, insights into our relationship with God come from living as a Christian in a fallen world where we work and engage with friends, family and community. Insight through direct revelation from God tends not to be an everyday occurrence. God speaks to us through Scripture, through others and through specific events and situations.

Revelatory preaching gives the realities reflected in a narrative due weight. The material situation and characters are not just springboards into what is regarded as the 'spiritual' meaning of the story. The material is not something to be left behind once the meaning is discovered. Revelatory preaching stays with the people, stays with the situation that gave rise to the insight. An example of an insight coming through the mundane is found in the story of the manna (Ex. 16). At the beginning of the chapter, we are told the Israelites have been walking for about a month. This is often overlooked in the push to get to the miracle of the manna. Walking across a wilderness for weeks is boring. Weeks of nothing but: walk, eat, sleep, repeat. The often-boring nature of everyday life can erode faith, it is probably the biggest danger many Christians face. A revelatory sermon on Exodus 16 would put the miracle in the context of weeks of boring walking across a wilderness and the effect on faith.

> These were people who had seen God act
> and they entered the wilderness with confidence.
> Wildernesses, however, evaporate confidence.
> Deserts do not need spectacular miracles.
> They do not need seas to part or rivers turned to blood.
> Deserts just require that you cross them,
> they just need you to keep going.
> ......
> All the Israelites know is wilderness,
> mile after mile of desert.
> Each day is the same:
> get up, walk, sleep, repeat.
> Life has become mundane, ordinary.
> There is the reassurance of God's presence,
> a cloudy pillar by day,
> a fiery glow at night,
> But now is not the day of big miracles,
> now is the day of small things,
> when all that is required is to keep going.
> All that is required is to hold onto faith when life is repetitive:
> get up, walk, sleep, repeat.
> The desert poses a threat to the Israelites,
> to us,
> not hunger and thirst
> but monotony,
> the times when nothing spectacular happens,
> when all that is required is that we stay faithful,
> when life is repetitive, ordinary:
> get up, work, sleep, repeat.

This could have been a story of two very different miracles:
the 'miracle' of people staying true to God when life is mundane
[make " " gesture]
and God's miracle of provision of food.
After weeks of walking food and faith are short.
They have seen God do spectacular miracles.
The Israelites know God can part seas, turn rivers to blood, etc. etc. etc.
They know he holds the power of life and death,
they saw that in Egypt,
but does God do small stuff?
Does he do daily bread?
Can he be the God of ordinary life?
Is God for everyday
or just Sundays?
Does he only do big stuff, religious stuff –
creating a world,
guiding a nation –
or is God also good at small stuff?
Is he the God of illness and worry,
of housing and work,
of friendships and heartache,
of daily food,
or is he too busy ruling the world
to be bothered with details?
The Israelites were about to find out.[6]

Erich Auerbach noticed that Bible stories are not just focused on the great and the good but relate the activities of daily life, not just the heroic.[7] This is important for it affirms the way most of us live and work out our relationship with God. If the preacher only focuses on what is perceived as supernatural, the congregation can feel their faith is not only different from the faith of biblical characters but inferior. Revelatory preaching is a 'ground up' style of preaching. The insights are not preached apart from the situations where they arise. It is an approach that starts and stays with the earthed specifics of the narratives, presenting the people and their physical, emotional and spiritual situation and allowing these to give the insights rather than abstracting them from the context.

Showing

The realities of a narrative (physical, emotional, relational, socio-economic, political and spiritual) are shown or displayed when the preacher lays these bare and holds up a slice of narrative life that contains an insight for the congregation to see and for people to recognize. David Schlafer likens this to drama that presents a slice of life; the preacher frames a situation for the congregation to observe.[8] For example, in the extract on the manna, people may recognize the effect mundane life has on their faith and concerns about God's involvement with the everyday. Recognition does not mean people need to have experienced the same situation, it can be a recognition of the reality of a situation, even if it is not one that they share.

Showing or laying bare a situation avoids reverting to abstract and general language, which can make relevance difficult. For example, it is easy to wax lyrical about the poetry of Ruth's promise and commitment (Ruth 1.16–17), but commitment is an abstract concept. Ruth's commitment was realized in hard work and poverty. Even words such as 'hard work' and 'poverty' are too general, they need translating into actualities: sweat, callouses, backache, anxiety, going to bed hungry. Long descriptions are not needed, just enough to anchor big ideas in reality. The insight that promises may be made in poetry but they are paid in pain is shown when the preacher holds up a slice of narrative life from Ruth to show the outworking of that promise. The showing exposes the realities: the cracked skin and the backache, the relationships and obedience to custom and law, the social and economic realities, the faith and the loneliness. These realities matter, for they are what happens to people in Ruth's situation, they sweat and worry like us. Ignoring these realities, particularly the physical realities, leaves biblical characters stranded in some spiritual neverland and they are not perceived as people like us, and if they are unlike us how are they relevant? The extract that follows exposes some of the physical realities (the full sermon can be found in Chapter 15).

> Ruth stands up and arches her back.
> She places her hands in the small of her back,
> and stretches.
> Her back aches from working bent double in the heat.
> Strands of hair stick to her forehead,
> her clothes are dark with sweat.
> She looks at her hands,
> the fingers are cracked from the rough stalks of barley.

Her apron is bulky with what she has collected
but she knows that by the time she has threshed it
there will be little to take home.
There will be just enough to make bread for her and Naomi.
It was good they arrived at harvest time,
she is glad to have work,
even if she does work apart from the others.
She recalls her promise:
'Where you go, I will go.'
And here she is, in a field in Bethlehem.[9]

This aspect of revelatory narrative is scenic and key scenes often carry the significance of a narrative. Showing paints a verbal picture, this can be biblical or it may be a contemporary scene that parallels a biblical scene. Alyce McKenzie, in her book *Making a Scene in the Pulpit*, gives detailed information on creating scenes.[10]

Exercise

What scene from the activity on Luke 19 would you include in detail in a sermon to show the insight you came to? Write or draw what would be in your scene.

Reduced suspense and closure

As there is no push to resolve a conflict, problem or ambiguity with a revelatory approach, suspense is reduced, but emotional and psychological tension are still present. The extract below begins to build the emotional tension present at the Last Supper.

They have just eaten a meal that became a farewell
and now they sit in silence.
They don't know what to say.
'Does no one ask where I'm going?' says Jesus.
'I have told you I am going away to the One who sent me.'
The disciples say nothing.
Peter had earlier asked the question, 'Where are you going?'
and had vowed he would follow.
Jesus had responded with a warning of Peter's failure.

Peter would deny him.
Maybe this made them cautious.
The disciples have not understood enough to ask the right question.
They still haven't got the plot.
The silence drags on.[11]

The reduced suspense of the revelatory plot is reflected in the Bible. Meir Sternberg observes that divine control tends to reduce suspense, although this is tempered by free will.[12] This is shown at key points in Israel's history; once God has promised the Hebrew slaves a land of their own the outcome is not really in doubt, what is open is how it will be achieved (Ex. 6.8). In the New Testament the promise of the Holy Spirit is given, his coming is sure, the manner of it is not. Jesus' followers wait without really knowing what to expect (Acts 1.1–8).

Revelatory sermons can end with some closure or possibilities that hold out hope, rather than ending with complete or tight closure. There are degrees of resolution, resolutions can be partial. Fred Craddock maintains that there can be a degree of incompleteness in preaching, allowing room for congregations to complete the sermon and giving them space for their own response. This reflects confidence in both the text and the guidance of the Holy Spirit that removes the need for closed conclusions for every sermon.[13] The first extract from a sermon on Joseph and his brothers ends with assurance but not closure. The second extract ends with more definite guidance.

Ending 1

'It does not have to be so,' says this story.
'It does not have to be so.'
Hearts of stone can crack.
Guilt can be forgiven.
'I will take away your hearts of stone and give you hearts of flesh,'
says God.
'But only if you see yourselves as I see you:
created, flawed, loved, mine.
I can change you.'[14]

Ending 2

He is God with us,
and he shows us how to be with others,
for it is easy to help those who are troubled

from a position of emotional security.
It is easy to counsel those whose life is a mess
from a position of feeling we have life sorted.
It is easy to sympathize with the weak
from a position of strength.
Such counsel will not truly help,
for it comes from a place that is distant, superior, safe.
We need to be aware of our own weakness,
to know what little it would take for us to become insecure.
We need to know our own vulnerability
and acknowledge that our lives get messy.
That way we close the gap,
stand beside people, forever saying,
'There but for the grace of God go I.[15]

Question

What advantages may there be in not having tight closure and a degree of openness? What disadvantages can you foresee?

Creative with time, movement and language

Revelatory narrative uses creative language such as metaphor, simile and word-images but the style is light and impressionistic, not a lapse into purple prose or long descriptions. In art, the impressionist painters suggested things with just a few brush strokes; similarly, impressionist writing uses just a few words to suggest something. Lengthy description is neither desirable nor helpful in a sermon. Sermons are comparatively short, there isn't time for long descriptions and too many adjectives and adverbs overload a sermon. The three examples that follow use small touches of creative language.

1 Power is slippery,
    it can trickle away like sand,
    it can build like a storm.
    And the clouds are gathering over Golgotha.

2 As the rich man built his walls
    a similar defence formed in his heart.

The walls of his heart hardened,
grew in height and width,
went down deep into his soul
until his heart was locked against a needy world.
The rich man stood surrounded by his barns,
they were his castle,
his fortress,
his defence against the world,
his surety for the future.

3   Jesus' cross was not detached,
not placed at a distance from the thieves.
His cross was not at the end of the row,
semi-detached.
His cross was in the middle,
a terraced death,
one with sinners to the end.

The Bible is replete with creative language: the lazy person is like vinegar to the teeth (Prov. 10.26) and the Kingdom of God is like a pearl (Matt. 13.45–46). Much is suggested in biblical description but with little detail. In life we do not see in detail, we don't see the whole of something, this means that too detailed a description may suggest unreality.[16] Just a few descriptive touches are needed.

Revelatory plots can get creative with time. Without the forward movement to resolve, the preacher can step sideways, look back, dip in and out of time. However, care needs to be taken that there are enough signposts for the congregation to follow. The following extract is Moses standing before the people just before they enter the Promised Land. The sermon moves back in time through Moses' memories.

He would catch himself reminiscing with people:
'Do you remember when the Nile turned to blood?'
'Do you remember when the Angel of Death passed over?'
'Do you remember when we walked dry-shod across the sea that parted?'
'Do you remember …?'
Then he would stop himself.
Of course, they didn't remember,
they weren't even born then.
Those who did remember were buried in the desert.[17]

A slower reflective pace with room for ambiguity/mystery

The revelatory plot tends to have a reduced pace, giving time for reflection. Luke 23.56 tells us that Jesus' disciples and the women rested on the Sabbath (Saturday). The congregation can be invited to reflect on what that might have meant.

> For us, Holy Saturday is a gap to be spanned,
> a ravine to be bridged,
> a valley to be crossed.
> For us, the other side is in view – Easter Sunday.
> But not for them.
> For them Saturday was a chasm,
> a black hole of grief,
> a cliff edge of despair,
> an abyss of sorrow no rope could span.
> For them, there was no other side,
> no knowledge of Easter Sunday to make Saturday bearable.
> He was not gone for a little while,
> he was gone.[18]

The Bible is often content with mystery and as preachers we cannot give more certainty than the text allows, though preachers can be forgiven for sometimes wishing the Bible would supply neat answers to the questions people ask. A sermon does not have to answer every question but it can end with assurance and hope for the gospel is good news. Sermons can challenge, assure and comfort but they should not end negatively. The story of the birth of Samuel leaves questions unanswered but assures us that our lives matter to God.

> This story does not answer the questions we have concerning why some prayers are answered and others appear not to be.
> Not every woman had Hannah's experience.
> The same is true today.

This story does, however, give us reasons to trust God.
It assures us God listens and remembers.
It assures us that God is concerned about everyday lives as well as world events.
This is a story about a God who took a woman's grief seriously and used an imperfect family to save a nation.[19]

The reduced pace of a revelatory approach gives people time to indwell a situation and get to know a character, a situation or an issue. David Day notes that Bible stories often move too quickly for people to feel their power, so the preacher slows the pace with detailed storytelling.[20] If preachers move too quickly to what can be learned, the congregation do not have time to identify with the characters, situations and issues or perceive their relevance. The congregation need to feel the full force of a situation. Moving too quickly to the overtly spiritual can have the opposite effect of what is intended; without facing the depth of the reality communicated in a biblical narrative a congregation may have difficulty realizing the extent of God's role.

Question

Think of a biblical story that you think would benefit from a reduced pace. Why would it benefit that story?

What are the problems with the revelatory plot?

The revelatory plot, like all sermon styles, has its weaknesses. Ways of avoiding or minimizing these will be followed up later in this book but they are summarized here.

Not for all texts

A revelatory approach works well on many biblical narratives but it is not appropriate for all texts. Some texts and contexts call for strong closure. Some biblical narratives contain sensitive material that may need a less immersive approach for pastoral reasons. The Bible has many different genres, which calls for preaching styles that are appropriate to the texts. Some epistles may call for a more expository approach. The revelatory approach is another style of preaching to add to the preacher's toolkit.

This enables the preacher to respond to the variety of texts in the Bible, letting the text decide the style of the sermon.

Too much ambiguity and mystery

Too much ambiguity and mystery can mean that a sermon lacks direction and purpose. Appropriate ambiguity and making room for mystery should not leave a congregation floundering. Revelatory plots can resolve to a degree, what they do not have is tight conclusions that tie everything up. Ending with possibilities should still give assurance and hope.

Slow reflective pace

The pace needs to be calculated for the text and context; too slow a pace can lose the congregation. The congregation may not recognize the approach as a sermon if they are not used to a reduced pace and reflective style. Changes in approach may have to be intentionally introduced. The slow pace may initially appear difficult for churches with a tradition of short sermons, but later chapters demonstrate how the approach can work with limited time spans.

Creative use of time and language

You may have noticed that many of the sermon extracts are laid out like poetry. This is a matter of personal style; it happens to be mine. Revelatory sermons do not have to be presented in this way. Creative prose works well in this style of preaching. For preachers who are good with language the revelatory style can be a temptation to use too many linguistic fireworks. There is nothing wrong with an artistic use of language but the degree of use is determined by the text and context. The creative use of time is another danger. Hopping backwards and forwards can be creative and enlightening, particularly moving between the present day and the biblical past, but the preacher will need to judge how much signalling their congregation needs; it can be easy to get lost.

The change can be difficult

Most preachers have a major style, this may be the result of personality, training, tradition or some other factor. David Schlafer in his book *Your Way with God's Word* helps preachers to determine what their major style is.[21] Whatever our major style, as preachers we need to be flexible in our approach in order to honour the text and be appropriate for the context. The Bible's many genres can't all be preached in the same way.

Conclusion

The revelatory plot is an alternative way of developing a sermon that addresses some of the weaknesses of the resolution plot and provides an open style that shows and has relevance built in from the beginning. It is earthed in the realities reflected in biblical narratives, creates the opportunity for people to identify with biblical characters and situations, and encourages congregations to reflect.

Notes

1 James Breech, 2007, *The Silence of Jesus*, Minneapolis: Fortress Press, p. 98.
2 Meir Sternberg, 1987, *The Poetics of Biblical Narrative*, Bloomington: Indiana University Press, p. 54.
3 Margaret Cooling, 'God Speaks to Joseph', *Preaching that Shows*, https://preachingthatshows.com/2018/10/10/god-speaks-to-joseph-hail-joseph/, accessed 14.11.2021.
4 James Joyce, 1993, *Dubliners*, London: Penguin, pp. 79–80.
5 Paul Scott Wilson, 1999, *Four Pages of the Sermon*, Nashville: Abingdon Press, p. 87.
6 Margaret Cooling, 'The Wilderness Wanderings', *Preaching that Shows*, https://preachingthatshows.com/2018/10/11/the-wilderness-wanderings/, accessed 14.11.2021.
7 Erich Auerbach, 1953, *Mimesis*, Princeton: Princeton University Press, pp. 21–2.
8 David J. Schlafer, 2004, *Playing with Fire*, Cambridge, MA: Cowley Publications, pp. 69–70.
9 Margaret Cooling, 'Ruth', *Preaching that Shows*, https://preachingthatshows.com/2018/10/11/ruth/, accessed 14.11.2021.
10 Alyce M. McKenzie, 2018, *Making a Scene in the Pulpit*, Louisville: Westminster John Knox Press.
11 Margaret Cooling, 'The Promise of the Holy Spirit', *Preaching that Shows*, https://preachingthatshows.com/2018/10/12/the-promise-of-the-holy-spirit-silence/, accessed 14.11.2021.
12 Sternberg, *Poetics*, pp. 209, 233–5, 267–8.
13 Fred Craddock, 2001, *As One Without Authority*, St Louis: Chalice Press, pp. 54–5.
14 Margaret Cooling, 'Joseph and his Brothers', *Preaching that Shows*, https://preachingthatshows.com/2018/10/11/joseph-and-his-brothers/, accessed 14.11.2021.

15 Margaret Cooling, 'The Baptism of Jesus', *Preaching that Shows*, https://preachingthatshows.com/2018/10/10/the-baptism-of-jesus-god-in-the-crowd/, accessed 14.11.2021.

16 Craddock, *As One*, p. 77.

17 Margaret Cooling, 'Moses Speaks to the People', *Preaching that Shows*, https://preachingthatshows.com/2018/10/11/moses-speaks-to-the-people/, accessed 14.11.2021.

18 Margaret Cooling, 'Holy Saturday', *Preaching that Shows*, https://preachingthatshows.com/2018/10/12/holy-saturday-the-other-side/, accessed 14.11.2021.

19 Margaret Cooling, 'Hannah', *Preaching that Shows*, https://preachingthatshows.com/2018/10/11/hannah/, accessed 14.11.2021.

20 David Day, 2005, *Embodying the Word*, London: SPCK, pp. 53, 57–9.

21 David J. Schlafer, 1995, *Your Way with God's Word*, Cambridge, MA: Cowley Publications.

3

Embodiment and the Language of Earth

This chapter considers an idea that is at the core of a revelatory approach and is integral to any showing style – embodiment. What embodiment means is discussed as well as how it is expressed in sermons. Four binaries lie at the heart of embodiment: material/spiritual, concrete/abstract, specific/general, particular/universal. These are demonstrated with sermon extracts, for understanding these binaries helps to keep the language of sermons earthed. Both religious language and the 'language of earth' are considered and possible problems arising from embodied language.

Embodiment: a range of meanings

I am a vegetarian, which makes me a bit of a pain to have to dinner. Some people find the concept of vegetarianism difficult and offer me fish. I resist explaining that a fish is not a vegetable as it sounds rather patronizing. If people are kind enough to invite me for a meal, I make a joke of being a vegetarian and give them a rule of thumb, 'If it has a face, I don't eat it.' Like most rules of thumb, it does not cover everything. (Do shellfish have faces?) A similar rule of thumb applies to preaching, 'If you can't give it a body, don't preach it.' The word 'body' covers anything that can be known through our bodily senses in some way, not necessarily a human body. Once again it is only a rule of thumb, it probably does not cover everything. Embodiment is giving something a 'body', a physical form that can be sensed. Embodiment is a crucial element of preaching for it stops sermons flying off into abstractions. Below are a series of ways of explaining embodiment.

- Embodiment is the way we are, we are people with bodies. We learn through our bodies and we experience the world through our bodies and its senses. We are embodied.

- Embodiment is a concrete expression of an idea, emotion or quality in a way that can be related to general experience of the world or sensed in some way. The following examples relate to the senses and experience.

> Looking at him curled on the sofa, his posture was the embodiment of despair. (Sight, body language)
> The perfume was the embodiment of sexuality. (Smell)
> Her mother let the biscuit melt on her tongue and knew that her daughter's love was embodied in that home-made biscuit. (Taste)
> The sound of the siren embodied all their fears. (Hearing)
> The rough feel of the uniform embodied all she hated about school. (Touch)
> Their hopes were embodied in that one word, 'tomorrow'. (Experience)

- Embodiment is something general or abstract expressed in a person.

> She was the embodiment of compassion.
> He embodied what it means to forgive.

You may still be wondering how this relates to preaching. A few examples may help.

> Saul embodied the idea of a king: he was young, handsome and head and shoulders taller than anyone else (1 Sam. 9–10).

> Ruth's commitment was embodied in working in the fields to support Naomi (Ruth 2).

> Jesus embodied service in the action of washing feet (John 13.1–17).

> The rich fool's values were embodied in big barns (Luke 12.16–21).

Spiritual insights are embodied in the Bible; when God wanted to show his love for humanity, he sent his Son who took on flesh (John 3.16). God's love was embodied in Jesus. When God speaks, it is through the words and lives of the prophets, poets and writers of the Bible who lived in specific places and experienced particular situations through their bodies. The Bible is not a collection of disembodied messages; it is the story of a people and their relationship with God, and it is the story of

Jesus Christ and the spread of his redeeming gospel across communities in the first-century world.

Exercise

Take one biblical story and say how a quality, emotion or idea is embodied within the story.

The four binaries

What follows are four pairs: material/spiritual, concrete/abstract, specific/ general and particular/universal. I have separated these for clarity but in practice they overlap. These binaries operate in every type of sermon but preaching styles differ according to what they emphasize. A revelatory approach, and a showing style, tends to emphasize the first part of each pair and that becomes a way of revealing the second.

Material/spiritual

Material is matter, the physical, the stuff that makes up the world. Embodiment is the revealing of the spiritual through the physical and the material things of this world. Embodiment is when biblical characters are presented as people with bodies as well as souls; they are people who live in a material world and it is often through the world and their bodies that people learn of God. Matter and spirit are not separated; the spiritual needs the material world to manifest itself. This can be expressed in preaching. Instead of talking about Jesus submitting to the will of God – a very spiritual statement – preachers can document how that submission was expressed physically.

> From the moment he said,
> 'Thy will be done,'
> Jesus changes from subject to object.
> Before he did things,
> now people do things to him.
> Before he spoke,
> now he is largely silent.
> Judas betrays him,
> guards bind him,

he is led away to trial.
Peter denies him,
the High Priest condemns him
and hands him over to Pilate.
Pilate questions him,
passes him to Herod
who mocks Jesus and sends him back.
Pilate tries to release him,
washes his hands of him,
condemns him,
gives him to soldiers who mock and beat him.[1]

We learn through our bodies and we live out our faith through our bodies in the material world. Barbara Brown Taylor states this explicitly, she speaks of the human body being a source of revelation because we are enfleshed people who learn through our bodies.[2] Embodiment is a feature of all narrative preaching but it is particularly important in revelatory preaching. It is endorsed by Eugene Lowry throughout his writings and Thomas Troeger literally gets physical: he advocates feeling 'the bodily weight of the truth', physically rehearsing some of the actions in the text such as kneeling and bowing.[3]

Concrete/abstract

Concrete is something that is solid, real, definite and tangible. It is the opposite of vague, theoretical and abstract. It is easy for preachers to drift into abstract religious language and forget that their congregations live out their faith in the office and factory, the home and the farm. The congregation has to translate abstract statements into a way of life. David Day notes how preachers can help congregations do this by making a deliberate choice for concrete situations, images and examples rather than abstract language. He asks if preachers can work backwards to the sense experiences and concrete situations that evoked the texts, which is an integral part of a revelatory approach as documented in Chapter 6.[4]

Jesus spoke in concrete terms, using images and examples from everyday life to communicate the message of the Kingdom. Following Jesus' example means that language used in preaching can root religious concepts in concrete situations without being seen as 'dumbing down'. Language that uses images from everyday life is not the poor cousin of abstract language. Bonnie Miller-McLemore notes that being able to think abstractly is often held up as a sign of maturity, particularly in developmental schemes that categorize stages of faith, but this attitude marginalizes the way many people learn.[5] The following extract takes Paul's words to the Ephesians concerning being enslaved to 'the ruler of the power of the air' (Eph. 2.2) and makes this abstract statement concrete, particularly as this was preached during the Covid 19 pandemic.

> When the spirit of 'I'm all right Jack' is at work – leading to a vaccine grab, or stockpiling loo rolls and resources – the ruler of the power of the air is being worshipped.[6]

This may seem a bit too down to earth for some people – shouldn't the sermon be more spiritual? I think the answer is no. Using abstract language may sound more spiritual to some people but spiritual is not rising above the things of this world, it is practising our faith in this world. The way we behave concerning toilet rolls in a shortage can be an expression of our faith. This is a concrete example of showing who we worship by our behaviour.

Specific/general

Specific is about being clearly defined, precise and detailed. General is being broad, generic and comprehensive. Painkiller is a general term, Aspirin, Paracetamol and Ibuprofen are specific painkillers. The Bible is often specific, Paul gives specific attributes of the general term 'love' (1 Cor. 13.4–8). The laws of the Old Testament cover all aspects of life and are very specific. Fred Craddock comments on the 'almost embarrassing specificity' of the Bible.[7] Specific rather than general language is part of a showing style. Words easily drift into broad generalizations and a conscious move is needed to make language specific as in the examples that follow.

General:	Compassion sometimes needs to get tough.
Specific:	Compassion getting tough includes us. We can nurture compassionate attitudes in ourselves and be tough on ourselves if we find hard-hearted attitudes within. As Christians we can get tough by refusing to purchase newspapers that foster hatred, whatever their source. We can be fair and just in our dealings with others and support organizations that help people out of debt. We can pray, for prayer changes things and we can gossip compassion and not join in with callous views when in conversation with others.[8]

General:	Naomi was grieving.
Specific:	These hands no longer cling to life,
	no longer cling to anything.
	I stare but do not see.
	I touch but do not feel.
	Grief numbs my senses.
	I make no eye contact.
	I dwell in a frozen land.
	Death has drained life.
	I am no longer Naomi,
	pleasant,
	I am Mara,
	bitter.[9]

General language can be translated into specific language by asking questions concerning what is involved in the general statement.

General statement:	From this point onwards (Luke 9.51) Jesus' ministry was a journey towards Jerusalem.
What is involved?	Walking
	The choosing of a particular direction
	The constant choice of that direction over a period of time even though there were many events and encounters on the way: healings, teaching, conflicts.
This becomes:	Day after day he walks,
	every step takes him closer to Jerusalem.
	But his course is not direct, there was no Google map showing the shortest route.
	The path to Jerusalem winds through Palestine taking in people in need of healing, men and women hungry for teaching, conflicts to be faced.
	Day after day he sets the compass
	and the needle always points one way,
	Jerusalem.

A revelatory approach is specific in its presentation of the biblical narrative. Keying into a specific situation to understand a larger and more general one is a well-known technique used in the media and the arts. An example of this is the girl in the red coat in the film *Schindler's List* (1993). Understanding the horrors of what happened to the Jewish people is initiated through focusing on one specific child. This is an approach that journalists sometimes use, they may tell the story of one family to help people relate to a distant situation, rather than talk in general terms. Ed Murrow, an American war correspondent posted to Britain in the blitz, once portrayed the atmosphere of an air raid by describing the way shrapnel drilled holes into tins of peaches rather than giving a general description.[10] This reflects the way we live, we live specifically; vegetarians do not eat vegetables, they eat broccoli and peas. Food, like most of life, is only experienced specifically and it is easier to identify with specific instances as this is the scale on which we exist.

Helmut Thielicke provided a striking example of specific language. He posited what might have happened if a Christian had protested at a Nazi rally. If there had been a Christian shouting 'Jesus is Lord' he or she would probably have been ignored. If this imaginary Christian had been specific and asserted not only Jesus' lordship but also denounced false lords such as Adolf Hitler, he or she would probably have been killed.[11]

Art is a form of visual language that is specific. Artists communicate via the specifics of their art form: the people, the setting, the gestures, the objects and the expressions. Preachers can learn from artists how to communicate the general through the specific, a subject explored in Chapters 4 and 5. Although preaching language needs to get specific, the specifics of a narrative need to be generalized at some point so that they relate to the hearer's lives and different situations. However, the general needs to be approached via the specific. In the sermon extract that follows the first section focuses on the specifics of the narrative – the man at the pool of Bethesda – and this leads into generalizing what is learned from it, remaining specific in practice, still relating to the man at the pool.

> To the pool of Bethesda Jesus came.
> There he met a man who had lain by the pool for thirty-eight years.
> The pool held out hope, yet failed him.
> It was always out of his reach.
> Always he was too late.
> For thirty-eight years he had rested on his bedroll.
> Over the years it had become shaped to his body,
> he knew its lumps and its sags, its stains and its familiar smell.
> Jesus came to the poolside and asked a question,
> a question so basic that the man should have laughed in his face,
> told him where to get off or refused to answer.
> Fancy asking a man who had waited thirty-eight years to be healed
> if he wanted to be well.
> Did Jesus think he laid there for fun?

Jesus asked a stupid question.
The Bethesda poolside was not a place people wanted to be
unless they had to.
But Jesus knew the heart of this man
and we see it in his reply;
there is no eager acceptance of a chance to be well.
This is a man whose bed was his prison
but also his place of security,
the only bit of the world that was his,
where he felt in control.
This is a man whose enthusiasm to be well
had been exhausted by continual disappointment.

It is this Jesus who still walks our world,
stopping by the factory floor,
the kitchen,
the office,
the school.
And he is still asking stupid questions:
'Is this really the way you want your life to be?'
'Do you want to change?'

And when we answer we do not have to worry
about being the right sort of person.
God is not fussy,
but we, like the man who was healed by the pool,
do have to be prepared to leave some things behind.
We have to accept the challenge that freedom in Christ brings.
That can be scary.

The command is clear, 'Take up your bed and walk.'
Take up whatever it is we rest upon,
whatever is comfortable and shaped to our lives,
not because resting or being comfortable is wrong,
far from it,
but sometimes we use it as an escape, an excuse.
We get used to the way we live our lives
even if we are disappointed and dissatisfied.
Like memory foam, habit creates a shape that fits.
To change, even for something better,
will require effort, courage, daring.

But the command is clear,
'Take up your bed and walk.'[12]

The difference between general and specific in terms of practice is something we encounter in daily life. General statements such as 'lose weight' are imprecise and are easy to evade, but a specific statement such as 'refuse the biscuits at coffee break' stands more chance of being practised. The same is true of sermons. Specific language can resonate with a congregation as it gives enough detail to build a picture of an event or person, and enough detail to give people pointers concerning how something may be lived. General statements that are exhortations, such as 'love more', are difficult to practise and may be ignored, or they may engender a vague sense of guilt – we know we ought to love more but are not sure how to do it.

If we find ourselves making general exhortations such as 'love more', 'pray more' it helps to add the word 'how'. If we cannot add any specifics or pointers, should we be preaching it? That does not mean we have to have all the answers, but it does mean we have to give some clues concerning how a general statement or principle may be practised. Furthermore, it needs to be borne in mind that practice includes feeling, thinking and being, as well as action. This subject is followed up in detail in Chapter 13.

Exercise

Look at a sermon you have preached. Locate any general statements. Do you give any specific pointers to ground the general statements in the practice of faith in daily life? Do you detail narrative specifics about people and situations? If not, adjust the sermon to include some of these.

Particular/universal

Jane Austen opens her novel *Pride and Prejudice* with the famous words, 'It is a truth universally acknowledged, that a single man in possession of a good fortune, must be in want of a wife.'[13] Unfortunately Jane Austen's statement does not qualify as a universal truth, for universal truths apply to all people, for all time, in all places, and not every single, rich male needs or wants a wife. Universal truths are not always universally acknowledged. For example, 'God is holy' is a universal truth held by

Christians but it is not universally acknowledged. Universal truths are big truths, and they are too big for us to understand except in particular instances. We may experience the holiness of God in the particulars of worship. Christians hold 'God is love' to be a universal truth, but we only know it in the particular, when we experience that love. When preaching universal truths, preachers can root them in particular experiences; they can also be grounded in the particulars of storytelling so that people see a universal truth lived out in the details of a narrative when a slice of narrative life is presented.

David Day suggests imaginative ways of presenting the particulars of a story. He suggests entering the story by envisioning it as a film or using Ignatian methods where the reader imagines themselves as part of a biblical story or as an observer. Both methods involve 'seeing' the situation and people in a biblical narrative, and that can be shown in a sermon. The emphasis on universal truths being expressed in the particulars of storytelling means the doctrines of Christianity can be preached in a narrative way, for real situations underlie many doctrines. The slave market underlies redemption, and a goat being driven into the wilderness is the basis for the concept of atonement. Day points out that before Paul wrote about justification, Jesus told the parable of the Pharisee and the tax collector (Luke 18.9–14). The truths of doctrine can be preached in an embodied form.[14]

In summary,

• the spiritual is revealed in and through the material and physical,
• the abstract is known through the concrete,
• the general is experienced in the specific,
• the universal is known in the particular.

The language of faith

The previous sections of this chapter looked at broad language use. This section looks at individual words. The language of faith is something we learn. Over the years we get to know how to handle religious words such as 'salvation', 'redemption' and 'faith' and we have a rough working knowledge of what these religious words mean. As preachers we may say that Abraham was a man of faith and the congregation may nod in agreement, as most people will know what is meant by that statement at a basic definition level (Abraham trusted God). However, the level of understanding may remain superficial *because* people know roughly what the word 'faith' means. The familiarity of certain religious words acts as a barrier or film that stops us going deeper; we register words such as 'faith' and move on, thinking we know what it means. We are, however, often unaware of the depths of meaning of a word and its implications. If a word is completely new, we stop and try to think through its meaning, not so with familiar words. Embodiment is what is needed to pierce the film of familiarity and to begin to work through what religious words mean and their implications. This is part of building relevance throughout a sermon. In relation to Abraham being a man of faith, (Heb. 11.8–12) it means more than just a general trust in God; faith had wide-ranging implications in Abraham's life. Abraham having faith in God meant his belief in the following.

- God had a purpose in calling him to leave home, even if he did not fully understand it.
- God could be trusted to keep his promises. Confidence in God's faithfulness and responding with a faithful life. Faith is relational.
- Faith is not just an inner attitude or assent to certain doctrines; it is trust in action. Faith is ongoing obedience and a way of life (James 2.20–24).
- Faith encompasses failure. Abraham failed spectacularly on several occasions (Gen. 12.10–20; Gen. 20). His faith in ever having a son wavered (Gen. 16.). Nevertheless, he retained his title and is still known as a 'man of faith'. He was not like athletes who have been found to have cheated and are stripped of their titles and medals. In a relationship of faith, it is not just us holding on to God; it is God holding on to us (Ps. 63.8). A relationship of faith can withstand failure.
- Faith can mean sacrifice. In Abraham's case it was committing to being strangers in someone else's land, never having somewhere they called home. Abraham and Sarah left their family as an act of faith in God's calling. That means they would not be there when family members died, they would not be there for the funerals. They would not be there to celebrate the marriages and births.
- Faith needs honesty. Faith is being able to face the truth about ourselves having faith that God can change us. It is facing the truth about the world and having faith that God's redemptive love triumphs in the end.

The language of faith, and the language of any of the doctrines, can be a problem unless doctrine is embodied and the implications are worked through. People may get used to using key words like 'salvation', 'redemption' and 'justification' without understanding their import. There is nothing wrong with learning the language of faith but such language left

unexplored can act as little more than a shibboleth, a password, signalling that we belong within the Christian community.

Exercise

What religious word is embodied in the story of Saul/Paul on the road
to Damascus (Acts 9.1–19)? How would you embody it in a sermon to
deepen a congregation's understanding?

Embodied language: the language of earth

Embodied preaching is about speaking the language of earth. Fred Craddock sums up this type of speech as language that reflects the world of the
text rather than just reflecting on it.[15] Embodied language gets physical
and it has a this-world quality, not an otherworldly one. Charles Rice
comments on how down-to-earth Jesus' language was; he referred to the
ordinary realities of earthly existence. Jesus' parables are about cooking
and landlords, muggings and family life. Jesus' stories and images are
about helping people to see God as present in the material world and in
human lives. Jesus had confidence in the stuff of everyday life to be the
way in which we come to know God, and the way in which God reveals
his presence.[16] Living a Christian life is not rising above the things of
this world or earthly existence, it is throwing ourselves into life, into the
world God made; it is what Jesus did.

   Familiarity, or the sacred aura that surrounds the Bible, may cause
its down-to-earth nature to be missed. The temptation is for preachers
to focus on what is perceived to be the explicitly spiritual aspects of
texts and ignore the physical circumstances that give it expression. In the
sermon extract on Ezekiel 37, the insight comes through the physicality
of the bones and their extreme dryness. These bones are beyond dead,
there is no trace of flesh left. Kate Bruce takes time to dwell on the nature
of those bones, the sounds and the sights, before moving on to a statement about God's power. If the extreme dryness of the bones had not
been entered into, the insight into God's power to bring life out of death
would not have had so great an impact.

   On the bleached white sea on which you stand you pick out skulls,
   tibias, fibulas, jawbones ... you spot the odd kneecap here and
   there ...

44

Bones. Bones. Bones.
Bones under your feet.
Bones as far as your eye can see.
Bones crunching underfoot ...
Standing amid a sea of bleached dry bones faced with the question,
'Mortal, can these bones live?' we might be tempted to say, 'Not
a chance. Are you mad! They are bones!' Really the situation is
hopeless, quite beyond help.
But God ...
But with God nothing is ever utterly hopeless.[17]

If sermons are to connect with people, they need to include the language
of earth, words like 'sweat', 'dribble', 'exhaustion' and 'mud' – whatever
earthy words are appropriate for the narrative. The Bible is not shy about
human physicality, it is happy to mix laws on worship and religious festivals with laws concerning toilets, food and sex (Deut. 12.1–32; 14.1–21;
16.1–16; 22.13–30; 23.12–14).

Exercise

Present the physicality of Mark 2.1–4.

The incarnational principle

David Day laments that too often the Word that became flesh is turned to
mere words again. He asks if ideas can be returned to a physical sensory
form, which he calls a preaching version of the principle of incarnation.[18]
It is the incarnation that gives preachers the freedom to speak of God
using the language of earth. Incarnational language is the language of this
world that reveals the spiritual world. We come to know the spiritual by
going deeper into the material and physical world because this is God's
world. When God wanted to reveal himself to humanity he came in flesh,
in Jesus, and we learn of his divinity through his physical life. Some
preachers may worry that using the language of this world in a sermon
may reduce the radical nature of the gospel. Richard Lischer notes that
it has the opposite effect. It is abstract religious language that can rob
preaching of its impact; it can make the amazing sound remote and irrelevant. Such language neither moves nor offends people, for it does not
reach them at any depth.[19]

If Jesus is fully human as well as fully God then certain things follow: his feet got dirty, rain would have plastered his hair to his head, his clothes would have got soiled when kneeling in prayer, and that soiling would have been the colour of local earth. These are things that can also happen to us, things with which people can identify because they are part of being human. For the reality of the incarnation to begin to communicate, we need to say more than 'Jesus was like us so that he could make atonement.' People need to see a little of that everyday likeness in order to identify Jesus as Emmanuel, God with us. If congregations do not see doctrines, such as the incarnation, in the small, sensed things, they are unlikely to comprehend them in the larger and more abstract ones, which is why embodiment is so important. To engage people in doctrine, the preacher needs to deal in the language of the senses for it is sensed details that act as guy ropes stopping the sermon flying off into unearthed abstraction. In the case of the story of Jesus walking on water (Matt.14.22–33), the text describes the wind causing the waves to buffet the boat. In the sermon extract that follows mention is made of the physical effect of the wind.

> On the hillside Jesus prayed alone,
> the wind swirling round him,
> whipping his hair into his eyes,
> the rain plastering his clothes to his body,
> but in prayer he reached a still point at the centre of the storm. [20]

If nothing were said about the physical circumstances or to say, 'untouched by the storm he looked across the lake,' the impression would have been given that Jesus was unlike us. Such a statement, or lack of physical circumstances, puts Jesus outside ordinary experience and he becomes an insubstantial figure untouched by reality. If doctrines such as the incarnation are to be perceived as relevant, they need to be sensed. Not every part of the narrative needs treating this way, for that would over-burden the sermon and make it too long, sometimes just small touches are needed.

First date with a text

Many preachers when they come to a text ask the question, 'What does it mean?' To start in this way is like asking about the meaning of life and the universe on a first date. Generally, couples ask each other small questions on a first date. (There are always exceptions!) Couples ask embodiment questions about person and place; they tend not to be abstract. These small questions help us to understand a person's character and background and place them in their situation. When we first encounter a text, similar 'first date' questions can be asked, about character and situation. Questions of meaning come after these initial inquiries.

Accepting the artist's bind

Earthed language that deals in the senses and specifics may be new to some preachers who are used to preaching in a more abstract manner. Artists who show biblical scenes cannot escape the need to make decisions concerning physical particulars that engage with the senses, it is not an option they have. Characters inhabit a definite space, wear particular clothes, express recognizable feelings and make specific gestures. Artists have to work within a physical space and they use colour, line, texture, and composition to evoke a range of senses. The artist must make decisions about specifics, such is the artist's bind. The preacher can learn from artists, accept some of that bind and refuse abstraction and generality that does not touch sensed reality.

Potential problems

Throughout the homiletical literature there is a call for embodied preaching, but there are potential problems relating to both the preacher and the congregation.

- Some preachers may be hesitant about becoming too specific, particularly about focusing on the physical as they, and their congregation, may be used to physical things being an illustration of something spiritual rather than being dwelt upon.[21]
- A congregation may question the spiritual status of the sermon that uses everyday language and focuses on the physical as a way of comprehending the spiritual. However, the use of abstract and general spiritual language also has its problems, it can be distant, difficult to relate to and could imply divine distance. The purpose of embodied language is not to shock or to sound contemporary, it is to serve the gospel.
- Using embodied language is not as easy as it sounds; it is easier to drift into the language of abstraction and generalities: 'sinners', 'commitment', 'salvation'.

- Not every general and abstract statement can be turned into specific tangible forms – a sermon would become overloaded and very long. It is a matter of focusing on a key term or important statements and earthing them. Over many sermons, abstract, general and spiritual language becomes earthed in specific concrete expressions and images.
- David Day recognizes that specific examples can leave part of the congregation feeling that it has nothing to do with them. However, sticking to abstractions, which may not relate to anyone, is a high price to pay to avoid some people being unable to relate to an example. He advises spreading examples across a range of life situations and characters. Examples also need to be credible. The use of exceptional Christians of the past may sometimes inspire but more often they seem beyond the reach of most Christians. When instances of love, faith, forgiveness and other Christian virtues are embodied in ordinary people, they are more likely to relate to the congregation and be perceived as relevant.[22] A suitable range of examples can be spread within a sermon or across sermons.

Conclusion

Throughout the preaching literature there is an affirmation that we come to know the general, abstract, universal and spiritual through the specific, concrete, particular and material. There is also an acknowledgement that there are difficulties in putting this into practice. The move to specific, concrete, particular and physical language may take time for preachers who are used to preaching in a more abstract style. Once the move is made, however, biblical stories come alive and doctrines gain flesh and blood.

Notes

1 Margaret Cooling, 'The Trials and Mocking of Jesus', *Preaching that Shows*, https://preachingthatshows.com/2018/10/12/the-trials-and-mocking-of-jesus/, accessed 14.11.2021.

2 Barbara Brown Taylor, 2001, 'On This Rock', in Roger Alling and David J. Schlafer (eds), *Preaching Through the Year of Matthew: Sermons that Work*, Harrisburg: Morehouse Publishing, pp. 143–7 (p. 143).

3 Thomas H. Troeger, 1990, *Imagining a Sermon*, Nashville: Abingdon Press, pp. 53–6.

4 David Day, 2005, *Embodying the Word*, London: SPCK, pp. 2–3.

5 Bonnie Miller-McLemore, 'Embodied Knowing, Embodied Theology: What Happened to the Body?', *Pastoral Psychology*, 62 (2013), 743–58 (pp. 749–51), doi.org/10.1007/s11089-013-0510-3.

6 Kate Bruce, *Freedom from the Locked-down Life*, unpublished sermon.

7 Fred Craddock, 2001, *As One Without Authority*, St Louis: Chalice Press, p. 52.

8 Margaret Cooling, 'Nehemiah', *Preaching that Shows*, https://preachingthatshows.com/2019/01/14/nehemiah-when-compassion-gets-tough/, accessed 14.11.2021.

9 Margaret Cooling, 'Naomi', *Preaching that Shows*, https://preachingthatshows.com/2018/10/11/naomi/, accessed 14.11.2021.

10 Jolyon Mitchell, 1999, *Visually Speaking*, Edinburgh: T&T Clark, p. 52.

11 Quoted in Richard Lischer, 1987, *Theories of Preaching*, Durham, NC: Labyrinth Press, pp. 300–3.

12 Margaret Cooling, 'The Man by the Pool of Bethesda', *Preaching that Shows*, https://preachingthatshows.com/2018/10/10/the-man-by-the-pool-of-bethesda-the-pool/, accessed 14.11.2021.

13 Jane Austen, 2021, *Pride and Prejudice*, London: Alama Classics, p. 3.

14 Day, *Embodying*, pp. 30–3, 59.

15 Craddock, *As One*, p. 63.

16 Charles L. Rice, 1991, *The Embodied Word*, Minneapolis: Fortress Press, pp. 74–5.

17 Kate Bruce, 2015, *Igniting the Heart*, London: SCM Press, pp. 189–93.

18 Day, *Embodying*, p. 2.

19 Lischer, *Theories*, pp. 300–3.

20 Margaret Cooling, 'Jesus Walks on Water', *Preaching that Shows*, https://preachingthatshows.com/2018/10/10/jesus-walks-on-water-he-calms-the-storm-sometimes/, accessed 14.11.2021.

21 Craddock, *As One*, p. 50.

22 Day, *Embodying*, pp. 74–91.

4

Art and the Sermon

Throughout the previous chapters I have signalled that art has a role in helping the preacher to employ a showing style. This chapter demonstrates ways in which art can be used at different stages of the sermon. A number of artworks are referred to, and these can be viewed online. Increasingly, art is being used by preachers alongside commentaries as a visual commentary and you can find some good examples online. The *Visual Commentary on Scripture* (https://thevcs.org/) gives access to art with commentaries on the paintings.[1] The website *The Text This Week* (http://www.textweek.com) has an art index to parallel biblical texts.[2] Resources such as the *Imaging the Word* series matches artworks to Bible readings.[3]

Art can give preachers examples and models of narrating in a revelatory style that engages, can be reflective and open while remaining earthed in the people and situations it reveals. Art is practical, it can help preachers prepare and it can sometimes help preachers through that terrible moment when you study a passage, pray over it and still nothing comes. Art can be used by the Holy Spirit to break through that frustration and give an insight into a biblical text.

The many roles of art

Art can function in many ways in a sermon. It can be the focus of a sermon or be used in preparation; it can provide information and inspiration. Art can fulfil many preaching roles.

- Art can provide an insight. Paolo Veronese's painting of the Last Supper provides an insight into its meaning. It shows Christ died for all and invites all types of people to Communion.[4]
- Art can provide information; for example, Millet's *Gleaners* shows just how back-breaking Ruth's gleaning was. It was the job of those at the bottom of society.[5]

- Art can help preachers to stay earthed as art is specific. Art does not work in generalities; artists must draw specific people wearing particular clothes doing certain things in a definite setting.
- Art can create an atmosphere as part of a sermon – where you are able to show it. Some art is contemplative and can contribute to creating a reflective tone.
- Art can be a visual commentary that the preacher uses but does not show or even refer to in a sermon.
- A painting can be described as a way of presenting a biblical narrative. People can look it up afterwards. (Note: ask the congregation not to get their phones out and look it up during the sermon unless you want to make time for people to do this.)
- Members of the congregation can be posed in the way characters are presented in a painting if insight lies in the composition of the scene. Simone Martini's 1333 *Annunciation* shows a frightened Mary twisting away from Gabriel. This body language is easy to recreate.[6]
- The preacher can demonstrate a significant gesture or body language from a painting. In El Greco's painting of *Christ Driving the Traders from the Temple*, one of Christ's hands is raised in judgement (the hand holding the whip), the other is raised in blessing.[7]
- Art can be central to a sermon. If it can be shown, the sermon can draw on the visual image to tell a biblical story, interpret it and reflect on it.
- Art can provide preachers with a model of narration that is revelatory and showing in nature.

Question

Look at the list of different ways of using art in preaching. Which are you most likely to use?

Insight

Art can help preachers see the significance of a narrative and nurture insights into the text. Below is the ending of a sermon on the Last Supper (Luke 22.14–23) that uses Veronese's painting *The Last Supper*. It takes people through the painting pointing out different people: 'There is ...', 'There are ...' The story behind this painting is that Veronese received a summons to appear before the Inquisition as they did not like the fact that he had included all sorts of people in his painting of the Last Supper beside Jesus and the disciples. Veronese included servants, merchants, soldiers, drunks, people fighting and a dog. The Inquisition gave him three months to make changes, to make it more religious and respectable, and to remove the dog! (The transcript of Veronese's trial is available online.) We do not know why Veronese painted so many people at the Last Supper, maybe he just liked painting parties, maybe it is his interpretation of the Last Supper, or maybe Veronese painted more than he knew.

Question

Look at the sermon extract that follows. In what ways does the art (Veronese's *Last Supper*) help to bring out the significance of the event?

There is Christ in the centre leaning over to talk to his disciples, having just broken the bread and blessed the wine. Around him is a riot of colour and people of different nations. There are people of various professions: servants, soldiers, a jester and rich merchants. The canvas is filled with all sorts of behaviour: some listening devoutly, some fighting, some laughing, some busy working, some definitely drunk. All are painted as local people; the sort Veronese would have met wandering around Venice. Veronese placed the Last Supper amid an everyday crowd at a feast. For us, it would be like Christ breaking bread at a party on a Saturday night when the guest list included some really dodgy characters. In this painting Christ breaks the bread and blesses the wine and maybe he is saying:

'This is my body broken for you, who look as if you never take life seriously, but underneath wonder what it is all about.'
'This is my blood shed for you, who have drunk too much but still can't forget.'
'This is my body broken for you, who look so tough but are crying inside.'
'This is my blood spilled for you, so busy with all the demands on you that you don't have time to think about what really matters.'

Veronese painted life with Christ at the centre of it.

What happened to Paolo Veronese? Well, he did not change a thing in his painting. The drunks still fight, the parrot still squawks and the dog still waits by the table hoping someone will drop some food. Veronese lived. He did not end up in prison. He did not die at the stake. He out-witted the Inquisition. He merely took his pen and crossed out the title 'The Last Supper' and wrote, 'Feast at the House of Levi', a feast that the Bible tells us included people that the religious authorities labelled as sinners. The Inquisition was satisfied. Somehow it was all right to have that sort of crowd at a party for sinners, but not at the Last Supper or at Communion that celebrates that event. Maybe they missed the point. Maybe that is what Communion is, a party for sinners who want to change. It does not matter whether we meet Christ at a party, in church, in daily life, or in bread and wine. When that meeting takes place, the change begins. And he will continue to change us if we let him.[8]

Art in preparation

Art can help preachers in both preparation and delivery of sermons. This involves learning the names of three types of art: monoscenic, synoptic and simultaneous. There is no agreed set of terms in the art world, publi-cations differ, but the terms I employ are in common use.

Monoscenic art

Monoscenic art is a single scene from a story, where characters and actions that are central to the scene appear only once. It is probably the most common type of artwork. Leonardo da Vinci's *Last Supper* is monoscenic.[9] The artist chooses a significant scene and communicates the insight through gesture, colour, position, expression, etc. Artists cannot use abstract words such as 'forgiveness', they have to show forgiveness. If there are projection facilities an artwork can be shown (subject to copyright) and the sermon can be a moving round the artwork showing the insight.

Exercise

Choose a Bible story and decide on one scene from the story that captures a significant insight. Imagine the scene as a painting. Describe your scene in a way that will show the insight. This can be done in words or a rough drawing – pin people with notes. Be specific concerning placement, gesture, expression, etc. How could this feed into a sermon in a showing style?

Once you have your 'picture' in your mind of a scene you can use the language of showing as part of presenting the scene to the congregation. You may invite them to imagine the scene with you. A scene based on John 8.1–11 might read as follows:

> There is the woman, her hair loose, her clothing dishevelled. She is kneeling, she is too frightened to lift her head, too ashamed. The men stand above her, they are not dishevelled, they wear the clothes of power. Their heads are up, secure in the knowledge that they are in the right. The Temple towers above them all.

Synoptic art

Synoptic art has more than one scene from a story in a frame or boundary of some sort and the scenes are not in the same order as the original story. Lorenzo Ghiberti's *Jacob and Esau* has seven scenes from the story in one frame but not in the order of the biblical story.[10] Preachers can use this style in preparation by noting the different scenes in a biblical story on pieces of paper and then arranging them in various ways to see what insights arise from different combinations. Not all the combinations need exploring and not all combinations will yield insights. Once you have a key combination that yields an insight, note how it is embodied.

Naboth's vineyard is a scenic story. The text can be divided into different scenes and different moments within scenes that can be paired in various ways. This exercise is just a starting point to stimulate thinking. Three examples of pairing follow with their insights and how they are embodied. Once the insight is achieved the process towards showing a situation would continue with the focus on the two major scenes.

A *Scene 1:* The palace. Ahab sulks because he is denied the vineyard.
  Scene 2: The vineyard. Ahab stands in the vineyard that is now his.
  Insight: Ahab gets what he wants but it turns to ashes in his hands because of the way it was obtained. This is embodied in body language, first the sulk, then the standing alone in the vineyard after Elijah departs.

B *Scene 1:* The palace. Ahab sulking.
  Scene 2: The palace. Jezebel acting, writing, sealing the document.
  Insight: Ahab had mental 'lines' created by God's law that he could not cross. He could not force Naboth to give up his vineyard as the

law was on Naboth's side. Ahab went home and sulked. Jezebel had no such lines so she acted. This is embodied in mental lines created in Ahab's mind by the law. These are metaphorical lines that can be expressed physically in a sermon by stepping either side of an imaginary line or drawing a line in the air. A metaphorical line may not be physical but it is real, it draws on the physical reality of a line.

C *Scene 1:* The palace. Ahab letting Jezebel act.
Scene 2: The vineyard. The doom pronounced by Elijah.
Insight: Doing nothing does not cancel responsibility. This is embodied in Ahab's clean hands. No ink stained his hands – he did not sign the death warrant. No blood stained his hands – he did not throw the stones that killed Naboth. But to God they were ink-stained, blood-stained hands. Hand gestures can be used by the preacher.

Note: Sometimes an insight is embodied in what is missing but possibly should be there, as in this last example concerning Ahab. In such cases it is the absence that is embodied – as it is in Ahab's clean hands. A sermon may open with a very physical reference to those hands and end with how God sees them in the light of Elijah's condemnation:

Exercise

Choose a biblical narrative with several scenes. Divide it into scenes (or differing moments within scenes) and pair them in various ways. What insights arise from the different combinations? Note how they are embodied.

Simultaneous art

This style often consists of a main image with images of one or more different stories included to indicate how the main story is to be understood. An example of this is Stanley Spencer's *The Resurrection with the Raising of Jairus' Daughter*.[11] By including the resurrection at the end of time in this painting Spencer invites us to read the raising of Jairus' daughter as a foretaste of the resurrection. It is the start of the rolling back of the domain of sin and death initiated by Christ's own resurrection but also indicated by his raising of the dead child.

Exercise

Choose a main story for your sermon and choose a significant scene from it. What other image from a different biblical story would you include to enrich the understanding of the main story and show how it is to be read?

Sermon critique

I have deliberately included a complete sermon here to encourage critical assessment of how an artwork may function within a sermon. In this sermon I drew on Rembrandt's etching of *Abraham Entertaining the Angels*.[12] I was able to show most of the artworks mentioned and they can all be viewed online. Only the figures of Abraham and Sarah were shown from the Rembrandt etching, not the whole artwork.

Exercise

Look at the sermon on *Abraham and the Three Visitors* and respond to the following questions thinking through reasons for your answers:

- How is art used in this sermon? (More than one use can be identified.)
- A number of artworks are referenced. Is it too many?
- Many of the artworks were shown, was that necessary? Could it have worked without showing them?
- How could the art have been used more effectively or differently?
- What do you think the artworks added to the sermon?
- In what ways might the artworks have detracted from the preaching on the biblical passage?
- Does the structure (prologue and long reflective epilogue) work or does it need a different structure?

SERMON: ABRAHAM AND THE THREE VISITORS, GENESIS 18.1–15

Prologue

The story of Abraham and the three visitors takes us back to around 1800 BC. It takes us into the story of an elderly, childless couple. The events take place in Mamre in the south of Canaan. Many years before, Abraham and Sarah had left their homeland to follow God's call with a promise that they would become a great nation. When they arrived in Canaan the promise was made more specific, this would be their land and they would have descendants, too many to number. The couple settled in Mamre for a while, a place shaded with trees, then they moved on. But Mamre was the place they returned to time after time, it is the place where they were later buried.

The years go by and the promise becomes a covenant but still no son, still no land to call their own. Abraham and Sarah continue to live a wandering life on the fringes of society. When Abraham is a hundred and still childless, God confirms his promise that Abraham will have a son, and Abraham laughs. It is after this event that our story occurs.

Pause.

It is the hottest part of the day and the sweat breaks on Abraham's skin; retreating from the heat he seeks shelter beneath the tree under which he has pitched the tent. Abraham sits in front of the tent, slumped forward, his elbows resting on his knees. Sarah rests inside the tent. They are grateful for the shade and this break in the day's routine. They have been on the move for twenty-five years, but they often come back to Mamre. The tree they rest under has seen them change over the years. It saw them in the early days, not long after they had left their homeland. They were full of hope then, for God had promised that they would be a great nation. The tree has seen them many times since. It has, no doubt, heard prayers of distress when no child came. It has seen hope rise each time God restated the promise, it has witnessed their hope grow weary. Now, after twenty-five years of waiting, Abraham and Sarah rest once more beneath a great tree at Mamre, an elderly couple reconciled to a life without children, their hopes tamed by time and disappointment. A blanket of resignation has settled over them.

Abraham does not see the strangers coming, he just looks up and there they are. They stand at a short distance, showing they pose no threat, waiting to be invited closer. Abraham snaps out of his reverie and runs to greet them; visitors are few and far between. He bows low, not so easy to do now; he has difficulty getting up. Abraham offers the customary hospitality of a wash, bread and water. The sleepy scene of minutes before becomes all action, Abraham rises, runs and hurries, he organizes the finest bread to be made, fresh meat, milk and yogurt – food that went way beyond the customary bread and water. He puts the feast before his guests, but this is not fast food, this is cooking from scratch Bedouin style. Hours must have passed but we are told nothing of that time. All we know is that Abraham and his visitors spent time together.

The meal over, the visitors speak and ask where Sarah is. Abraham does not ask how they know his wife's name; it has been slowly dawning on him that these are not ordinary visitors. 'In the tent,' says Abraham. The visitors knew of course, she was just behind them, listening to every word, ear close to the tent flap. The visitors tell Abraham that this time next year Sarah will give birth to a son. The words are directed to Sarah via Abraham, as was polite. Strangers would not speak directly to a host's wife. Abraham says nothing. It is momentous news, but Abraham greets it with silence. He has heard it all before. Sarah hears the words and laughs to herself, just as her husband had laughed on an earlier occasion. She is old, Abraham is old and worn out and her body is long past child-bearing. It's laughable, it is bitterly laughable. She had welcomed this promise twenty-five years ago, but now it is too late. The secret laughter is known to the visitors and they ask if anything is too hard for God. The question is left hanging. It is not answered.

Epilogue

We leave Abraham and Sarah watching the visitors go.
They have done everything a good host should;
they have shown lavish hospitality,
well beyond what was expected.
They have ticked all the boxes for being hospitable
except one.
They have not been hospitable to the news these strangers brought.
They had an open home
but they were no longer open to hope.
The message of hope was met with silence and bitter laughter.

Late in life Rembrandt drew this scene,
not one of his great masterpieces
but a small etching.
He drew an elderly Sarah behind a door that is almost closed,

she stands in darkness.
He drew Abraham as a man bowed down and weary.
This couple were worn out by waiting
and can we blame them?
If they dared to believe, it would dredge up hope again
when they had adjusted to disappointment.
They had made life bearable by reducing their expectations.

At the end of the visit, Abraham and Sarah are left with a question,
'Is anything too difficult for God?'
This story does not tell us their response.
If they answer, 'Yes, some things are too difficult for God,'
they are left without hope.
If they answer, 'No, nothing is too difficult for God,'
they run the risk of raising their hopes after they have adjusted to the
situation.
The question is left unanswered by the elderly couple,
but it is answered by God.
A year later Isaac is born.

Rembrandt drew Abraham and Sarah when he was at rock bottom.
The drawing is dated 1656, the year he was declared bankrupt:
he lost his house,
all his goods were sold at auction,
he no longer owned a single one of his paintings.
This disaster came at the end of a long and difficult time for Rembrandt:
his wife had died,
he was ageing,
he had been in trouble with the authorities,
his biblical painting went out of fashion,
he was hounded by his creditors,
he was completely broke.
Everything came to a head in 1656,
the year he created the drawing of Abraham and Sarah.
Bankruptcy must have felt like the final nail in the coffin of his career.
But some of his greatest paintings were created after 1656,
paintings that often focus on relationships:
The Return of the Prodigal Son, *Jacob Blessing the Sons of Joseph* and
the incredibly tender *Isaac and Rebecca* also known as *The Jewish
Bride*.
Hope was born for Rembrandt in a time of despair, anxiety and grief.
We see that despair in the way he drew Abraham and Sarah.

If God had sent an angel to Rembrandt in 1656 to tell him that he
was about to enter his period of greatest creativity, I think Rembrandt
would have laughed, and it would have been bitter laughter. Such
a message would have felt like mockery. Like Abraham and Sarah,
I doubt he would have welcomed the message.

Hope spoken too brightly when we despair
only serves to underline our broken state.
When we feel hope-less, hope sometimes needs to be whispered.
It needs to be offered gently
or even silently, a squeeze of the hand, an arm round the shoulder.
A shy hope can be nurtured in the heart
and allowed to grow quietly.[13]

When we are at rock bottom,
exhausted,
at the end of our resources,
God sometimes calls us to the emotional risk
of accepting the hope he offers.
This is not easy when all we want to do is rein life in,
reduce our expectations
and settle for less.

Probably two of Rembrandt's most hopeful paintings
were painted after 1656.
They are *The Return of the Prodigal Son*
and *Simeon in the Temple Praising God*.
The painting of Simeon was still on Rembrandt's easel, unfinished,
when he died.
The painting is a bit of a mess,
but we can still see Rembrandt's work.
Rembrandt paints Simeon with eyes half-closed,
we get the impression his sight is almost gone.
This is a man who has waited for this moment all his life.
He finally sees the Messiah, Jesus.
Hope radiates from him in light,
for the hope of the world is embodied in the child in his arms.
Rembrandt restricts the colours he uses,
and those he does use are soft and glowing,
nothing dazzles.
The figures are misty, nothing is clearly outlined.
This is not an image that confronts us,

this is shy but deep hope in paint.
If we look closely, Simeon does not embrace the child,
his hands point forward,
open in praise.
The baby merely rests on his arms.
This is hope accepted but not grasped.

Hope takes courage.
It is daring the future to be different.
It is not made of grand gestures;
we do not all paint pictures like Rembrandt,
or found nations like Abraham and Sarah.
Hope is the way we live in the world day by day.

When the Israelites were at rock bottom,
in exile, far from home,
mourning the loss of loved ones and nation,
God told them to live hopefully.
He told them to do ordinary things,
to plant, to marry and have children.
These are hopeful acts that look to the future.
Hope is not necessarily something we feel,
it is something we do.

We are called to live hopefully,
to build relationships,
to engage in activities that look to the future –
of this world and the people in it.
Despair turns us inward.
God's hope turns us outwards.
How we live today
shows the world we believe in God's tomorrow.[14]

Exploring art

Many people feel baffled when viewing an artwork, and that is fine. All that is needed is a commitment to look. The looking involved is not the brief glance that happens in galleries, but the long look, the detailed look of contemplation and prayer. This can be followed by research into the painting, there are lots of art websites that help in researching an artwork. When beginning to explore an artwork some of the questions below may help. Not every question relates to every artwork, select what you think applies to the artwork you are exploring.

Exercise

Choose an artwork that relates to a biblical story and research it online. After spending time in prayer and contemplation with the biblical text and the artwork, select some questions that you feel relate to it. When you have done this think of questions the text and the artwork may be asking you. Some questions to ask of an artwork are listed below, only a few will apply to any particular artwork, select which ones are appropriate to the work you have chosen.

To begin
What are your first impressions?
Does anything surprise you? What do you find perplexing?
Does the image trigger any associations?
How may this image help you understand the story it depicts?
What questions may the image be asking? How do you respond?

Relationships
How is power (or the lack of it) expressed in this image?
What do expressions and body language tell you? (Recreate some of them.)
What do the clothes convey?
What relationships can you detect?
What speech or thought bubbles would you add to show what people are thinking or saying?

Composition
Are there dominant colours? What effect do they have?
What mood has the artist created?
Locate some details that you think may be significant.
Does the image form a meaningful shape or is it from a particular viewpoint?
In photographic terms, is it a close-up or a long shot?
What is to the fore and highlighted? What is in the background and hidden or in shadow?
Look closely at the centre and the edges. What is going on in these spaces?

Is the setting natural or is it of human construction? How would you describe the setting?

Note the weather and the season. What role are these playing?

Does the way light and shade are used tell you anything?

Conclusion

Art can have many roles in preaching and preachers do not have to be well versed in art to use it. It can contribute to preaching at any stage, from preparation to delivery. Art can help preachers show a narrative, an idea or a quality; it can bring depth and add a reflective aspect to preaching.

Notes

1 *The Visual Commentary on Scripture* (2018), https://thevcs.org/, accessed 14.11.2021.

2 Jenee Woodward, *The Text This Week* (1997–2020), http://www.textweek.com/, accessed 14.11.2021.

3 Jann Cather Weaver et al., 1994, 1995, 1996, *Imaging the Word*, 3 vols, Cleveland: United Church Press.

4 Paolo Veronese, *The Feast in the House of Levi* (oil on canvas, 1573; Gallerie dell' Accademia, Venice).

5 Jean-Fran François Millet, *The Gleaners* (oil on canvas, 1857; Musée d'Orsay, Paris).

6 Simone Martini, *Annunciation with St Margaret and St Ansanus* (tempera and gold on wood, 1333; Uffizi Gallery, Florence).

7 El Greco, *Christ Driving the Traders from the Temple* (oil on canvas, c.1600; National Gallery, London).

8 Margaret Cooling, 'The Last Supper and the Feast at the House of Levi', *Preaching that Shows*, https://preachingthatshows.com/2018/10/12/the-last-supper-and-the-feast-at-the-house-of-levi-the-party-for-sinners/, accessed 14.11.2021.

9 Leonardo da Vinci, *The Last Supper* (tempera and oil on plaster, 1495–8; Santa Maria Delle Grazie, Milan).

10 Lorenzo Ghiberti, *The Gates of Paradise: Jacob and Esau* (gilt bronze relief panels, 1425–52; Museo dell'Opera di Santa Maria Del Fiore, Florence).

11 Stanley Spencer, *The Resurrection with the Raising of Jairus' Daughter* (oil on canvas, 1947; Southampton City Art Gallery, Southampton).

12 Rembrandt, *Abraham Entertaining the Angels* (etching, 1656; Rijksmuseum, Amsterdam).

13 'A shy hope in the heart' is a phrase coined by Gary D. Bouma, 2006, *Australian Soul*, Cambridge: Cambridge University Press.

14 Margaret Cooling, 'Abraham and the Three Visitors', *Preaching that Shows*, https://preachingthatshows.com/2019/07/21/abraham-and-the-three-visitors-whispered-hope/, accessed 14.11.2021.

5

Every Picture Tells a Story?

Throughout this book I refer to art as a source and model of the rev-elatory plot and ways in which art can help preachers create narrative sermons in a revelatory manner. There is, however, a question mark concerning art's ability to tell a story. If art can't narrate then it can't be used as a model for revelatory preaching, which is a narrative form. Two types of art have already been mentioned: sequential (such as comics and paintings in a series) and continuous (such as the Bayeux Tapestry). Few people would doubt that these styles of art tell stories. The question mark hangs over the three types of art encountered in Chapter 4: monoscenic, synoptic and simultaneous. Can these styles of art tell stories? This chapter explores the issues this question raises and some of the hesitancies that preachers may feel about using art as part of preaching.

Telling a story visually

Stories can be told in many ways: they can be told through drama, oral storytelling, dance, music, written word and art. Each form has its own unique way of narrating. When encountering visual narration, it helps to begin by engaging with it on its own terms rather than starting by comparing it with written or oral narration. Any assessment of visual narration of biblical stories comes after the initial engagement.

Telling Naomi's story

Before discussing the issues or looking at the hesitancies some people may have concerning using art in preaching, it may help to see visual storytelling at work. By experiencing visual storytelling, you can begin to judge the ability of art to narrate.

In 1795 William Blake painted two watercolours: *Christ Appearing to the Apostles After the Resurrection*[1] and *Naomi Entreating Ruth and Orpah to Return to the Land of Moab*.[2] Look at these images online. The painting of the risen Christ and the Apostles depicts the moment when Jesus says, 'Behold my hands and feet.' The painting of Naomi is the scene where she begs her daughters-in-law (Ruth and Orpah) to return to their families. Look closely at the two images. What do you notice? Look at Naomi's stance and look at Christ. Blake paints Naomi and Christ in the same pose. The risen Christ bears the marks of sacrificial death on his hands and feet. Naomi's hands are scarred by hard work; they have dug graves for her husband and sons. Her feet are those of a refugee who has walked from her homeland when famine struck. Blake has realized something significant about the book of Ruth.

By painting Naomi in the stance of the resurrected Christ, Blake asks us to read the story of Ruth in a different way. He asks us to see it as Naomi's story, a story of death, sacrifice and metaphorical resurrection. It is a story of deprivation, sorrow and death that ends in new life. Blake has painted the moment when Naomi frees Ruth and Orpah of any responsibility to look after her. This is her moment of sacrifice. In the scene that Blake paints, all Naomi knows is loss and grief, she does not know that her sacrifice and Ruth's commitment is the turning point of her life. From now on death will not be the defining experience of her existence. She will now experience a life surrounded by a new family, friends and eventually a grandchild. Naomi sees this moment of returning to Bethlehem as an end, she feels rejected by God, but with God ends can become beginnings. Naomi is about to experience a form of resurrection. God often works in ways we do not expect. God has far from abandoned Naomi, he brings hope and new life, but he does it through a foreigner, her daughter-in-law, Ruth. Blake only shows us the moment of self-sacrifice and Ruth's commitment, but Naomi's resurrection stance tells us that new life is about to begin.[3]

Question

How is the art telling Naomi's story? Is it doing anything more than just telling the story?

Telling a story and more

It may help to put the use of Christian art in its historical context. Historically, narrative art was used in worship, for teaching, for interpreting
a text and for contemplation. Religious instruction was often in visual
narrative form but it was not just telling the story, it had an interpretive
role. In medieval manuscripts sometimes the art gave the basic storyline
and the text drew out the spiritual significance. At other times, the position reversed with the art interpreting the text's spiritual importance.[4]

With the artist Giotto (1266–1337), a change began. He emphasized
empathy and emotional engagement. This reflected a new imaginative and
meditative way of reading the Bible. With Giotto, painting became like a
stage where the drama of human relationships and feelings were played
out and people were invited to join in emotionally.[5] Giotto's *Lamentation*
is probably the most well known example of this style.[6] Narrative biblical painting also began to reflect the world more realistically; people
saw biblical characters dressed in clothes like theirs, in street scenes
they recognized. This enabled people to identify with the characters and
situations, perceiving their contemporary significance. An example of this
approach is Pieter Bruegel the Elder, whose biblical paintings are set in
ordinary Flemish villages and towns. In *The Census at Bethlehem*, Mary
and Joseph are no bigger than anyone else, they do not have halos, there
is no spiritual glow. They are just a peasant couple in a crowded town.[7]
Sometimes trying to find the sacred figures in Bruegel's paintings is like a
'Where's Wally?' puzzle. The theological significance lies in the ordinary
nature of Bruegel's scenes; it demonstrates God's choice of the powerless.
Bruegel did more than tell the story.

Biblical narrative art developed roles that were a combination of teaching, contemplation and interpretation. Despite a decline in biblical art
in the late seventeenth and eighteenth centuries, visual biblical narration continued. In the nineteenth and twentieth centuries, artists such
as Holman Hunt, Harriet Powers, Ossawa Tanner, Marc Chagall, John
Muafangejo and Sadao Watanabe all produced biblical narrative artworks. It may feel that biblical art is in decline in many parts of the
Western world but the baton has passed to artists in Asia, Australasia,
Africa and the Americas. The Australian Bible Society's *Our Mob, God's
Story* tells the biblical story from Genesis to Revelation in aboriginal art.[8]
History affirms a complex role for art that goes beyond repeating the
storyline but still asserts that art can narrate.

The original question

We are now back to the original question: Can art tell stories? The debate concerning art's ability to tell stories revolves around three types of art that were introduced in Chapter 4: monoscenic, synoptic and simultaneous art. Can these forms really narrate? You may wonder about the relevance of this debate for preaching, but if art is to be one of the models for revelatory narrative preaching it needs to be demonstrated that it can tell stories. There are five challenges to the ability of monoscenic, synoptic and simultaneous art to narrate.

- Monoscenic art is a single moment. How can monoscenic art, which is about one moment and one scene, tell a story that is made up of many moments and scenes?
- Art is taken in at a glance, everything is seen at once, but stories are told in sequence with one scene following another.
- Art can't express time, it cannot say 'before' or 'after' or indicate time passing. Stories are about things happening in time.
- How can synoptic art, which often muddles the original narrative order, tell a story?
- Simultaneous art contains more than one story in a single frame. How can two or more images, often separated by time and geography, tell a unified story?

A *single moment*

Many people would agree that art is a single moment captured by the artist and therefore art can't narrate. However, this idea is a matter of debate. The question of the single moment goes back to the fifteenth century when Leon Battista Alberti suggested that artists should draw a quadrangle on the canvas to represent an open window and then paint their subject as if seen through a window.[9] The idea of the single moment was born and with it the doubts that paintings of a single scene could tell stories.

Anthony Ashley Cooper, third Lord Shaftesbury (1671–1713), took up this idea and developed it. He maintained that painting represented a single moment and once the artist had chosen that moment all other actions beyond that point were off limits. Despite this, Shaftesbury conceded that the artist could indicate past and future. The artist could show the marks left by tears, pointing to the past action of crying. The future could be shown in various ways, such as showing a character in the act of deciding and indicating the way the decision will go.[10] Over time, the idea that painting *should* only show a single moment became entrenched, leading to people thinking that a painting *could* only show a single moment.[11]

The idea that a painting represents a single moment may seem obvious but a closer look reveals a complex situation. The problem lies in using the standards of photography to judge art. Photography comes much closer to a single moment in time. However, Ernst Gombrich argued that the whole idea of a single moment in time is difficult to achieve, even with cameras, and human beings are not cameras. Every moment is informed by what has just happened and what will follow. When we are reciting one line of text, we are getting ready for the next. The future is, to a degree, present in our minds. The same is true of the past. After we have seen or heard something, both light and sound linger for a while and there is a form of immediate memory before something is stored or lost.[12] Imagine the following situation:

> You are chatting with someone over coffee and for a moment you lose your concentration and drift while they are speaking. They ask you a question and you realize you have missed the last few seconds. Fortunately, you can reach back into your immediate memory and retrieve what was missed and make the appropriate response.

Caravaggio, in his painting *The Supper at Emmaus*, shows what appears to be one moment in time, a moment of recognition when Jesus breaks the bread.[13] Lorenzo Pericolo notes that Caravaggio asks viewers to go beyond that moment and think about the before and after by his dynamic portrayal of the scene. Our knowledge of the story behind the painting and our general experience of life enables us to complete the actions depicted in the painting – art sets still actions into motion.[14]

Art shows characters involved in situations that embody previous decisions and result in future actions. A painting may show neither the decision nor the resulting action. Jack Greenstein notes that paintings of the circumcision of Christ only show a knife. Viewers understand the earlier decision of Mary and Joseph to fulfil the law and they know the ritual that will follow. In this way time is understood as 'folded' into an artwork.[15] It is as if the whole story is drawn on a large piece of translucent paper and folded many times until only one small rectangle is left showing (the scene in the painting), but the rest of the story is faintly visible. The artist decides what piece of the story is left showing but there is still an imprint of past and future. The idea of the single moment, which looked so obvious, is far more complex than it initially appeared to be.

At a glance

Another popular notion is that art can't tell stories because artwork is perceived at a glance, all at once. In contrast, stories are told one scene after another. This is a position taken by Eugene Lowry who maintains that forms that present all at once are not narrative by definition. He underlines the difference between arts of space and arts of time. Painting and sculpture are arts of space. Arts of time are stories, music, poetry and drama. Lowry links the sermon to arts of time: for Lowry, the sermon is in a 'wholly different category' to painting.[16]

Lowry's ideas go back to Gotthold Ephraim Lessing (1729–81) who stressed the differences between arts of time and arts of space, and he thought that each should keep to its own territory. He saw painting's territory as description because it deals in bodies and objects and shows a single 'pregnant' moment. In contrast, the arts of time are about action with one thing following another.[17] This long-held contrast between arts of time and arts of space is now a matter of debate. We may initially perceive an artwork as a whole, creating a first impression, but viewers then scan paintings section by section. This is more like 'reading' a picture. The initial overall impression acts as a frame, into which viewers assemble the parts.[18] This is a little like doing the outside edges of a jigsaw first.

A glance may not tell us much about a painting. Klaus Speidel notes that sometimes artists hide things they want viewers to see last because they are significant and cause viewers to rethink. An example of this technique is Pieter Bruegel the Elder's hiding of Icarus in his painting *Landscape with the Fall of Icarus*. Without the title most people would miss Icarus' drowning and the dead man in the bushes. Viewers admire the pastoral scene that they perceive at a glance and it is only with close inspection that they discover its darker side. The first glance does not tell the whole story.[19]

Question

Look at Bruegel's painting of *Landscape with the Fall of Icarus* online. What is your first glance impression of the painting? Now find Icarus and the dead body. How does it change your understanding of the painting?

Art can't express time

This is another argument that seems obvious; how can art tell the consecutive events of a story when it cannot say 'before' or 'after' or show time passing? Once again, a closer look reveals the situation to be complicated. Art has its own time conventions; pictures may not be able to say 'before' or 'after', but they can show time passing by showing seasons, ages and changes in people and nature. Artists can lead viewers through a story using colour, light, size, and other elements of art. When Nicolas Poussin painted *The Israelites Gathering Manna in the Desert*, he created a painting that could be 'read'.[20] The Israelites in the painting show the different stages (times) of the story in a single image. Some people are hungry, some complaining to Moses, some collecting manna, others praising. The different moments of the story are all there.[21]

Speidel sums up the idea of art not being able to show time by referring to Mandarin Chinese. To insist that a painting can't show time is like saying that sentences in Mandarin Chinese are always referring to the present as it does not have a past and future tense. Mandarin Chinese has its own ways of indicating time that are as natural as English conventions. Art, too, has its own ways of communicating the passage of time.[22]

Muddled order

In synoptic art the scenes are not often in narrative order. Paul Barolsky maintains that any form of synoptic art takes liberties with the timeline of a story. He locates this problem in the different aims of the artist and the narrator. The artist is concerned with making a beautiful composition, whereas the narrator is concerned with telling the story. Ghiberti's *Jacob and Esau* has seven episodes from the story, which are not arranged in the order of the original narrative. They are presented in different ways: some are in high relief (raised), some low; some are large, others small; some are in full view, others are partially hidden. In one sense Barolsky is right, there is a radical disordering of the storyline. Ghiberti's artwork also includes a group of women who are not in the biblical account and puts these in high relief, nearest the viewer, whereas Esau selling his birthright (an important biblical episode) is in low relief and barely visible.[23]

Exercise

Look up Ghiberti's *Jacob and Esau* online and locate:

- Rebekah praying to God.
- Rebekah giving birth.
- Esau selling his birth right for a bowl of lentil stew.
- Isaac asking Esau to hunt for his favourite food.
- Esau going to hunt.
- Rebekah plotting with Jacob.
- Jacob deceiving Isaac with Rebekah looking on.

Synoptic art does muddle the order of narratives but this is common in drama; films would be boring if they had to tell stories in a straightforward manner without flashbacks and flash forwards. Preaching on a narrative does not always follow the order of a biblical story. The main aim of narrative art was not necessarily to tell the story as a sequence of events in the correct order. Artists saw their role differently; they were concerned with meaning, significance, emotional engagement and contemplation. These aims influenced the way they painted; they also overlap with preachers' aims. Synoptic art is not tearing the story apart but rearranging it to explore its depth, to enable the story to be read differently. The example of Ghiberti's artwork may demonstrate the value of synoptic visual narration. The scenes can be connected in different ways. For example, the telling might move vertically downward on the righthand side, moving from Rebekah listening to God, to Rebekah plotting with Jacob and finally to her watching the act of deception.

- The first image evokes the Rebekah who was a woman of faith (Gen. 24; 25.22–23) and the image portrays the moment when she listens to God who tells her that the younger son will take precedence over the older twin.
- The second image fast-forwards to an older Rebekah who is now prepared to plot with her favourite son to *make* the promise come true.
- The third image shows a cold Rebekah watching her son deceive her blind husband.

Connecting the images invites a question, 'What happened to Rebekah to create this change?' It invites questions concerning trying to grasp at what is promised rather than waiting for God's timing and how, as a result, Rebekah loses Jacob who must flee his home.

James Elkins observes that there are two ways of reading an image: there is deductive reading and associative reading. It is the difference between treating a narrative as a puzzle to be solved by analysing it (deductive) or meditating on it allowing associations to be formed in different ways.[24] Both ways of reading can be used at different stages of preparing a sermon.

How can different stories in the same frame tell a unified story?

Artists sometimes put two or more biblical stories in the same painting and those stories may be separated by time and geography. Fra Angelico, in his [Madrid] *Annunciation*, placed an image of Adam and Eve being expelled from Eden in his painting of the angel Gabriel coming to Mary.[25] The artist leaves the viewer to work out the connection. In the case of Fra Angelico's *Annunciation*, the including of Adam and Eve's expulsion from Eden could be indicating Christ as the second Adam (1 Cor. 15.45–48) and could be asking the viewer to 'read' the story of the annunciation in this light.

The doubts concerning the ability of monoscenic, synoptic and simultaneous art to narrate assumes that the main role of art is to tell the story. Once this assumption is challenged and art is allowed to narrate in its own way, while also fulfilling its other roles, many of the problems concerning art's ability to narrate diminish or disappear.

Art and preaching

Some people's first reaction to using art in a preaching context may be negative, which is understandable, for it raises questions such as the ones that follow. Look at the speech bubbles. Do any of these apply to you or members of your congregation?

If any of the responses are yours, this section may help you consider how art can contribute to preaching. If you already use art in preaching, continue with this section, for some members of your congregation may feel hesitant about art being used in sermons and this section explores negative feelings around this issue.

I look at a painting and don't know what I am supposed to feel or think

You may feel that there is something about you or the way you were educated that stops you engaging with art, but art is not some mysterious form of knowledge that only the initiated can appreciate. The art world must take some of the blame for people feeling this way. Some art professionals have created an aura around art that makes people feel that only experts can engage with it. Sometimes it feels like an elitist area that is not for ordinary people, though modern TV programmes on art are dispelling some of those perceptions. We can learn from experts and with a little help we can all engage with art. This chapter is for ordinary preachers, not art experts. Art is for all; it is part of God's gift to the world.

Doesn't the Bible ban art in worship?

The second Commandment appears to take a very negative stance towards art and it is wide ranging:

> You shall not make for yourself an idol, whether in the form of anything that is in heaven above, or that is on the earth beneath, or that is in the water under the earth. You shall not bow down to them or worship them. (Ex. 20.4–5).

The word 'idol' ('graven image' in other translations) is sometimes interpreted as a ban on art in church in case it results in idolatry. This commandment was initiated in a culture where nature worship was an issue, which has led to the tradition of imageless worship within Judaism. The Bible balances the second Commandment with positive attitudes towards art. In Ex. 31.1–11 God gives artistic ability to Bezalel and Oholiab. Both the tabernacle and the temple were artistically decorated (Ex. 25—29; 31.1–11; 1 Kings 6) and some synagogues (Huqoq and Dura-Europos) have been discovered that are decorated with paintings and mosaics of biblical stories.[26]

Art is found in Christian contexts from the third century but there were several controversies concerning the use of images. In AD 787 the Council of Nicaea decreed that the humanity of Jesus could be represented in churches and Mary, angels and saints and the Scriptures could be presented artistically. The Council distinguished between worship that belonged to God alone and reverence that can be due an image. The Christian Church has been a major art patron for most of its history.

Most art is copyright and we can't afford to pay for it

This is correct, a lot of art is subject to copyright laws. However, increasingly galleries are releasing some of their works under open access/public domain or other forms of free non-commercial usage. The Victoria and Albert Museum, the Rijksmuseum, the National Museum of Sweden, the Getty Educational Open Content Project are just a few examples. Look up their terms of use. Often an email to a gallery will clarify the terms of use if it is at all unclear. Always check.

We rely on the Bible, not art

The statement 'We only use the Bible' may be spoken as a genuine concern to stay biblical, however, no one *only* uses the Bible; preachers draw on their own understanding, scholars and other Christians. Only using the Bible seems to imply that the Holy Spirit is no longer active, whereas many Christians will bear witness to the Spirit inspiring hymn writers, artists, poets, scholars and musicians. An artist's interpretation of a text always needs evaluating against Scripture, but that is true of commentaries, the lyrics of Christian songs and many other sources that preachers draw on.

We don't have the facilities to show paintings in our church

Not every church has the facility to project art. This need not be a barrier; learning from artists – past and present – is not necessarily about showing the image to the congregation. Preachers do not generally show commentaries they have used when they preach. Assuming art has to be shown may reflect an assumption that art's role is illustration. This is the way many preachers use art – a visual image to sit alongside text, something to brighten up a sermon. The art is not there in its own right. Art, however, can have a number of roles in preaching that go beyond illustration to include interpretation, contemplation, emotional engagement and information. Art can illuminate.

> ## Question
>
> Which of the objections above are likely to be a factor for you or your congregation? If you wanted to use art, how would you overcome people's hesitancy?

Conclusion

Monoscenic, synoptic and simultaneous art narrate but they do this on their own terms. Visual narration is complex and engages viewers in interpretation and contemplation as well as storytelling. Art is seldom a straightforward rehearsal of the storyline; narrative art is an invitation to active engagement not passive viewing.

Notes

1 William Blake, *Christ Appearing to the Apostles After the Resurrection* (watercolour print, ink and varnish on paper, *c*.1795; Tate Gallery, London).

2 William Blake, *Naomi Entreating Ruth and Orpah to Return to the Land of Moab* (fresco print on paper with watercolour, 1795; Victoria and Albert Museum, London).

3 'William Blake and the Book of Ruth', unpublished talk. See also Margaret Cooling, 'Naomi', *Preaching that Shows*, https://preachingthatshows.com/2018/10/11/naomi/, accessed 14.11.2021.

4 Herbert L. Kessler, 1994, *Studies in Pictorial Narrative*, London: Pindar Press, pp. 25, 35–6.

5 Hans Belting, 'The New Role of Narrative in Public Painting of the Trecento: "Historia" and Allegory', *Studies in the History of Art*, 16 (1985), 151–68 (pp. 151–3) https://www.jstor.org/stable/42617840?seq=1, accessed 14.11.2021.

6 Giotto, *Lamentation* (fresco, 1304–1306; Scrovegni Chapel, Padua).

7 Pieter Bruegel the Elder, *The Census at Bethlehem* (oil on wood panel, 1566; Royal Museums of Fine Arts of Belgium, Brussels).

8 Louise Sherman and Christobel Mattingley (eds), 2017, *Our Mob, God's Story*, Sydney: Bible Society Australia.

9 Leon Battista Alberti, 1966, *On Painting*, New Haven: Yale University Press, pp. 56–8.

10 Anthony Ashley Cooper, 1790, *Characteristics of Men, Manners, Opinions, Times*, Basil: J. J. Tourneisen and J. L. Legrand, pp. 294–7.

11 Klaus Speidel, 'Can a Single Still Picture Tell a Story? Definitions of Narrative and the Alleged Problem of Time with Single Still Pictures', *Diegesis*, 2/1 (2013), 173–94 (p. 185). https://www.diegesis.uni-wuppertal.de/index.php/diegesis/article/view/128/159, accessed 14.11.2021.

12 E. H. Gombrich, 'Moment and Movement in Art', *Journal of the Warburg and Courtauld Institutes*, 27 (1964), 293–306 (pp. 297–300). https://doi.org/10.2307/750521.

13 Caravaggio, *The Supper at Emmaus* (oil on canvas, 1601; National Gallery, London).

14 Lorenzo Pericolo, 2011, *Caravaggio and Pictorial Narrative*, London: Harvey Miller, pp. 6–7, 79–81.

15 Jack M. Greenstein, 1992, *Mantegna and Painting as Historical Narrative*, Chicago: University of Chicago Press, pp. 150–2.

16 Eugene L. Lowry, 2012, *The Homiletical Beat*, Nashville: Abingdon Press, pp. 1–3, 8, 46.

17 Gotthold, Ephraim Lessing, 1887, *Lacoon*, Boston: Roberts Brothers, pp. 16–17, 21, 59, 91–2; 109–12.

18 Lew Andrews, 1995, *Story and Space in Renaissance Art*, Cambridge: Cambridge University Press, pp. 48–53.

19 Speidel, 'Can a Single Still Picture Tell a Story?' pp. 189–90.

20 Nicolas Poussin, *The Israelites Gathering Manna in the Desert* (oil on canvas, 1637–1639; Louvre, Paris).

21 Pericolo, *Caravaggio*, pp. 79–80, 89–90, 101.

22 Speidel, 'Can a Single Still Picture Tell a Story?', pp. 185–6.

23 P. Barolsky, 'There Is No Such Thing as Narrative Art', *Arion*, 18 (2010), pp. 49–62 (pp. 49–57, 60). www.jstor.org/stable/27896816, accessed 14.11.2021.

24 James Elkins, 'On the Impossibility of Stories: The Anti-Narrative and Non-Narrative Impulse in Modern Painting', *Word & Image*, 7 (1991), pp. 348–64 (pp. 354–5, 358–9). http://dx.doi.org/10.1080/02666286.1991.10435883.

25 Fra Angelico, *The Annunciation and Expulsion of Adam and Eve* (tempera and gold on panel, 1425–6; Museo del Prado, Madrid).

26 Jodi Magnes et al., 'Explore the Huqoq Mosaics' (2019), *Biblical Archaeological Society*, https://www.biblicalarchaeology.org/%20scholars-study/more-on-the-mosaics/, accessed 14.11.2021. Hagith Sivan, 'Dura-Europos Synagogue Paintings' (2019), *The Torah.com*, https://www.thetorah.com/article/retelling-the-story-of-moses-at-dura-europos-synagogue, accessed 14.11.2021.

6

Creating Sermons that Show

This chapter looks at creating sermons that show using a revelatory approach. A revelatory approach could suggest a range of sermon designs but this chapter develops just one that brings three key characteristics to the fore: character, insight and showing. Other characteristics tend to follow or can be included as appropriate for each sermon. The way the sermon begins and ends is covered in the next chapter. This sermon design involves three processes as part of sermon preparation, but the resulting sermon does not have a particular structure to work through.

- Creating a living text: unfolding or unpacking the text to expose the realities of the characters and the situation in which they exist.
- Locating an insight: discovering an insight and noting how it is embodied, how it is known through the senses.
- Showing: selecting and crafting material from the living text that will deliver the insight and show it for the congregation to see.

Extracts from sermons are used to demonstrate the process throughout this chapter. Central to any sermon preparation is prayer and sensitivity to the work of the Holy Spirit. This frames the whole process and is assumed. Although this process works backwards to an original event, parables can be preached in this way even though they make no claim to be historical. Parables often paint vivid pictures of real life that can be re-presented in a sermon while making it clear that it is a parable.

Creating a living text

Creating a living text has two stages: exposing the realities followed by scholarship and reflection. The initial stage exposes the realities embedded in the text, these may be physical, social, emotional, spiritual, political and economic. The process works backwards to an original event that caused the text to be written, where the text signals that, without assuming that we can know *exactly* what happened. The focus is on the event as presented in the text. The second process involves stepping back to engage with scholarship and taking time to reflect.

1 *Exposing the realities*

The initial process starts with immersion in the biblical narrative, reading it slowly and many times, trying to see what is there. This type of seeing does not come naturally but takes practice, as we are used to skimming. Starting in this way roots preparation deeply in the text. The preacher works backwards from the text to the event that the narrative reflects, the event that caused the narrative to be written. This is creating a living text. It returns biblical narratives to lived realities including the people, settings, textures, actions, smells, tastes, sounds and other narrative aspects available to the senses. This means going through the narrative many times and asking questions such as:

- What is happening?
- What could be sensed in terms of smells, sounds, sights, textures and tastes?
- Describe the setting.
- What is the mood?
- What are people doing, saying, thinking?
- What emotions may be present?
- What might have been the spiritual impact on the characters? How is this sensed? What is it in the texts that lets you know what the spiritual impact is?
- What might have been happening to relationships, including the relationship with God? How is this made known?

Notice that questions that particularly relate to meaning come towards the end. It is the questions that help us to get to know the character in their physical setting that are asked at the beginning. The questions will change depending on the different types of narratives but they should expose the characters and the physical, socio-economic, emotional, relational, political and spiritual realities of the situation they are in. Not all aspects may be present in every narrative but many may be.

What Jochebed knew

The position from which the preacher works matters. If we ask questions of the text from outside a narrative, we can end up with a scenario that is very different to that experienced by the characters. When we engage with a narrative, we have the privilege of an overview and hindsight, both of which can lead to simplifying issues and circumstances. The characters in stories have neither overview nor hindsight – they don't know the ending and they experienced the events amid the detail of daily living. With an overview we can see what is significant and what isn't. The characters had no such view.

In the story of the birth of Moses (Ex. 1.22—2.10) we are told what was happening to the slaves in Egypt through focusing on one family. What Jochebed (Moses' mum, named in Ex. 6.20) knew was limited by her situation and what she could perceive within the plethora of detail that is daily life. There was no one whispering in her ear saying, 'Don't worry, it all ends well.' For Jochebed, significant events did not come with emojis signalling their status. The important moments may have been obvious but, like us, she would have had to work out the significance of most happenings within the busyness of life. Questions should be asked of a narrative from within the narrative, addressing the characters in their situation bearing in mind what they could know and what they experienced. This only needs rough notes as below. The rough notes may be more explicit than the final sermon. Pastoral concerns are a priority.

> General: Not many places to hide a baby in a slave home, it would not have been large. Shift system to take care of the baby. They could not let the baby cry. Did they plan what they were going to do during the pregnancy? Did they hope for a girl?

> Jochebed: Constant rocking and soothing. Exhausted mother continually breast feeding. Sleeping lightly, awake at the first sound. Terrified of the sounds of soldiers coming through the settlement, banging doors, shouts, the sobbing of other parents. Where was God in this? Urgent prayers to God to save her baby. Making most of every day with the baby as she doesn't know how long she will have him.

A living text is not an attempt to get behind the text to the author's world, as that could be different to the world reflected in the text. However, author direction in the form of stylistic and descriptive details and comments may indicate ways in which the narrative may be unfolded. Careful attention is paid to what is happening to characters as whole people: body, mind, spirit and emotions.

A word of warning

The story of Moses contains violence against children. The threat should not be ignored, but it should be approached sensitively, through the fear of the parents rather than any detail concerning violence done to children. To dwell on the violent and sexual nature of some biblical stories would be pastorally insensitive. This is not about avoiding difficult texts; it is about how they are handled and how far someone enters a story or what parts of the story they enter. There are some stories that need a more distanced approach for pastoral reasons.

Exercise

Bearing in mind Miriam's role in the story, what would Miriam have known and experienced? Make a few rough notes.

Unfolding

The word 'unfolding' is used to describe what the preacher does to a biblical narrative to create a living text. Biblical narration is often compressed and lacking in detail – sometimes just a few words may cover a large part of a story. Such shorthand in narration would not have been a problem for a biblical audience, as many people shared a common culture and way of life and there would have been little need to fill in details. The same assumptions do not apply to a modern congregation.

The compact biblical narration needs to be unfolded or expanded; otherwise congregations read across a narrative rather than being drawn into it. An instance of this is Exodus 2.2b where it says of Moses' mother that 'she hid him for three months'. Members of a congregation would understand the words to the extent that they could probably repeat it and could say what the statement means in terms of definition. Nevertheless, the level of understanding could be shallow unless the verse is unfolded and its realities exposed, showing what it would mean to hide a baby for three months. Reading across a narrative means that people register it but do not penetrate a narrative at any depth, the eye or ear travels on to the next part of the story. With the revelatory approach, forward movement – so characteristic of the resolution plot – is often checked and the moment expanded to understand what a statement would mean in real terms.

Recreating the mess

The family must have lived through the practicalities of hiding a baby: the physical exhaustion, the boring repetitive actions of soothing and rocking, the physical effects of constant breast feeding, plus still having to work – I doubt slaves got parental leave. Most of all they would have lived with constant fear, maybe feeling that God had abandoned them. Moses' family, like modern believers, lived amid the detail that is daily life. Life is messy and seeing the hand of God at work is not easy. Creating a living text recreates a little of the mess and detail; it gives the preacher the raw material to craft into a finished sermon later. A sermon that creates a little of the real-life detail allows the congregation to see the full humanity of biblical people. The characters step out of the tunic and sandals stereotype and are freed to speak across generations, one exhausted mother to modern exhausted people, one father feeling helpless speaking to others who know a little of that feeling, even though the context may be very different. Creating a living text does not make the text relevant; it begins to reveal the relevance that is already there.

This story is often preached as an example of providence but that is the privilege of hindsight. It is doubtful that Moses' parents said, 'this is all part of God's plan' when facing such a terrible situation. Sometimes sermons present a simplified version of life that can be pastorally unhelpful. The combination of hindsight and simplification can increase the disconnect between the biblical text and modern life.

More practical help

None of the details in my example of rough notes are in the text, but they are implied in the text. How do preachers draw out those implications? Well-known writers in this area have a number of practical suggestions.

- Paul Scott Wilson suggests bringing out the implications by asking questions such as 'who, what, why, when and where' and questions related to the senses.[1]
- Thomas Long suggests exploring categories such as cognitive elements, emotional elements and behavioural elements.[2]
- Thomas Troeger suggests physically going through some of the movements and actions recorded in the text.[3]

Richard Swanson suggests asking placement questions about each scene in a biblical narrative, because where people are and what they can see and hear matters. He asks:

- Who is present in this scene?
- How are they arranged?
- What do people see or hear?
- What physical contact happens?[4]

Whatever method is used, the narrative reality can be turned into a living text by the preacher asking, 'what would this mean in real terms?' The word 'real' covers the physical, emotional, spiritual, relational, socio-economic and political realities – whatever is appropriate to the passage.

> **Exercise**
>
> Using the story of Jairus' daughter (Mark 5.21–43), write the name of each character in the story on separate pieces of paper. The crowd can be represented as a group on one piece of paper. Read through the text moving the character papers about to represent the movement of the characters in the story. Ask yourself some of the questions suggested in this chapter as you move the characters around. What do you notice?

Example

Below are some questions to ask of the story of Jesus' baptism (Luke 3.1–22) as part of creating a living text. Luke states that Jesus was baptized along with others; it was not a private ceremony. This means that Jesus waited with others on the bank of the river. Taking just this initial scene, preachers can ask a range of questions.

- Who came to be baptized?
- Why did they come? What might have been weighing on their hearts?
- Not all would have been dramatic sins, what mundane wrongs may have motivated people to come to John?
- What might have been their body posture?
- How might they have responded to one another? Do some try to keep their distance, not wanting to be associated with certain members of the crowd? Do some cling together?
- How might Jesus have responded to the people around him while he waited?

We don't know exactly why people came to John except that it was for baptism for forgiveness of sins. Just labelling people 'sinners' is too general; it is difficult to relate to a general group and the word 'sinners' immediately sends a signal to Christians not to align with them. The text indicates some sins; others can be suggested to bring a sense of real people in real situations facing real issues. Is this just speculation? This raises the issue of adding details not given in the text, a subject discussed in the next chapter.

2 Scholarship and reflection

Immersion in the text is followed by stepping back and drawing on scholarship relevant to the text, using commentaries and books on cultural and political background. It is impossible to unfold a text without exploring the narrative in depth, including its socio-economic and political background as well as its theological import. Background includes ways of thinking, believing and attitudes, not just customs and lifestyle. This roots the narrative in time and place, always bearing in mind it is the narrative reality that is the focus. The academic research may cause a revision of the initial rough notes that constituted the living text, as modern assumptions may have been made. It also adds to the notes aspects preachers may have missed. Art can be used alongside written scholarship as a visual commentary. The standing back from immersion also allows time for the preacher to reflect, which needs a certain amount of distance.

Locating an insight

As the living text is created insights tend to be revealed, but the whole story should be turned into a living text as more than one insight may be present. Insights reveal a little of the true nature of something as already noted.

- A gesture may give an insight into what someone is feeling.
- An action may tell something about a person's character.
- An object may be full of meaning.
- A sound or speech may communicate an insight into an issue.

Insights are embodied in things reflected in texts: in the physical situation, in bodies, in objects, in relationships and in things that can be sensed. We only perceive these things by words when we read a text but, to differing degrees, people can imaginatively 'hear', 'see', 'touch', 'smell' and 'taste' what is read or heard. In the extract from the 'The Wise and Foolish Bridesmaids' the sensation of heavy eyelids and dribbling in sleep are details the congregation may imaginatively be able to sense or at least relate to.

> They wait.
> Boredom sets in.
> Conversation runs out.
> Eyelids become heavy.
> They sleep.
> The dresses crease,
> the make-up shines,
> the hair tumbles forward,
> they dribble.[5]

Insights can also be embodied in atmospheres and feelings detected in texts, but these are usually transmitted through something that can be sensed either directly or indirectly. Even silence can be sensed. It is easy to drift into generalities at this stage, the focus needs to stay on how the insight is embodied. When an insight is revealed, how it is embodied can be located by the preacher asking how they came to recognize the insight. Insights are seldom neatly spelled out in narratives.

In the story of the infant Moses, the insight may be that God's working is often far from clear in the detail of daily living; sometimes people only see the hand of God looking back over their lives. That insight is embodied in the realities of hiding a baby, which probably made it hard to detect what God was doing. Maybe only looking back on the events of Moses' first few months would his parents have seen the hand of God at work. At the time it must have been all fear and hard work. Christians often have similar difficulties in seeing the hand of God at work in the messiness of life. To preach the Moses story as God's providence, without engaging in the realities and ordinary human responses, could leave the congregation thinking that Moses' parents viewed the experience that way. It is hard to imagine a family facing that situation and just calmly sailing through it. This would make the narrative difficult to relate to, the characters become people unlike us, they are no longer fully human and the story slips into irrelevance.

Insights come in various ways; they all result in something specific and earthed rather than generalized abstract statements. Insight may come through:

- Sensed details.
- A theme woven throughout.
- An image triggered by the text.
- Art or a visual image.

Insights through sensed details

It is frequently small details that can be sensed that reveal an insight; the insight that the crossing of the Jordan river (Josh. 3) was a test of faith and a magnification of God's power comes through the textual detail of 'three days' (verse 2). This is not a general statement such as, 'the waiting three days tested their faith'. It is about the physical reality of waiting by a fast-flowing river for three days knowing they needed to cross it with children, the frail and the elderly and all their possessions. They fell asleep to the sound of a raging river, they woke to its noise and stood on its banks staring at its turbulent surface. The preacher can take the people through the three days, one day at a time if needed.

Insights through a theme woven throughout

Insights are not always located in individual details; sometimes they are woven throughout a narrative. However, it is still important to locate how the insight is embodied. An insight into the story of the woman taken in adultery (John 8.1–11) may be that judgement is overtaken by mercy. Judgement is embodied in the fingers in the text, both physical and metaphorical: the pointing fingers that accuse, the finger of judgement, the pointing finger of self-recrimination. Mercy is embodied in the finger with which Christ wrote. His finger is not pointed in judgement. Each finger in the text is specific and can relate to a physical action in a way that can be demonstrated by the preacher. Although some of the finger pointing is metaphorical it is not unreal, as anyone who has experienced unspoken disapproval will testify. The issue of how the metaphorical relates to the physical is discussed in Chapter 9.

Insights through an image triggered by the text

Sometimes an insight comes through an image or word-picture triggered *by* the text rather than located *in* the text. Superficially this looks like an exception, it's not a physical action or object in the text. However, word-images, metaphors and similes are rooted in the physical world. The image of fighting with one hand behind your back may be triggered by the Sermon on the Mount (Matt. 5.21–26, 38–48). It relates to a physical gesture that expresses vulnerability and disadvantage. The insight that followers of Jesus are in a vulnerable position as they seek to live by the values of the Kingdom of God in a fallen world can be expressed by this image.

'Do not be angry,' says Jesus,
going straight for the wellspring of violence.
'Be reconciled.'
And maybe we should add:
'Don't let others stir up hatred and anger in you,
don't let hearts be led by headlines.'
Hate makes simplistic slogans,
it's the lazy option
relieving us of the obligation to think.
Love is complicated,
it admits the tangled state of life.
Headlines don't do nuance.
Love fights with one hand behind its back ...
But if that hand clasps the hand of God
we are holding onto the one with the real power.
We are likely to get hurt.
We will be bloodied and bruised
and we will get disheartened.
But God has assured us
that love triumphs in the end,
for that is his name.[6]

Insights through art and visual images

Visual images that relate to a text may also reveal an insight. This book particularly looks at paintings but other forms of images may trigger insights. Artworks, even representational artworks that re-present a scene or person, do more than represent reality. Artworks can help people see the world in a different way and that includes the world of a biblical narrative. Simone Martini's 1333 *Annunciation* painting shows Mary keeping her thumb in her Bible.[7] Traditionally, Mary has the Bible open at a page predicting the Messiah; in this painting, however, the Bible is almost closed and maybe her thumb is in such a place. Alternatively, Mary's thumb could be keeping her place so that she can carry on reading once the angel has left, indicating Mary's freedom to say no. Such a gesture could also embody keeping options open. Such insights can be developed into sermons.[8]

As noted in Chapter 5, synoptic art can bring insights by placing scenes from a story in non-chronological order and juxtaposing various scenes. Simultaneous art can also bring insights by placing scenes from two different stories together that relate in some way. Artworks do not always have to match the text; sometimes the insight is on the general human condition. For example, Nehemiah 5 can be paired with Masaccio's *The Expulsion of Adam and Eve from the Garden of Eden.*[9] The insight is embedded in a sound. Masaccio paints Eve's mouth wide open in a howl, that terrible sound of pain and suffering. Eve howls as she realizes what she has lost and she grasps that life will now be a struggle in a world marred by sin and death. We have been howling ever since. Howls of grief and anguish were heard across Nehemiah's Jerusalem as corruption and greed destroyed families and wrecked lives. People lost their land, their homes and were forced to sell children in lieu of debt. A sermon on this text can then go on to relate what Nehemiah did to silence the howls (termed outcry in Nehemiah) and what we can do today. Staying with the sound would be important and the picture of Eve is so dramatic that it takes little to imagine the sound.

Question

Using the story of Jairus' daughter (Mark 5.21–43) what insights did you find within the text? What senses were involved and how were they embodied?

Showing

When the living text has been created and insights located, one or two insights can be selected for the sermon. This part of the process involves showing the situation, holding up a slice of life from the narrative that contains the insight or insights to show to the congregation. As the approach requires detailed presentation of some scenes, a sermon could become overburdened with too many insights. Being selective means the preacher can return to the text and different insights can be presented at a future date.

With a significant insight located, how the sermon is to be delivered becomes paramount, which means a careful selection of material from the living text that contains the insight. This stage is about developing and crafting the sermon. Some preachers write the sermon in detail; others think through the sermon in detail but only use headings and key reminders in delivery. The scene that contains the main insight may be delivered in detail and other parts delivered more briefly so that time moves faster in some parts of the sermon than others. The key scene can be used to interpret the rest of the narrative. This extract from a sermon on Jesus' baptism (Luke 3.21–22) puts the spotlight on Jesus waiting with others on the bank of the Jordan to be baptized. The extract takes the rather abstract insight that Jesus identified with sinners and embodies it in Jesus' relationship with the crowd as well as in his baptism.

> Among the crowd stands one who is different,
> but you would not know it.
> He wears the clothes of a working man,
> he is jostled by the crowd,
> he makes contact with his neighbours with eye and word.
> He smiles at the white-collar sinners,
> the blue-collar sinners
> and those with no collars at all.
> No T-shirt slogan declares him innocent.
> No halo marks him as holy.
> His clothes emit no glow.
> ......
> God in the crowd looks like the man next to him,
> who could be a con man.
> His feet are as dirty as the woman to his right,
> who could be a thief.
> He does not avoid the pimps.
> He rubs shoulders with the ordinary sinners,
> those guilty of mundane sins, everyday betrayals,
> the liars, the greedy and the hard of heart.[10]

This scene happens to come at the beginning of the biblical narrative, but sermons can start with a key scene from any part of the narrative, a sermon does not have to follow the order of the text. Sometimes an insight is not focused on one scene but woven throughout the narrative, which will need a different type of presentation. It will mean weaving the insight throughout the sermon as the narrative unfolds, drawing attention to the insight in *its embodied form*, not isolated from the situation of the narrative. In the case of the woman taken in adultery (John 8.1–11), an insight is that judgement is overtaken by mercy. This is embodied in fingers – physical and metaphorical. This insight and its embodiment can be woven throughout. That means talking about 'pointing fingers of accusation' not just 'they accused her'. It means describing what was going on in terms of fingers. 'Now in their mind's eye they saw the finger of judgement pointing at themselves' not just 'they felt guilty'.

Going back to the birth of Moses, if the insight that God working in a situation is hard to see in the detail of daily life, then some of that detail needs to be shown. Some of the rough notes from the living text can be crafted to present that slice of life as part of weaving the insight through a sermon as in the extract that follows.

The family work together to hide the child ... Miriam is still young, but she has a part to play, you grow up quickly when surrounded by danger. She knows her baby brother must not cry and alert the soldiers. They must be given no reason to search the house. He must be kept a secret from Egyptian neighbours who might betray them to the authorities. At the slightest cry baby Moses is fed and rocked. He must not give away his existence. At night they sleep lightly, rising at the first whimper.[11]

Exercise

Continuing with the story of Jairus' daughter (Mark 5.21–43), craft a small part of a sermon that communicates your insight.

Looking at art based on the text may help in presenting the narrative, for artists have to be specific, they have to show a situation. The following extract from a sermon on the conversion of Saul/Paul draws on a painting of that event by Caravaggio, *The Conversion on the Way to Damascus*, 1601.[12] The artist has Paul on horseback as the text talks of him falling.

Towards the end it happens,
almost at the gates of Damascus,
a light brighter than the sun,
the Light of the World himself.
The horse rears,
Saul falls, sprawled on his back,
helpless.
The horse's hooves hover above his body,
the sword lies at his side,
useless.
The letters lay crushed beneath him.
Everyone is higher than Saul now
as he lies on his back in the dirt.
His servant is confused,
he hears a sound but doesn't know what it is.

He sees the light, but is so bent on calming the horse
that he does not look at Saul.
Saul lies on the ground.
A man on a horse is powerful.
A man on his back in the dirt is not.
Lying there, helpless,
Saul hears the words from heaven that he least expected:
'I am Jesus.'
This is the Jesus who had been pursuing him ever since Stephen.[13]

Laying bare a situation and showing it is about bringing people face to face with what is happening and holding it up for people to see. It is taking time to display a narrative rather than report it. If preachers move too quickly to what can be learned, people do not have time to identify with the characters, situations and issues. In order to appreciate the relevance of the biblical narrative, the preacher needs to stay long enough in the world displayed in the text for the congregation to feel the full force of a situation and its effects on characters. Moving too quickly to the explicitly spiritual can have the opposite effect of what is intended; without facing the depth of the reality communicated in the narrative, a congregation may have difficulty realizing the true extent of God's role.

Conclusion

The process of creating a revelatory sermon is deeply rooted in the Bible and insights are earthed in the realities of the world revealed in the text. This chapter has explored one way of creating revelatory sermons; preachers can experiment with other ways while keeping a focus on character and insight and a showing presentation.

Notes

1 Paul Scott Wilson, 1988, *Imagination of the Heart*, Nashville: Abingdon Press, pp. 64–6.

2 Thomas Long, 1983, 'Shaping Sermons by Plotting the Text's Claim Upon Us', in Don M. Wardlaw (ed.), *Preaching Biblically: Creating Sermons in the Shape of Scripture*, Philadelphia: Westminster Press, pp. 84–100 (p. 89).

3 Thomas H. Troeger, 1990, *Imagining a Sermon*, Nashville: Abingdon Press, pp. 53–66.

4 Richard W. Swanson, 'Moving Bodies and Translating Scripture: Interpretation and Incarnation', *Word and World*, 31/3 (2011), 271–8 (p. 276). https://wordandworld.luthersem.edu/issues.aspx?article_id=1566, accessed 14.11.2021.

5 Margaret Cooling, 'The Wise and Foolish Bridesmaids', *Preaching that Shows*, https://preachingthatshows.com/2018/10/12/the-wise-and-foolish-bridesmaids-bothered/, accessed 14.11.2021.

6 Margaret Cooling, 'The Sermon on the Mount', *Preaching that Shows*, https://preachingthatshows.com/2018/10/10/the-sermon-on-the-mount-you-have-heard-it-said/, accessed 14.11.2021.

7 Simone Martini, *Annunciation with St Margaret and St Ansanus* (tempera and gold on wood, 1333; Uffizi Gallery, Florence).

8 Margaret Cooling, 'The Annunciation', *Preaching that Shows*, https://preachingthatshows.com/2018/10/09/the-annunciation-marys-thumb/, accessed 14.11.2021.

9 Masaccio's *The Expulsion of Adam and Eve from the Garden of Eden* (Fresco, 1425; Santa Maria del Carmine, Florence).

10 Margaret Cooling, 'The Baptism of Jesus', *Preaching that Shows*, https://preachingthatshows.com/2018/10/10/the-baptism-of-jesus-god-in-the-crowd/, accessed 14.11.2021.

11 Margaret Cooling, 'The Birth of Moses', *Preaching that Shows*, https://preachingthatshows.com/2018/10/11/the-birth-of-moses/, accessed 14.11.2021.

12 Caravaggio, *The Conversion on the Way to Damascus* (oil on canvas, 1601; Santa Maria del Popolo, Rome).

13 Margaret Cooling, 'The Conversion of Saul-Paul', *Preaching that Shows*, https://preachingthatshows.com/2018/10/12/the-conversion-of-saul-paul-from-human-certainties-to-divine-assurance/, accessed 14.11.2021.

7

Issues, Beginnings and Endings

This chapter continues the subject of creating sermons that show, with a particular focus on ways of starting and ending sermons and ways of combining explanatory and creative language. The final stage of creating a revelatory sermon holds up a slice of narrative life for the congregation to see; it lays bare a person, situation or insight. This final stage raises issues that need addressing, these are: adding details, non-physical realities and learning to see.

Adding details

A showing style needs a detailed presentation in parts of the sermon, if not the whole. This often means going beyond what the text states. In the previous chapter there is part of a sermon on Jesus' baptism where details have been added. Luke only relates that Jesus was baptized at the same time as other people (Luke 3.21–22). This was expanded and details added that are not in the text. Is this just speculation? What is the warrant for expanding the text in this way? Adding details can be justified in the following ways.

- What is implied but not stated.
- Other texts.
- Human experience.
- Magnification.
- The trajectory of the text.

Implied

Sometimes the details are implied even though they are not given in the text; people at the time would have taken certain details for granted, so there was no need to state them. This is not true of a modern congregation. The text says that Jesus was baptized when the people were – he did not ask for a private ceremony. The text does not say Jesus queued with sinners but it is implied. The text records that crowds came to John (Luke 3.7–8) and John's baptism is described as baptism for forgiveness of sins (Luke 3.3). This implies that Jesus stood alongside sinners.

Other texts

I have said that Jesus was jostled as he queued on the banks of the Jordan. This is likely considering other texts such as Mark 5.31, where the text specifically says the crowd pressed in on Jesus. I have indicated that Jesus mixed with the crowd. Other texts show Jesus' character and behaviour: he welcomed sinners and accepted their touch (Luke 7.36–50), he mixed with people disapproved of by the religious authorities (Luke 15.2). Mixing with the crowd is likely given Jesus' customary behaviour towards people.

Experience

John's response to the questions asked by some of the people in Luke's account of the baptism suggests some sins (Luke 3.7–14) but I have added others. From human experience we know that it is not only people who feel guilty about dramatic sins who come to God wanting forgiveness. Sometimes the ordinary wrongs weigh heavy: the lack of love, the ordinary betrayals of trust, the lack of compassion.

Magnification

The expansion of the text is a form of 'magnification', to use Paul Scott Wilson's term. Within a text God's actions may be significant but they are often presented in a terse manner and their significance is not always perceived. Preachers can bring out significance by magnifying God's actions. This may involve adding details but imaginative details are not freely invented but are rooted in the meaning of the text, what Paul Scott Wilson calls the 'Godsense'.[1] In the example of Jesus' baptism, to magnify what Jesus was doing in identifying with sinners, details have been added of people who queued with Jesus and his response to them.

Trajectory

The term 'trajectory' is helpful in describing both the freedom to develop
a text and its guiding role in that development. The text decides the
trajectory (direction) for the development of details. In a sermon on
Moses at the end of his life (Deut. 30), I wrote:

> Moses was an old, old man,
> the muscles slack upon the bone,
> the skin loose upon the flesh.
> No longer a prince of Egypt,
> No longer a wiry shepherd,
> No longer the courageous opponent of Pharaoh,
> No longer the tough, desert commander,
> No longer young.
> Moses was an old, old man and death was closer than his shadow.

I added physical details as a specific embodiment of Moses' age, drawing
on human experience of ageing in a way that indicated weakness. Unfortunately, these details did not follow the trajectory of the wider text that
says Moses retained his strength into old age (Deut. 34.7–8). I corrected
this so that any details I added worked with the trajectory of the text. It
now reads:

> Moses was an old, old man:
> No longer a prince of Egypt,
> No longer a tough desert shepherd,
> No longer the courageous opponent of Pharaoh,
> No longer young.
> His sinewy frame tells of a strength not yet gone.
> But death is closer than his shadow.

Exercise

Read Matthew 2.13–15. What details would you add to show the
situation, bearing in mind the above guidelines?

Non-physical realities

Showing a situation includes the non-physical aspects of a narrative, the emotional, relational and spiritual realities. How does the preacher show these realities? Sometimes these are indicated in the text, sometimes actions and responses enable preachers to work out what people are feeling and experiencing and what social factors are operating. At other times, preachers may have to infer them based on other parts of Scripture or common human experience. Care needs to be taken not to ascribe emotions to a character based on modern thinking. The extract that follows is from a sermon on Exodus 2.1–10. I refer to the parents praying. Is this just speculation?

> Hands that felt the kick of a baby are lifted in prayer. The God they have worshipped all their lives has surely not forgotten them. Where is God in this danger? Where is God in this fear?[2]

None of the above details are mentioned in the text, but Hebrew parents were likely to pray when their child was in danger. Many people pray in extreme circumstances, even if they do not identify as believers. Would Moses' parents not wonder where God was in their situation? The warrant for this comes from other parts of Scripture. David prayed when his baby son was dangerously ill (2 Sam. 12.16). Naomi thought God was against her when she lost her husband and sons (Ruth 1.3–5, 20–21). Comparable situations in Scripture can act as guides for non-physical aspects of narratives alongside human experience.

Ascribing emotions to characters in texts has its dangers because we risk getting it wrong, though the guidelines detailed above limit the risk. An example of a common mistake is interpreting biblical marriage in modern terms, which tends to see romantic love as the only acceptable basis for marriage. Preachers are faced with a choice: to add emotional tone to a narrative, doing their best to stay true to what the narrative implies, or to present characters without emotions unless they are spelled out in the text. There are risks both ways. Preachers may sometimes get it wrong, but to refrain from engaging with the emotional lives of biblical characters leaves them distant and unlike us, difficult to learn from, irrelevant.

Learning to see

A key skill in turning a biblical text into a living text, and then showing a situation, is learning to see. The preacher perceives the situation in a narrative by focused attention on the biblical text. This can be difficult in a society where we are bombarded by text and we have learned the art of skimming. What is needed is a disciplined approach that goes beyond the surface of the text to see people and situations and enter their stories as appropriate. It is turning the words we read into realistic situations in our mind's eye. This type of imaginative seeing starts with reading the text slowly, as if for the first time, for familiarity means we glance over what is there and miss much. We do not notice what we do not notice. This type of seeing takes the text slowly and tries to imagine what it would mean in real terms. Later, when the preacher presents the sermon, he or she helps the congregation to see the situation in a text by a showing style. Seeing is also helped by making the familiar strange, showing the narrative from a different perspective or just getting down to the physical realities of a situation.

Exercise

Read Judges 11.1–2. What do you see in this situation? Imagine the scene visually. What might be the dialogue?

Beginning a sermon: prologues

Revelatory sermons draw people into a situation and show it rather than explain it. That is fine, but sometimes there are things that a preacher needs to explain. It breaks the narrative flow if the preacher keeps interrupting a narrative to explain some piece of history or cultural background. One way of dealing with this issue is to use a prologue. A prologue is a separate section that introduces a play. Several of Shakespeare's plays start with a prologue. In *Romeo and Juliet*, the prologue tells the audience the backstory, the location and what will happen.

Chorus: Two households, both alike in dignity,
            In fair Verona, where we lay our scene,
            From ancient grudge break to new mutiny,
            Where civil blood makes civil hands unclean.

From forth the fatal loins of these two foes
A pair of star-cross'd lovers take their life;
Whose misadventured piteous overthrows
Do with their death bury their parents' strife.
The fearful passage of their death-mark'd love,
And the continuance of their parents' rage,
Which, but their children's end, nought could remove,
Is now the two hours' traffic of our stage;
The which if you with patient ears attend,
What here shall miss, our toil shall strive to mend.[3]

The audience, on hearing this prologue knows the lovers are going to die. At first glance it looks like a spoiler, but the audience does not leave and demand its money back because the prologue does not ruin the play. The prologue primes the audience (we are ready with the tissues). Shakespeare uses a technique that was part of classical drama and is also found in the New Testament. The Gospel of John opens with a prologue (John 1.1–18) that gives the reader the cosmic, spiritual context within which to understand the life of Jesus and his significance. John's prologue tells the reader how to read the rest of the Gospel. A preaching prologue can fulfil a number of functions.

- Prologues orientate a congregation geographically, stating where the story takes place.
- They locate the story historically, stating when it takes place and giving the historical background.
- They locate the story narratively, showing where it fits in the larger narrative of the Bible.
- Prologues situate a story culturally, introducing the congregation to the biblical world.
- They set the tone emotionally.
- They bring the central issue to the forefront so that the congregation is primed theologically.
- Prologues outline the narrative.
- They prepare a congregation to listen in a particular way.

An example of preparing a congregation to listen in a particular way is the story of the anointing of David after Saul is rejected as King. The prologue asks the congregation to listen to this as a story of God weaving human choices into the divine design.

God stands by the people's choice to have a king, for he made them with freedom to choose. God works with that choice for kingship, even though it is not what he wanted for his people. The choice of kingship is woven into God's design for Israel. God sends Samuel to anoint another king, David.[4]

Prologues can set the mental stage and arrange the emotional furniture to create an atmosphere and guide expectations. They can familiarize a congregation with the basic information they need to fully participate in the rest of the sermon. This is a response to the criticism that is sometimes made of narrative preaching, that it only functions well with a congregation that has a good knowledge of the Bible. With a prologue, the preacher can supply information the congregation may need, which leaves the preacher free to be creative in the rest of the sermon without breaking narrative mode to explain matters. In some sermons, having a brief outline of the biblical narrative in the prologue can help a congregation navigate the rest of the sermon, which may be more detailed and less sequential. A different situation is the congregation that is well-informed biblically; they feel they have heard it all before. A prologue can introduce a different slant on a story and defamiliarize it. The extract that follows recasts the story of the feeding of the 5,000 as part of a duel.

This is the story of a duel, not pistols at dawn but a power-duel with two kings showing what their power can do. It looks unequal at first, Herod has all the big guns: kingship, military might, dungeons and the power of life and death. Just a word from him and you can lose your head. Jesus fights back with compassion shown in healing and feeding the hungry. It looks like water pistols against cannons, but victory is not always obvious. We can listen to the story again seeing it as a duel between two kings.[5]

Transitions

Transitioning from prologue to the main body of the sermon can be done in various ways. In each case there is a brief pause at the end of the prologue.

Transition sentence

In a sermon on the Emmaus Road the preacher may signal the change between prologue and the main body of the sermon by a transition sentence such as, 'We can walk that road with the two disciples.'

A move in content

The subject that ends the prologue leads into the subject that opens the main part of the sermon.

> When Christ returns, we can hope to hear his words, 'Well done, good and faithful servant.' Until that day we live in a busy world, a world that needs lists.
> *Pause.*
> We are a people of lists:
> shopping lists,
> to do lists,
> urgent lists,
> packing lists,
> prayer lists,
> wish lists,
> fifty things to do before you die lists.[6]

General to specific

There can be a move from the general nature of the prologue to the specific opening of the main body of the sermon as in this extract from a sermon on the shepherds.

> Once and for all God gave us the assurance he is by our side, come among us in Jesus. He breaks into our loneliness as he broke into the night-time watches of the shepherds. *Pause.*
>
> The night was cold,
> the stars frost-bright.
> The air was clear,
> the silence deep.
> Blowing on their fingers,
> stamping their feet,
> the shepherds huddled in their coats.[7]

Exercise

Read the story of the call of Matthew (Matt. 9.9–13). Look at the different functions of a prologue and decide how you would use a prologue if preaching on this text. More than one function can be chosen.

Twice-told narratives

Another way of using two styles of language in a sermon (explanatory and creative narrative language) is the recounting of the same story in two ways. This is found in the Bible, the most well-known examples being the parting of the sea (Ex. 14.1—15.20) and the defeat of Sisera (Judg. 4—5). In both cases the story is told in both prose and poetry.

The Exodus 14 prose account gives details of the flight of the Hebrew slaves before Pharaoh's troops and the parting of the sea. Brevard Childs notes that the second account, the song of Moses and Miriam, does not follow the order of the first account and it puts the event in a wider cosmic context emphasizing that the battle was between God and Pharaoh. The second telling shifts the emphasis and tone to one of praise, highlighting God the deliverer, which becomes a theme in Israel's story. The second telling interprets the first and the two together create a single theological narrative.[8] Much of the detail in the first telling is omitted in the second and the language of the second telling is full of creative imagery: 'At the blast of your nostrils the waters piled up', 'the deeps congealed in the heart of the sea', 'they sank like lead in the mighty waters' (Ex. 15.8, 10).

In Judges the story of the defeat of Sisera is told twice but the second telling has details not included in the first account; in the second account we see Sisera's mother anxiously waiting for him to come home and the decisive nature of God's intervention in sending rain. There is a cosmic quality to it – Deborah sings, 'the stars fought from heaven'. Some aspects of the first telling, such as the oppression by the Canaanites, are omitted from the second account. The second telling is more poetic, and this is most noticeable in the account of the death of Sisera. The prose version just says, 'he died' (Judg. 4.21). The poetic has sensory detail, rhythm and repetition which reinforces his death.

He sank, he fell,
　He lay still at her feet;
At her feet he sank, he fell;
　Where he sank, there he fell dead.
(Judg. 5.27)[9]

A twice-told sermon draws on this biblical pattern, with the first telling being more explanatory than the second. Not every detail in the first telling will be covered in the second. What is touched on in one may be more detailed in the other and the second telling may be more interpretive and creative and have a different tone. The extracts below are from a sermon on the conversion of Saul/Paul.[10] The opening of the first telling is more explanatory than the opening of the second telling.

Opening of the first telling

It is AD 34, or thereabouts, and several years have passed since the crucifixion of Jesus. In Jerusalem, the followers of Jesus are growing in number. Not everyone welcomes this new sect; some are indifferent, some opposed, some take the 'wait and see' option. The religious rulers of Judea, however, believe they can no longer tolerate this sect called 'The Way', for that is what they call the followers of Jesus. No one has used the word 'Christian' yet. The authorities have tried threats, arresting the leaders, and telling them to keep quiet. That hasn't worked. Then it gets bloody. Stephen, a leader among the Christians, is arrested and condemned to death by stoning.

Opening of the second telling

Men range in a circle around the crouched figure of Stephen,
arms raised, aiming stones at his body.
Bones break under the rain of rocks,
the best he can hope for is a merciful blow to the head.
Yet the bloody mess that is Stephen prays for his persecutors.

Question

Think of a biblical narrative that could be preached in a twice-told manner. What would be the benefit of narrating that story in this way?

Open endings

Revelatory sermons can end in a variety of ways but do not end with *tight* closure. Paul Scott Wilson claims that it is seldom necessary to tie up all the ends in a sermon; preachers can often trust the meaning of the story to be apparent. Simple reminders are sometimes enough.[11] The text and the nature of the insight control the degree of closure alongside the context of the congregation. The way the sermon relates to the congregation's lives does not always need pointing out. Often the narrative is powerful enough to make relevance apparent. Eugene Lowry admits that preachers can be tempted to explain too much.[12] Sermons can have an invitational and open form of ending by finishing with possibilities where that is appropriate to the text. Some texts, however, call for the significance and implications to be made clear and that can be done without tight closure.

Three examples of endings without tight closure follow. The first ending is from a sermon by Kate Bruce on John 21 where she makes it clear to the congregation that they provide the ending. Sermon 2 is on Luke 24.13–24, the Emmaus Road; this sermon holds out a possibility in terms of being 'on the road again' with Jesus after retreating from hurt and disappointment. Sermon 3 on temptation has more closure in the sense that some of the implications of the text are drawn out.

Sermon 1

I can't finish this sermon ...
Because it's a doorway,
It's a threshold.
It's an invitation.
I want you to work on the next part of the sermon.
I want you to take away the next image.
and complete it yourself.
Spiritual homework if you like ...

Imagine the opening shots of a film.
We begin with a close-up on something.
It's an orangey colour.
The camera pulls back and we see
it has bits of black in it,
and flecks of grey.
The camera continues to pull back
and we recognize it as a fire,
a fire on a beach, by a lake.
Dawn is breaking.
There are two people near the fire.
See Jesus.
See the other person.
Look closely. It's you.

See Jesus, cooking bread and fish.
See yourself.
You know you have let him down;
You know you have thought
and said things contrary to his love;
You know you have denied him.
Just as I have.
He calls you over and places
warm bread in your hand
And offers you some fish.
He looks at you with great love.
'What matters most to you?'
He asks?
Tell him …

Take some time every day this week
To revisit this scene.
Tell him where you are
Listen to his response to you.
Only you can move the sermon on …
It's a doorway to a fireside conversation.[13]

Sermon 2

We have all done it,
walked away from a problem,
a disappointment,
a situation that fills us with despair.
Our Emmaus may be the TV,
music,
the pub,
anything that will allow us to forget for a while.
Our Emmaus is our place of escape,
time out from troubles
……
Our Emmaus can be a place of retreat
but it should not be our home.
It may be the place we meet Christ
but he sets us on the road again, finding our way back,
knowing in our hearts the promises are true.[14]

Sermon 3

Like Christ we can face the temptation
to live the Christian life according to the proofs demanded by others,
by ourselves
or even the proofs we think God demands.
Our calling is to live the life God desires for us,
as his children,
as followers of Jesus.
No ifs.
No buts.
Secure in our identity as children of God
we can step out of the dock
and stop the exhausting effort of proving we are worthy.
We aren't.
We never will be.
But we are loved, and we can change with God's help.
God is about transformation,
not accusation.
Life doesn't have to be lived
in the accusative.[15]

Epilogues

Epilogues, like prologues, have a long history in the theatre. Epilogues are one way of ending a revelatory sermon, but they are not needed for every sermon. Epilogues can leave people with ways to be, feel, think or act. Not every sermon needs to end in pointers for action: being, thinking and feeling often need to change first. Epilogues are not about adding a moral conclusion to the sermon or pointing out the meaning in a didactic fashion. Reflecting on the significance of a narrative feels different to a didactic or moralistic ending, although the same content may be covered. Tone is important. Sermon epilogues may fulfil several functions.

- They may reflect on the meaning and significance of the narrative and its implications for people today. One way of doing this is by having a character reflecting on what happened in the narrative.
- They can suggest what may happen in the future.
- Epilogues can put the narrative in a broader context theologically and narratively.

- They may help people step out of the narrative, going from close-up to a long shot.
- They can create a 'leave taking' of the characters.

Examples

This section of an epilogue from a sermon on Hannah combines leave-taking with reflection. A 'leave-taking' is taking a last look at characters and where they are at the end of the narrative.

> We leave Hannah now a mother.
> We leave Elkanah a little puzzled as to why they are suddenly blessed with a son when all their previous attempts had failed.
> We leave Peninnah rather put out now that her favourite sport of taunting Hannah has ended ... It is no accident that the first book of Samuel, a book about a nation, opens with a story about a woman's depression and childbirth. This area of life is not labelled 'private', it is not dismissed as 'woman's business' and of no consequence, it is not dismissed as too earthy to be spiritual. The quiet calling of Hannah to motherhood is central to the nation's story and is as spiritual as any other story in the book of Samuel. A spiritual life is just a life lived to God and it does not matter if that life is of a mother or a king.[16]

Sermons can end with a more focused reflection on the significance of the central issue for today. Although the meaning of a story is often apparent, sometimes the implications need drawing out in a reflective epilogue.

> When it came to the exercise of power,
> Ahab could but didn't.
> Jezebel could and did.
> 'Because I could.'
> The cry of the powerful when asked to answer for their actions.
> Why did they lie, abuse, cheat?
> 'Because I could,
> because power made it possible.'
> We all have power that makes things possible;
> power conferred by status, age, ability, wealth, education.
> But these are the obvious forms, power is subtler than that.
> Beauty, relationships, fitness, popularity, even spirituality
> can confer power.
> Misused, they can give us the power to make others feel
> inferior, guilty, unloved, isolated.

Jezebel had no lines that could not be crossed,
for power tends to erase lines.
It is hard to say, 'I can, but I won't.'
Much easier never to have power in the first place.
But we all have power.
No one is excused this struggle.
We learn to draw lines for ourselves that we will not cross,
lines not made by laws
but by living according to Christ's way of love.[17]

A character can reflect on the significance of an experience. The following
is a reflection by Luke who accompanied Paul on some of his journeys.

Looking through my notes there are things I did not record
but are vivid in my memory,
time slowed down for us, the senses heightened.
I can see us walking side by side, feel the heat, taste the dust.
I walked with a man following the Master's footsteps,
knowing where it would lead but caring more about building up others.
I saw Jesus in Paul.
I learned much in those weeks of travelling.
I saw the cost of obeying the Spirit
but also the fruits as churches were strengthened and encouraged.
I began to see the world through God's eyes:
I saw those tiny, insignificant churches as lights for Christ in a very
dark world.[18]

An ending can reduce closure by looking forward to the future and offering hope and possibilities.

Joshua surveys the scene. He sees the people lined along the west bank,
standing on the Promised Land. The people that wandered in the desert are now a nation ready to go forward. He sees the priests carrying
the Ark with a wide space around them. God went before them into
the waters. God went before them into the unknown. God is still with
them. To the west he sees the towns of Canaan, the future. To the
east lies Moab and the desert, the past. The wilderness years are over.
Between past and future lies the river Jordan, which they have crossed
with God. They will face the future with God, as will we.[19]

> **Exercise**
>
> Look at the sermon on Anna in Chapter 15. It is deliberately missing an epilogue. Write an epilogue for this sermon.

Conclusion

This chapter has developed ways of beginning and ending revelatory sermons. The issue of how explanatory and creative language can work together in a sermon is addressed through prologues and twice-told sermons. The word 'application' has not been used and some preachers may be worried by this but this issue is addressed in detail in Chapter 13. The emphasis on showing and detailed presentation may also sound alarm bells for preachers whose churches have a tradition of short sermons and some narratives would take too long to present in this way. Fear not, the next two chapters look at ways of creating vivid sermons with limited time.

Notes

1 Paul Scott Wilson, 2004, *Broken Words*, Nashville: Abingdon Press, pp. 22–3, 32–3.

2 Margaret Cooling, 'The Birth of Moses', *Preaching that Shows*, https://preachingthatshows.com/2018/10/11/the-birth-of-moses/, accessed 14.11.2021.

3 William Shakespeare, 2007, *Romeo and Juliet*, in *The Complete Works of William Shakespeare*, Ware: Wordsworth Library Collection, p. 245.

4 Margaret Cooling, 'David is Anointed', *Preaching that Shows*, https://preachingthatshows.com/2018/10/11/david-is-anointed/, accessed 14.11.2021.

5 Margaret Cooling, 'The Death of John the Baptist and Feeding the Five Thousand', *Preaching that Shows*, https://preachingthatshows.com/2018/10/10/the-death-of-john-the-baptist-and-the-feeding-of-the-five-thousand-the-duel/, accessed 14.11.2021.

6 Margaret Cooling, 'No One Knows the Hour of his Coming', *Preaching that Shows*, https://preachingthatshows.com/2018/10/12/no-one-knows-the-hour-of-his-coming-lists-2/, accessed 14.11.2021.

7 Margaret Cooling, 'The Shepherds', *Preaching that Shows*, https://preachingthatshows.com/2018/10/10/the-shepherds-watchers/, accessed 14.11.2021.

8 Brevard S. Childs, 1974, *The Book of Exodus*, Philadelphia: Westminster Press, pp. 224–33, 248–53.

9 Antony F. Campbell, 2004, *Joshua to Chronicles*, Louisville: Westminster John Knox, pp. 87–9.

10 Margaret Cooling, 'The Conversion of Saul-Paul', *Preaching that Shows*,

https://preachingthatshows.com/2018/10/12/the-conversion-of-saul-paul-from-human-certainties-to-divine-assurance/, accessed 14.11.2021.

11 Paul Scott Wilson, 1988, *Imagination of the Heart*, Nashville: Abingdon Press, p. 225.

12 Eugene L. Lowry, 1997, *The Sermon*, Nashville: Abingdon Press, p. 87.

13 Kate Bruce, *John 21*, unpublished sermon.

14 Margaret Cooling, 'The Emmaus Road', *Preaching that Shows*, https://preachingthatshows.com/2018/10/12/the-emmaus-road-a-road-without-rainbows/, accessed 14.11.2021.

15 Margaret Cooling, 'Jesus is Tempted', *Preaching that Shows*, https://preachingthatshows.com/2018/10/10/jesus-is-tempted-stepping-out-of-the-dock/, accessed 14.11.2021.

16 Margaret Cooling, 'Hannah', *Preaching that Shows*, https://preachingthatshows.com/2018/10/11/hannah/, accessed 14.11.2021.

17 Margaret Cooling, 'Ahab, Jezebel and Naboth', *Preaching that Shows*, https://preachingthatshows.com/2018/10/11/ahab-jezebel-and-naboth/, accessed 14.11.2021.

18 Margaret Cooling, 'Paul's Journey to Jerusalem', *Preaching that Shows*, https://preachingthatshows.com/2018/10/12/pauls-journey-to-jerusalem-the-farewell-tour/, accessed 14.11.2021.

19 Margaret Cooling, 'Crossing Jordan', *Preaching that Shows*, https://preachingthatshows.com/2018/10/11/crossing-jordan/, accessed 14.11.2021.

8

The Language of Showing

This chapter explores ways in which language can create a showing style for preaching. Lyrical language is also included to enhance a showing style by adding another sense. This section looks at issues that relate to this area: manipulation, ethical patience, different types of precision and the low-key language biblical writers often use when writing about God.

The practicalities of showing

There are specific types of language that help to show rather than tell. This section looks at five language techniques for showing:

- Tenses.
- Direct speech.
- Framing.
- Creating a world.
- Light touch language.

These different forms of language are used at the final stage of preparation when material that reflects the insight is selected from the living text to be crafted into a sermon. Some preachers write a detailed sermon manuscript, others think through the sermon in detail then write headings with notes underneath. The notes can be reminders of key words and phrases that are crafted for meaning and impact using some of the techniques that follow.

Tense: the historic present

The historic present tense (also known as the dramatic present or the narrative present tense) is when the present tense is used to talk about the past. Putting a biblical narrative into the present tense may make more of a connection with the congregation as they are not constantly being presented with the distant past. It can also hold up a situation and show it to a congregation rather than report it. In this sermon extract on Isaiah's vision a biblical historical event is related in the present tense.

> King Uzziah is dead
> and life is beginning to change,
> Assyria, dormant for so long, has finally woken up
> and is looking in Judah's direction.
> Assyria has already attacked other small nations
> and Judah is beginning to get the idea that was just for starters.
> They have the uncomfortable feeling they might be the main course.[1]

The historic present tends to be used for vivid and exciting events, but there is some debate concerning how this tense functions. Does it make events vivid and exciting or is it just used for exciting events? Deborah Schiffrin's research indicates that it adds dramatic energy, moving past events into the present. The historic present tense can intensify narratives and give a sense of immediacy. The preacher does not have to maintain a single tense throughout a sermon; there can be a switching between tenses, as in the following extract from a sermon on Acts 20.7–12.[2]

> Paul held Eutychus in his arms and saw:
> Elijah holding the widow's lifeless son, and the child living,
> Jairus' daughter rising at a word from the Lord,
> and Lazarus walking from the tomb.
> God had done it before.[3]

Moving past events into the present by the use of tenses may communicate that the past has something to say to us today. Not every text will be suitable to be treated in this way, but if preaching on biblical narratives is *always* in the past tense, it can sound as if preachers are forever talking about ancient history. This tense can also function as a defamiliarization technique, reducing the predictability of well-known narratives.

Exercise

Retell the story of the healing of Blind Bartimaeus using the historic present tense. What difference does it make?

Direct speech

Direct speech refers to what is spoken in a narrative:

> 'Take up your bed and walk.'
> 'Father, forgive them; for they do not know what they are doing.'
> 'Choose this day whom you will serve.'

Direct speech can be part of a showing style, particularly when combined with the present tense, though even in the past tense it can strike a note of realism and immediacy.[4] Small amounts can be added to a sermon without burdening it with long quotations that increase its length. Direct speech can be paraphrased providing it is true to the meaning of the text. Small sections of direct speech from Matthew 5.27–30 are included in the extract that follows, some of which is paraphrased.

> 'You have heard it said,' says Jesus.
> (In by-gone days. In times, so unlike ours
> that we imagine sex was not an issue.)
> 'You have heard it said,
> "Do not commit adultery."'
> This command seems a little closer,
> for adultery, like murder, comes in subtler forms;
> betrayal is a matter of the mind
> as well as the flesh.
> Faithfulness is a matter of the heart
> as well as the body.
> Lips do not have to touch.
> 'Do not lust,' says Jesus,
> going straight for the root of infidelity.
> 'Guard your eyes and your hands.'[5]

Framing

Another showing technique that aids engagement and reflects the embodied nature of revelatory preaching is framing. Framing roots a biblical narrative in a real-world context. This may be its historical context, or a modern context if the story is updated. The framing can include a definite place or time and other concrete particulars, along with language that gives sensory and emotional resonance. Framing gives a context that allows a congregation to imaginatively see a person and their situation. The first example below is framed, giving time, place and cultural context. It also gives the community context and emotional resonance by the description of the man among the tombs.

> Welcome to the East bank of the Sea of Galilee in the first century, the Gentile side, a place of Greek towns, a region of culture and sophistication. However, there is a blot on the horizon, the local cemetery, the haunt of a man who frightens his fellow citizens. Maybe he once lived in one of those sophisticated towns but now he is naked, wild, homeless and living among the tombs. He is captive to forces beyond his control. He is in the grip of powers that are so many, they are called 'Legion'. A regiment of evil. The local people fear him. They keep their distance, though his condition is extremely rare and no threat to them. They fear his lack of restraint.[6]

By way of contrast, the summary example that follows has no time and little emotional resonance. There is a low level of context and little engagement of the senses. The expression 'controlled by an evil spirit' does not communicate the desperate nature of the situation. The lack of detail makes it hard for people to see the situation.

> Jesus crossed the sea of Galilee and arrived at the Gentile side where he was met by a man who was controlled by an evil spirit. This man lived among the tombs and frightened the local people.

A biblical narrative can be framed in a sermon, giving details of time, place, action and emotional colour. This enables a congregation to experience events on a human scale, the scale at which life is lived, the scale at which faith is practised.

Exercise

Write the opening of a sermon on Acts 10. How will you frame it?

Creating a world

Revelatory preaching tends to create a world and show it rather than explain it. The Bible shows us a little of the world of the biblical characters in narratives. Using language that shows, preachers can recreate a little of that biblical world in a sermon that people can enter. Showing language draws people into the biblical world rather than telling them what the biblical world was like. Ronald Allen comments that in the ancient world the listener/reader did not have a text explained; they entered its world.[7] From inhabiting the biblical world we can look at our own world differently. Consider the following examples.

Explanatory: In the first century, women were considered to be of lower status than men. Boys were deemed to be more important than girls and age rather than youth conferred status.

Showing: Mary walks with her head down; she is used to lowering her eyes, she is, after all, only a girl, the least important in the group; men, boys and older women take precedence over her.

Explanatory: The Israelites waited for three days by the Jordan river.

Showing: Day after day they stand on the banks of the river. Night after night they fall asleep to its sound. On the third day …

Not all preaching language can be showing, time constraints may mean a mixture of styles. Explanation can be accommodated by a prologue if needed. For example, preachers may want to explain the status of women if they think that showing Mary's status in her world could be misunderstood as an endorsement of it.

Exercise

The two sentences that follow are part of an explanation concerning Mary's visit to Elizabeth (Luke 1.39–56). Turn this explanatory language into showing language.

Elizabeth's home was several days' journey for Mary. The journey crossed the hill country, where the land is steep and stony.

Light touch language

The language style of revelatory writing is sometimes described as 'impressionistic'. Impressionist painters could suggest something by just a few brushstrokes. Similarly, just a few words can be enough in a sermon rather than a long and detailed description. For preachers, the art lies in creating a vividly portrayed scene with a limited number of words; sermons are not novels, time is limited. These light touches of description work not only by what the words *indicate* but also by what they *activate* in terms of the senses. Kate Bruce evokes grief with just a short statement, 'The sound of earth falling on a coffin lid.'[8] Light touch description is true to reality. In everyday life, when we see something, we tend not to note every detail. The most realistic description is not necessarily the one with the most detail.

Exercise

Look at the following light touch descriptions, what do they indicate and what do they activate?

* She weaves her prayers around a troubled situation.
* They paint a scene of love around their kitchen table.[9]

Lyrical language: adding another sense

Lyrical or poetic language is a language style that works with revelatory forms of preaching and a showing style. This does not mean the preacher needs to become a poet in the traditional sense. Lyrical language is language with emotional resonance and sound patterning that contributes to the overall impact of showing a narrative. Such language is felt in the body, heart and mind. The sound patterning of speech can be part of presenting the narrative, for how something is said affects how it is perceived.

Walter Brueggemann calls for poetic speech, but he uses the term broadly to refer to language that is artistic, dramatic and evocative.[10] It is language that uses imagery, draws on the senses, reduces the use of adjectives and adverbs and layers description to build up the effect. Such language uses repetition and rhythm and other musical aspects of language that can be highlighted in delivery so that the effect is not lost.[11] Lyrical language does not have to be laid out as poetry, it is a matter of personal preference, it can be presented as prose, as in the extract that follows.

Below the cross the relatives grieve; others watch from afar and soldiers dice. Above their heads a cosmic drama is played out that will affect the whole world. Above their heads a personal drama is played out; three men are dying together. One of them is the Son of God.[12]

Lyrical language appeals to the whole person, not just the mind. The primary purpose of lyrical language is to invite people to respond, rather than communicate information and doctrine or to explain or prove things, though all of these may also happen. Lyrical language is not the language of relentless logic that funnels people into a binary response – accept or reject. Part of lyrical language is sound patterning. Our minds expect sound patterns such as rhythm, alliteration, rhyme and assonance.

Rhythm

Language in many forms has rhythm – it is not restricted to poetry. Rhythm is built into the universe: day and night, the seasons, the rhythm of the tides. Derek Attridge notes that rhythm is hard to escape, for our bodies are centred on the rhythms of heart and lungs. Poetic rhythm is something that we feel as well as hear; our bodies respond to the beat. Rhythm in language creates expectations: the rhythm of one line sets up expectations of the next and an onward movement is generated that can be felt. Meaning can be experienced through mind, heart and body.[13] We respond to rhythm and there is a felt dis-ease when an expected rhythm is missing. Rhythm can intensify language, signal beginnings and endings and important points.

Repetition can be used to create rhythm in sermons but it is important to know when to break the rhythm and stop the repetition. Sometimes a more prolonged repetition works, but it needs to be tested by ear and for meaningful impact.

> Not a hint of thanksgiving.
> Not a suggestion of welcome.
> Not an iota of joy.
> Not a whiff of excitement.
> Only fear.[14]

Prose can have its own rhythms. As an oral art, preaching can draw on language's natural rhythms to connect with the congregation and aid memory. Winston Churchill, Martin Luther King and Barack Obama all understood and used the rhythms of language.

Rhyme

True rhyme is when end sounds are the same, even if they are spelt differently and if other parts of the word are different. 'Bough' and 'how' are true rhymes so are 'fire' and 'hire'. Rhyme is unusual in a sermon but can be used occasionally to highlight an important point or signal an ending. Near rhyme can also be used. Near rhyme or half rhyme is when end sounds of words are similar but not identical. The end consonants may be the same but the vowels may be different. Sleep and slip are near rhymes as are hut and hat. Rhyme is not planned, it is often something that happens as a sermon is written, though sometimes people go back over a draft and tweak words using some of the techniques detailed in this section.

True rhyme

> Did they notice the lack of weight in their ears,
> no longer heavy with **gold**?
> Did they feel the lack of movement as they turned their heads?
> We are not **told**.

Near rhyme

> Careless of their brother's **life**,
> their father's **grief**.

Alliteration

Alliteration is when words share a sound at the beginning of a word. Most people experience alliteration in sermon points. A sermon on the Prodigal Son may be delivered under the following points.

- Rebellion.
- Repentance.
- Reconciliation.

Alliterated words do not have to start a line; they can be used within a line. Narrative preaching tends to avoid points but alliteration can still be used, but sparingly – too much can sound forced or comic. The example that follows uses alliteration within the lines but changes the initial sounds from F to D, W and M. If all the lines had used words beginning with D it would have sounded comic. (It is the sound rather than the letter that is important.)

Flawed, frightened and foolish people
Are invited
To name their deepest desire
To wrestle with God
God who weaves himself
Into the fabric of our mess and muddle.[15]

People often have an unconscious expectation of alliteration. An example of this is the pairing of the 'the lion and the lamb' by Christian lyricists rather than the wolf and the lamb of Isaiah 11.6.

Assonance

Assonance is harder to detect but can create a mood by using vowel sounds that echo one another. Sleep and feet, sack and fat, high and guide are all examples of assonance as each pair shares a vowel sound. The 'e' sounds in this sentence creates a dirge-like sound suitable for the story of Jairus' daughter, 'The death sentence enveloped them all.' Sound patterning of various kinds can be an integral part of preaching, highlighting certain parts of a narrative, creating different moods.

Lyrical language in the Bible

The use of lyrical language is supported by the Bible. Large sections of the Bible are poetic, not just the psalms. However, much of the poetry is presented as prose in English Bibles, though some modern translations seek to correct this. The lyrical language of the Bible is rich in images, is sometimes alliterative in its original form, but it does not rhyme. Much of the Bible's rhythm, assonance and alliteration are lost in translation. Parallelism is one of the most notable features of Hebrew poetry. A thought may be expressed two or three times in parallel. Hebrew parallelism is complex; what follow are examples of the simplest form where two or three lines echo each other.

The heavens are telling the glory of God;
    and the firmament proclaims his handiwork. (Ps. 19.1)

The flood would have swept us away,
    the torrent would have gone over us;
then over us would have gone
    the raging waters. (Ps. 124.4–5)

W. F. Dobbs-Allsopp comments on the irregular nature of Hebrew poetry. Hebrew poetry has rhythm that it is unique to each poem but the rhythms may vary. Psalm 19 is an example of this: verses 7–10 have a regular rhythm that is broken before and after.[16]

> The Law of the LORD is perfect,
>   reviving the soul;
> the decrees of the LORD are sure,
>   making wise the simple. (Ps. 19.7)

The rhythms of the Bible can inform our own sermon writing but when rhythm develops in a sermon it does not have to be continued throughout; rhythms can be broken as they are in the Bible. The techniques discussed in this section can engage a congregation but they need using with care, bearing in mind the context and aims of a sermon. A preacher aims for a response that combines head, heart, body and will, not just an emotional response. An over-emotional approach as well as an overly logical one can become coercive. These techniques are instinctive for some preachers, others have to consciously think about incorporating them into a sermon. For preachers who do not use this type of language automatically, it is a matter of going over a draft and adjusting some of the language. Small changes can make big differences.

Manipulation

As with any use of effective speech the danger of manipulation is present, particularly when it is used by a person perceived to have authority. Misused, people could be swept along to agreement by techniques that get past the mind's defences. Are the techniques discussed in this chapter manipulative?

Effective communication works with the way people learn, that is not manipulation, it is acknowledging how God made us and working with it. Manipulation is about power and control and involves a distortion of communication for those ends. It involves intellectually or emotionally overwhelming people, leaving them feeling that they must assent.

Manipulation can often be avoided by only using techniques that are warranted by the text and appropriate for communicating its meaning. Preachers do not have to use every technique they know to communicate a text; we can learn from artists like Rembrandt who did not use all the colours available to him but he was still effective.

Appropriate language techniques can encourage people to willingly use their senses to imagine scenes. It can send people back to the text and provoke discussion. Used well, language techniques can fulfil Augustine of Hippo's three functions of preaching: to delight, instruct and move.[17] The key to distinguishing between appropriate use and manipulation lies in intent. Asking the following questions may help to distinguish appropriate use of language:

- Does the sermon include the preacher or is it only speaking to the congregation?
- Is the movement all in one direction, the direction of assent?
- Are the techniques used warranted by the text or are they being used to impress or control?

Preachers want a response but the response should always be invitational. This may mean the preacher refraining from presenting an argument too tightly or appropriately limiting the emotional impact of the sermon so that listeners are left with freedom to respond in their own way. Preachers can resist the temptation to fill every gap so that the congregation has room to deliberate on their own questions raised by the text. Generally, as Walter Brueggemann has noted, people do not change by coercion. Congregations do not need sermons filled with 'oughts' and 'musts' that do not help them live the gospel.[18]

Aggressive tones or inducing guilt or fear to control people is also manipulative. The revelatory plot with its reflective nature and lack of tight closure creates an invitational tone. Linda Clader stresses that the preacher can share his or her insight into a text without forcing others to see it in the same way.[19] One way of testing for manipulation is for the preacher to consider how the sermon would feel if she or he were sitting with the congregation. Is there a sense of freedom for people to respond in their own way?

Ethical patience

Before making judgements, congregations need time to face the material and spiritual reality of a situation exhibited in a narrative and the personal and relational reality of the characters. To use Michael Dyson's phrase, 'ethical patience' is needed. This is an attitude that takes the trouble to stand alongside the characters and their situation before judging.[20] For the preacher, this attitude of ethical patience means using language that delays judgement, that signals a need to wait. Stereotypical characters and simplistic representations of situations can lead to quick-fire judgements, which means people can distance themselves from certain characters in biblical narratives early in the sermon, as it is made clear with whom the congregation is meant to align.

An instance of the need for ethical patience is the story of the making of the golden calf (Ex. 32.1–6). It is easy to censure the Israelites who made the golden calf but that is unlikely to resonate with people in any real sense as it is a situation outside the experience of most congregations. We can condemn with impunity as it is unlikely to include us. Closer attention to the specifics of the situation changes things. The Israelites were in an unknown wilderness and Moses, on whom they relied for leadership and direction, had been missing for days. They were geographically and emotionally beyond anything they knew. As slaves they had been controlled and suddenly they are on their own. Gaining freedom of mind and spirit is not instantaneous, it does not happen as soon as the chains fall off. The emotions experienced by those ex-slaves was so great that they were willing to sacrifice the earrings given to them by the Egyptians, probably the first things of value they had ever owned. They needed a sense of control in a situation that was new, frightening and disorientating. In making an idol they exercised control.[21]

Taking the time to show the realities of a situation means the actions of the Israelites cease to feel distant and unrelated to modern living; most people know the panic of being in situations where they feel a lack of control and everything is new and scary. Many in the congregation may recognize the desire for control, for a safe God who will bless us but not lead us into the wilderness. Although empathy is not right for every situation, often people need to come alongside characters before they can see the relevance to their own situation and before verdicts are uttered.

Precision

Language of all types tries to capture meaning, but each does it in its own way. Aristotle recognized that there were different types of precision.[22] Lyrical and explanatory language have different ways of being precise. Grief, for example, can be defined precisely in medical terms with all its aspects and stages but Shakespeare's poetry on grief has a different form of precision; it captures its experiential impact. Both are accurate but in different ways.

Constance: Grief fills the room up of my absent child,
Lies in his bed, walks up and down with me,
Puts on his pretty looks, repeats his words,
Remembers me of all his gracious parts,
Stuffs out his vacant garments with his form;
Then, have I reason to be fond of grief?[23]

Revelatory preaching uses lyrical language and poetic precision as part of a showing style, but the use of prologues allows the different precision of explanatory language to be incorporated.

The biblical writer's low-key language

For believers, God is part of the real world and the Bible presents God and Jesus as the central characters in its overall story. However, in some narratives God is not mentioned; Esther and the Song of Solomon do not have direct references to God. This does not present a problem for preaching as God is shown as deeply involved in human affairs through-out the Bible and, in the Gospels, God is incarnate in Jesus. This leads to an expectation of experiencing God through people and events, through creation and history. Generally, the everyday experience of God comes through the material world. This 'horizontal' relationship with the world and its people contains within it the possibility of a 'vertical' relationship with God, an issue discussed in Chapter 14. The rather relaxed position that some of the biblical writers take on mentioning God is possible for narrators who take for granted the presence of God in the world and throughout history.

This low-key language frees preachers to present situations and char-acters naturally. The actions of God can be magnified but this should not be forced. The story of Joseph (Gen. 37; 39—50) does not have to be peppered with the language of God's providence. It is extremely doubtful that the teenage Joseph was calmly thinking 'this is all part of God's plan' while standing on a block in a marketplace in Egypt being sold as a slave. To present it as such would not face up to the realities of Joseph's situ-ation. God's actions can be magnified as characters look back, as the text does in Joseph's story (Gen. 50.19–20). Pastorally, situations peppered with the language of God, when the text does not warrant it, could leave a congregation feeling that their experience of God is not only different to that of biblical people but inferior.

Conclusion

This chapter has documented certain language techniques that contribute to a showing style and enable a congregation to see a biblical narrative. Lyrical language adds another sense dimension to enrich the experience. Not every preacher will be comfortable using all these techniques, but most people will be able to use some, such as moving to the historic present tense instead of the past or using touches of lyrical language. If anyone needs convincing of the power of such language, ask the congregation about lines they remember from hymns and Christian songs. It tends to be the particularly lyrical lines that stick in the memory, that come back during the week and in difficult times. Those lines could probably be summed up prosaically, but I doubt they would be remembered in the same way.

Notes

1 Margaret Cooling, 'Isaiah's Vision', *Preaching that Shows*, https://preaching thatshows.com/2019/05/21/isaiahs-vision-what-god-did-not-say/, accessed 14.11.2021.

2 Deborah Schiffrin, 'Tense Variation in Narrative', *Language*, 57/1 (1981), 45–62 (pp. 46, 51–2, 57–8), doi:10.1353/lan.1981.0011.

3 Margaret Cooling, 'Paul's Journey to Jerusalem', *Preaching that Shows*, https://preachingthatshows.com/2018/10/12/pauls-journey-to-jerusalem-the-fare well-tour/, accessed 14.11.2021.

4 Schiffrin, 'Tense Variation', p. 58.

5 Margaret Cooling, 'Sermon on the Mount', *Preaching that Shows*, https:// preachingthatshows.com/2018/10/10/the-sermon-on-the-mount-you-have-heard-it-said/, accessed 14.11.2021.

6 Margaret Cooling, 'The Gadarene Demoniac', *Preaching that Shows*, https:// preachingthatshows.com/2018/10/10/the-gadarene-demonic-the-mathematics-of-love/, accessed 14.11.2021.

7 Ronald J. Allen, 1983, 'Shaping Sermons by the Language of the Text', in Don M. Wardlaw, (ed.), *Preaching Biblically: Creating Sermons by the Shape of Scripture*, Philadelphia: Westminster Press, pp. 29–59 (p. 34).

8 Kate Bruce, 2015, *Igniting the Heart*, London: SCM Press, p. 178.

9 Kate Bruce, *Creativity*, unpublished sermon.

10 Walter Brueggemann, 1989, *Finally Comes the Poet*, Minneapolis: Fortress Press, pp. 3–6.

11 Bruce, *Igniting*, pp. 57–62.

12 Margaret Cooling, 'Crucifixion', *Preaching that Shows*, https://preaching thatshows.com/2021/07/19/crucifixion-2-too-much/, accessed 14.11.2021.

13 Derek Attridge, 1995, *Poetic Rhythm*, Cambridge: Cambridge University Press, pp. 1–5, 23.

14 Bruce, *Igniting*, pp. 187–8.

15 Bruce, *Exodus 32*, unpublished sermon.

16 F. W. Dobbs-Allsopp, 2015, *On Biblical Poetry*, New York: Oxford University Press, pp. 98–103, 126–7, 136, 155.

17 Augustine, 'On Christian Doctrine, IV', *New Advent*, https://www.new advent.org/fathers/12024.htm, accessed 14.11.2021.

18 Brueggemann, *Finally*, p. 84.

19 Linda L. Clader, 2003, *Voicing the Vision*, New York: Morehouse Publishing, p. 96.

20 Michael Eric Dyson, 2011, *Can You Hear Me Now?*, Philadelphia: Basic Civitas Books, p. 232.

21 Margaret Cooling, 'Leaving Egypt and the Golden Calf', *Preaching that Shows*, https://preachingthatshows.com/2018/10/11/leaving-egypt-and-the-golden-calf/, accessed 14.11.2021.

22 Aristotle, *Nicomachean Ethics*, tr. W. D. Ross, http://classics.mit.edu/Aristotle/nicomachaen.1.i.html, accessed 14.11.2021, book I, para. 3.

23 William Shakespeare, 2007, *The Life and Death of King John*, in *The Complete Works of William Shakespeare*, Ware: Wordsworth Library Collection, Act III, sc. iv, ll. 93–8.

9

A Big Issue

This chapter focuses on issues and the thinking around the way we use language in sermons. It looks at a big underlying issue; how can preachers show the realities of biblical people and their situation when they only have words to do this? Sermons are made up of words, whereas life (including the life reflected in narratives) is multi-dimensional, rich and complex. Can mere words present the realities of biblical narratives in all their richness and complexity? The answer is 'yes' but it all depends on the relationship of the words to reality and the type of words we use. Words can relate to the reality of the world we live in and to the reality of the world reflected in biblical narratives but they do this in a variety of ways. The following sections explore seven ways in which words relate to reality.

- Basic reference/denotation.
- Connotation.
- Exemplification.
- The fabric sample.
- Sensed description.
- The reality effect.
- Creative relating to reality.

Basic reference/denotation

At a basic level, the words we use in a sermon refer to things in the world, either the world of the text or the world we live in. Words refer to things about which there is some level of agreement or common understanding. In English-speaking countries there is an agreement that the word 'dog' refers to a particular type of four-legged animal. This is the simplest form of reference, which is called 'denotation'. Denotation tends to be what we get when we Google a word. In a sermon we use words in this basic way, we refer to things and people in the world of the text: sheep, disciples, mountains. However, at this basic level words act like a dictionary definition and although they may refer to things in the world of the text, they do not have much depth and sermons need language that has depth to cover something as complex and multi-dimensional as a biblical narrative. Denotation leaves a sermon one-dimensional; it takes the next form of relating to reality – connotation – for language to begin to gain depth.

Connotation

Connotation is when the meaning of a word or phrase gains depth and complexity by association, by the emotional and cultural connections people make rather than a word just referring to something. The same word may have different connotations for various groups. The word 'rain' means the same in Britain and Namibia, but the connotations are different. Britain experiences too much rain, it is something to escape; Namibia experiences too little rain and it is welcomed as life-giving. Many words work by a web of connections created by the connotations a word has.

Exercise

Think of the word 'Internet'. What connotations does this word have for you? What connections do you make? Are the connotations positive, negative or mixed?

Connotation allows words not only to refer to something, but also to carry a large amount of information about human experience of the world. Connotations dwell in people's minds or in a community where a particular set of connotations is shared; these are often determined by culture, tradition and history. An example of this is Queen Elizabeth II: for many people in Britain, reference to the Queen has connotations of dedication and duty. Connotation can help preachers, for it means we can use words that come with a range of connections that may involve many senses and experiences. Words with connotations have possibilities for presenting a biblical narrative, they are words with depth and richness. There is a word of warning, however: some words may have different connotations for different groups and guidance may be required if unsuitable connections could be made.

Exemplification

Can language go even further? Can it gain even more depth, complexity and richness in its relationship to reality? Nelson Goodman explored ways in which meaning can be deepened by something he calls 'exemplification'. Goodman defines exemplification as display (showing). To exemplify something is to possess it and display it rather than just refer to it. Exemplification can be expressed as reference plus possession equals showing/presentation. We engage with exemplification in everyday life even if we have never heard the word before. Goodman uses the example of a paint chart.

A paint chart
A patch of colour on a paint chart labelled 'midnight blue' does not just refer to a colour, it possesses it and therefore can show it. It exemplifies it. In contrast, just the label giving the name of the colour would not exemplify the colour as it refers to it but does not possess it and therefore cannot show it.[1]

There are other examples of exemplification that we meet in daily life.

A perfume tester
A perfume tester labelled 'sandalwood' exemplifies a scent, as it possesses the scent as well as refers to it and therefore can present it. It exemplifies it. In contrast, an advert for the perfume in a magazine or online does not exemplify the scent as it refers to it but does not possess it.

Goodman describes two types of exemplification, literal and figurative. In art, to exemplify a quality an artwork must possess it and be able to show it. An artwork can literally exemplify sadness by including a person with a sad expression. It possesses sadness and can show it. Alternatively, an artwork could figuratively exemplify sadness by using greys and blues, as these colours indicate sadness in some cultures. (We talk of 'having the blues'.) A blue-grey artwork can possess and show sadness figuratively.[2]

Question

Think of an example of exemplification in everyday life. Is it literal or figurative?

How would exemplification work in the language of a sermon? Can language possess something of the nature of the thing it speaks of rather than just refer? Can words possess and show? Nelson Goodman often likened descriptive language to art and applying his thinking to language could mean a sermon both refers to a story and possesses some of its qualities. If it were a sad biblical story the language of the sermon could show the people, situations and relationships in the story using a form of language that captured the tone and qualities of lament. It could exemplify it. A sermon on a sad story that referred to the people and situation in the story but had an upbeat presentation would not possess its qualities; it would not exemplify it. In speaking of the crucifixion, language can figuratively possess something of the nature of the grief experienced by those at the event by word-choice, using a slow pace, rhythm and repetition.

> Soldiers dice,
> oblivious to the misery.
> Life goes on,
> despite the agony –
> now as then –
> in his pain and ours.
> We feel that time should stand still,
> to salute anguish.
> The world should bow its head,
> in acknowledgement of grief.
> But children still play.
> Work still has to be done.
> The body still demands food.
> Soldiers still dice.[3]

Exemplification has possibilities for presenting the many dimensions of a biblical text. With exemplification, language is no longer a flat depiction, it moves into a more multi-dimensional presentation by possessing some of the qualities that the texts reveal – it exemplifies.

Exercise

Look at the story of Jesus entering Jerusalem (Luke 19.28–40). Decide on its qualities. If you were preaching on this text, how could your language possess some of those qualities? How could you exemplify it?

The fabric sample

Goodman's concept of exemplification has advantages beyond being able to give language depth and richness, it also helps with relevance. Goodman uses the illustration of a fabric sample to explain this. A sample of cloth exemplifies weave, colour, pattern and texture; it displays/shows certain qualities of the fabric.[4] Once a person gets to know a sample, they can recognize it even when it is made into articles as different as cushions and a dress. The articles share the qualities that the sample possessed, even though other factors are very different. Getting to know a sample allows people to recognize other things with some of the same qualities in different contexts. In preaching, the sample is what is shown and it may be a sample of behaviour, emotion, situation, relationship, a concept – such as forgiveness – or a doctrine in action.

This relates to revelatory preaching that shows part of a narrative, a slice of life in language. Taking time in a sermon to display characters and situations acts as a sample as it helps congregations to recognize other characters and situations that share some of the same qualities, even though the context may be different. This aids congregations in linking one biblical story with another and recognizing modern situations and relationships that share some of the qualities displayed in a biblical narrative. The people and situations in the biblical story are, however, still presented in their own right even though they may also act as a sample. This form of relevance involves active participation by the congregation developing their skills, all the application/implication is not left to the preacher.

Is there a contradiction at the heart of this? Getting to know one person or situation should narrow relevance, for it is commonly assumed that people must share an experience for it to have relevance. If this is true, the very specific nature of the revelatory plot approach should hinder wider application but if it acts like a fabric sample the opposite is true. Dwelling on specific people and situations in a narrative means that members of the congregation can recognize those qualities in very different situations. In the extract below, you don't have to be female and living in the first century to recognize the situation based on Philippians 4.2–3. This extract happens to be in the first person but it could have been expressed differently.

My name is Syntyche, my friend Euodia and I work alongside the men sharing the good news of Jesus. We worked together as a team, gladiators for the gospel. Recently Euodia and I have quarrelled and distance has developed between us. We still meet at Lydia's house for worship but we avoid making eye contact. We speak, we are polite, but we don't know how to overcome the barrier between us. We sit close to each other at church but there could be a continent between us.[5]

You may have experienced how the sample works if you have ever read or watched Agatha Christie's detective stories that feature Miss Marple. Miss Marple lives in a tiny village and she knows her village and its occupants well. It is this deep knowledge of a small community that enables her to solve crimes at a national level. The village acts as a sample.

Sensed description

Marcel Proust uses description in a way that moves words into a three-dimensional scene. Proust describes how the taste of a madeleine dipped in tea caused a scene from his past to rise 'like a stage set'.[6] His description of this three-dimensional scene enables his readers to see it. Description is another way in which language gains depth and richness in its presentation of the biblical world. It can help preachers present a narrative scene that is multi-dimensional. This is not about indulging in 'purple prose' but using description that taps into the senses. Some preachers may query why such sensed description is needed as biblical narratives are not replete with this type of language. There is descriptive language in the Bible: the young David (1 Sam. 16.12) is described as handsome and with beautiful eyes and the Promised land is described as 'flowing with milk and honey' (Josh. 5.6). Generally, biblical stories did not need much in terms of sensed description as the original audiences needed little to prompt the formation of mental images. We are not given vivid descriptions of Ruth toiling in the fields because listeners knew what gleaning was like. In modern cultures, particularly urban ones, references to ancient agricultural life will fail to build scenes as most people have few connections with the type of culture the Bible reflects. Including sensed descriptive language in a sermon can help a congregation connect with a biblical narrative. The sensed language in this extract relates to touch, sound and sight.

It is dark inside the cell; precious light is not wasted on prisoners. Paul and Silas' cell is particularly dark being deep inside the prison ... Paul and Silas cannot change what has happened to them, but they can choose how they respond. Against all the odds, they choose to pray and to sing praises to God. What a strange sound in the dark, their voices bouncing off prison walls. Other prisoners listen in silence. The gaoler,

however, sleeps. They feel the earthquake before they hear it. The
trembling beneath their bodies, the vibrations in the walls. The sounds
gather, and they hear doors swinging open, chains rattling as they fall
to the floor. Dust powders their hair as the roof shudders, but it holds.[7]

The reality effect

The reality effect is a form of sensed description that is impressionistic. The
impressionist painters could suggest something by a few brush strokes,
in a similar way just a few words can suggest reality. The term 'reality
effect' was coined by Roland Barthes who championed small touches of
description that sometimes get dismissed as 'padding' or just there to add
artistic value. He asserts the significance of these insignificant touches of
description. He quotes Michelet's description of Charlotte Corday in her
prison cell waiting to be executed during the French Revolution. Charlotte
is sitting in her cell and 'after an hour and a half someone knocked softly
at a little door behind her'. In terms of the plot, the descriptive details
are not necessary, nothing depends on them. The reader does not need to
know the size and location of the door or the softness of the knock, but
these small details signal 'we are real'.[8] Small descriptive details can also
build atmosphere. Using the example of Charlotte Corday, if someone
had hammered on a large door in front of her the atmosphere would have
been very different.

In terms of preaching, small touches of the reality effect announce to
the congregation the reality of biblical situations and characters, which
can facilitate identification and signal relevance. The descriptive touches
may not be *exactly* what happened, which cannot be known, but they
can describe what was probable. Their role is to trigger a sense of reality.
Often the reality effect is created by just a few words, which is helpful in
churches with a tradition of short sermons.

> Onto the scene comes Jesus.
> No fanfare,
> no salute,
> just a boat grinding onto the beach.
> No red carpet,
> no elegant descent,
> just Jesus wading to the shore,
> wet clothes dragging at his limbs.[9]

The grinding of the boat and the feel of wet clothes move the narrative into sound and touch. They are both examples of the reality effect, which can help people relate to other times and cultures and help them to identify with the people and situations shown in a sermon. Most people in a congregation know the experience of wet clothes dragging at limbs, even if they have never jumped off a boat into shallow water. Many people have heard the sound of a boat grinding on the shore, it's a sound they have probably heard in TV dramas if not in real life. These short descriptive phrases signal real life. The sense of the real is created by what is triggered in the different senses of the listener, helping to create a visceral connection between the congregation and the text. To varying degrees, people can imaginatively 'hear' the noise of the boat and 'feel' or remember the sensation of wet clothes.

> **Question**
>
> If you were preaching on the story of Martha and Mary (Luke 10.38–42), what touches of the reality effect would you use?

Adding description to sermons raises the issue of faithfulness to the text as description is not usually about exact correspondence to what happened. Description can, nevertheless, be faithful. An example from art may make this clearer. A painting can be faithful to the reality it represents without being literal in a conventional sense. Some people decried J. M. W. Turner's paintings, which had none of the realism of conventional art. But Turner was faithful to his subjects, capturing the true essence of storms, steam, sea and landscapes. His *Rain, Steam, and Speed* captured the new experience of rail travel.[10] Edvard Munch's painting *The Scream* is faithful to a particular experience but it is not literally realistic.[11] A sermon can be faithful in the way a Turner painting is; it can capture the truth and meaning of a narrative without necessarily being literal in presentation.

The congregation may have set ideas about what constitutes faithfulness. Some may think in terms of following the passage verse by verse or they may think that the number of biblical references is important. Revelatory sermons are deeply rooted in the text but the text is not necessarily quoted. The congregation may be listening for the biblical quotes and be puzzled when they do not hear 'verse 27 says ...' Revelatory preaching intentionally draws people into the biblical situation and *shows* them the reality of the text; there is no need to quote it because they are seeing it. Just quoting verses or following the structure of a biblical passage does not guarantee faithfulness. A sermon with many biblical references can still miss the point. The test of faithfulness lies in the relationship of the sermon to the meaning of a text, not the style of delivery. The revelatory approach is not less biblical because it does not often quote texts. The revelatory approach is about immersing people in the text.

Creative relating to reality

Revelatory preaching uses creative language such as word-images, metaphor and simile. Figurative (metaphorical) language is sometimes dismissed as decorative and distant from the real world; however, cognitive linguists such as Raymond Gibbs, George Lakoff and Mark Johnson demonstrate ways in which figurative language relates to reality. Figurative language uses real-world experience and the human body to understand the more abstract aspects of life. An instance of this is the way we use the word 'see' to indicate understanding, 'Now I see what you mean'. We borrow a word from physical vision for intellectual understanding.[12]

Lakoff and Johnson highlight the role of the body in thinking because our access to the world is through our bodies and the way we reason is shaped by our bodies, physical existence and the environment.[13] They demonstrate how many of the basic metaphors we use for thinking are rooted in the physical world. The word 'up' tends to be used for happy, 'down' tends to be used for sad because when we feel sad, our bodies droop. People tend to use down for sad and up for happy because that best reflects our experience of life.[14] Figurative language uses things from the physical world to communicate abstract ideas by connecting two apparently different things. We understand our life as a journey by drawing on physical journeys. This is a common metaphor that shapes our thinking about life; we talk of being at a crossroads and not knowing which road to take in life. This image is used by the Psalmist, Jesus and John Bunyan.[15] The following extract from a sermon on Mary visiting Elizabeth refers to a physical path and a figurative one. Describing Mary taking a certain path in life is no less real than Mary walking a certain path to get to Elizabeth's village. Both literal language and figurative language can refer to reality and reveal insights about life.

> The next day Mary separates from the group who are going direct to Jerusalem. Her *path* veers round the hillside and she continues up the steep trail alone … She has no idea what the future may hold, but if God has chosen a different *path* for her life, then she will walk it and not keep looking back.[16]

Using creative, figurative language can increase the depth and complexity communicated by words. Goodman points out that when considering truth, it does not matter whether language is literal or metaphorical (figurative), both can be true in different ways, both are part of the actual.[17] Figurative language can capture the meaning of an experience to the extent that a paraphrase cannot. John Donne's 'No man is an island' cannot be paraphrased as 'We are not self-sufficient' even though the basic meaning is the same.[18]

Figurative language enables words to relate to the world in new ways. When Jesus wanted to communicate the reality of the Kingdom of God he chose figurative language – the parables. The Good Samaritan is not true in the sense that Jesus does not claim that the Samaritan was a particular historical figure, but the parable tells the truth about life. In the extract that follows Kate Bruce explores Peter's promise to stand by Jesus and his failure to keep that promise when he denies Jesus. She uses creative language to link this to her congregation using the image of sandals figuratively to help the congregation see the relevance of Peter's story.

Perhaps we have known such failure.
Promising to live one way
We fail and live another.
Promising to forgive, or at least to try,
Until ...
the sharp retort springs from our lips.
Promising to look to Christ as the centre
We find we have enthroned something else.
For all our best intentions ...
We have failed.
Self-interest has reared its head;
And like the mist that goes away early,
all our promises have evaporated.
Perhaps Peter's sandals
Are not unfamiliar to us.
Perhaps the fisherman's sandals fit
surprisingly well.[19]

The extract below uses the metaphor of a stock market crash to communicate what happened when Paul expelled the spirit from the slave girl who told fortunes in Philippi (Acts 16.16–19). The congregation may not own stocks and shares but stock market crashes are part of the news and part of general experience.

As the spirit leaves, so do the owner's profits. All those who have shares in this girl watch the share price tumble. Their stock market has just crashed.[20]

Some preachers may be anxious concerning difficulties in understanding metaphorical language. Is it harder to process than literal language? The work of Anthony Sanford and Catherine Emmott have shown that metaphor permeates our language and standard metaphorical language is processed automatically, though new or unusual metaphors may slow processing.[21] Slowing processing can be positive, as it gives time to think. Timing is important; people need to be able to reflect on new metaphors or hear the preacher reflecting on them. Too many metaphors used close together do not give the congregation time to dwell on them and feel their power.

The understanding of metaphorical language is guided by tradition within a community. Within the Christian community people know that when Jesus is referred to as 'The Good Shepherd' they are not meant to understand that he was low paid and worked nights. Metaphors need interpreting and they are always partial. No single metaphor captures Jesus' role; multiple images are needed (King, Judge, Shepherd etc.). Metaphors are part of the preacher's toolkit for presenting rich, complex narratives that have depth of insight. Metaphors, should, however, be used appropriately; too many metaphors can pull attention in different directions, blurring meaning.

Question

Think about sermons you have preached or have heard. What metaphors or word-images stuck in your mind?

Conclusion

This chapter has considered ways in which language that shows relates to reality. In particular, the use of connotation, exemplification and Roland Barthes's reality effect. These ways of using language earths preaching in lived experience and can move it out of one-dimensional reference into a multi-dimensional experience. The use of creative language earths it deep in the physical world rather than distancing language from reality. The careful use of figurative language and varied forms of reference can make narratives, and the doctrines they encapsulate, live.

Notes

1 Nelson Goodman, 1976, *Languages of Art*, Indianapolis: Hackett, pp. 52–5.

2 Goodman, *Languages*, pp. 50–2, 68–9, 77.

3 Margaret Cooling, 'Crucifixion', *Preaching that Shows*, https://preachingthat shows.com/2021/07/19/crucifixion-2-too-much/, accessed 14.11.2021.

4 Goodman, *Languages*, pp. 51–9, 88.

5 Margaret Cooling, 'Trouble at Philippi', *Preaching that Shows*, https://preachingthatshows.com/2018/10/12/trouble-at-philippi-divided-sisters/, accessed 14.11.2021.

6 Marcel Proust, 1992, *In Search of Lost Time*, New York: The Modern Library, p. 64.

7 Margaret Cooling, 'Paul and Silas in Prison', *Preaching that Shows*, https://preachingthatshows.com/2018/10/12/paul-and-silas-in-prison-choices-and-responses/, accessed 14.11.2021.

8 Roland Barthes, 1982, 'The Reality Effect', in Tzvetan Todorov (ed.), *French Literary Theory Today*, tr. R. Carter, Cambridge: Cambridge University Press, pp. 11–17 (pp. 11–12, 16).

9 Margaret Cooling, 'The Woman with a Haemorrhage', *Preaching that Shows*, https://preachingthatshows.com/2018/10/10/the-woman-with-a-haemor-rhage-dance-macabre/, accessed 14.11.2021.

10 J. M. W. Turner, *Rain, Steam, and Speed – The Great Western Railway* (oil on canvas, 1844; National Gallery, London).

11 Edvard Munch, *The Scream* (tempera and crayon on cardboard, 1893; National Museum, Oslo).

12 Raymond W. Gibbs Jnr, 1994, *The Poetics of Mind*, Cambridge: Cambridge University Press, pp. 7–8, 16, 158–60.

13 George Lakoff and Mark Johnson, 1999, *Philosophy in the Flesh*, New York: Basic Books, pp. 5–6.

14 George Lakoff and Mark Johnson, 1980, *Metaphors We Live By*, Chicago: University of Chicago Press, pp. 14–15.

15 George Lakoff and Mark Turner, 1989, *More Than Cool Reason: A Field Guide to Poetic Metaphor*, Chicago: University of Chicago Press, pp. 3–4, 9–10.

16 Margaret Cooling, 'Mary and Elizabeth', *Preaching that Shows*, https://preachingthatshows.com/2018/10/10/mary-and-elizabeth/, accessed 14.11.2021.

17 Goodman, *Languages*, pp. 51, 68–9, 80.

18 John Donne, 'Devotions on Emergent Occasions, Meditation XVII', *Black-mask Online* (2002), http://www.public–library.uk/ebooks/28/27.pdf, accessed 14.11.2021, p. 36.

19 Kate Bruce, *John 21*, unpublished sermon.

20 Margaret Cooling, *Preaching that Shows*, https://preachingthatshows.com/2018/10/12/paul-and-silas-in-prison-choices-and-responses/, accessed 14.11.2021.

21 Anthony J. Sanford and Catherine Emmott, 2012, *Mind, Brain and Narrative*, Cambridge: Cambridge University Press, pp. 58–9.

10

Imagination

This chapter explores the role of imagination in an approach that shows rather than tells. Imagination is involved in preaching at every stage, particularly in a revelatory approach. It needs imagination to turn the text of a biblical narrative into a living text, it needs imagination to present an insight in a biblical narrative in a way that the congregation can see. This section looks at the different aspects of imagination and then engages with the hesitations some preachers may feel concerning its use in preaching. This involves a whirlwind tour of Christian history and how imagination has been viewed across time. God's imagination in creation and imagination expressed in the Bible are also considered and how much freedom the preacher has in using his or her imagination.

What is imagination?

Some people have a limited idea of what imagination is. Imagination is a broad concept and this section considers four of its aspects:

- The ability to create mental images.
- The ability to reveal new realities.
- An ability to make the absent present.
- An ability to see the 'more' in life.

Mental images

One definition of imagination is the ability to produce images in the mind; this may vary in people to a degree but most people form some sort of picture in their mind when they read or hear. This is sometimes called 'inner sight' but Garrett Green stresses that this is not actually inner sight, it is *like* inner sight. The issue for religious imagination is whether the pictures we form in our minds are appropriate: do they reflect the gospel as rendered in Scripture?[1]

Question

How easy do you find it to create mental images in your mind when hearing descriptions?

New realities

Another aspect of imagination is the way in which it can reveal something new. This can be seen in the Kingdom of God parables. Jesus used everyday images to reveal a new understanding of the Kingdom. Walter Brueggemann stresses the ability of the imagination to create visions of reality that are not about the world as it is but as it could be.[2] Martin Luther King's 'I have a dream ...' speech was about America as it could be.

Making the absent present

Garrett Green considers an important aspect of imagination: the ability to make the absent present. That sounds rather vague, but it is something we do all the time.[3]

Time

Things that are in the past or future are absent to us, but imagination can make these things present. With imagination we can travel to the past and with imagination we can project the future. Imagination makes time travellers of us all.

Space

Imagination can make present things that are absent because they are distant. With imagination we can travel to places far away. We can imagine a wilderness, Mount Sinai and the lake of Galilee.

Invisible

The imagination can also make present things that are perceived as absent because they can't be detected by our senses. With imagination we can envisage a soul and other aspects of life deemed real but invisible.

Logical

There are things we do not know yet; they are logically absent. Scientists use their imaginations to create hypotheses. A hypothesis is based on what is known and theorizes about what is not yet known about the universe. Scientists made the possibility of black holes present to our minds long before they were proven to exist.

Size

Some things appear to be absent because they are too big or too small for us to directly observe. The imagination can make present the universe and sub-atomic particles.

Seeing the more in life: sacramental imagination

Kate Bruce talks of sacramental imagination as the ability to see the 'more' in life.[4] We exercise this aspect of imagination when bread and wine are taken as the body and blood of Jesus, and the waters of baptism as rising to new life. To others they may be just bread, wine and water. This is a key function of the imagination in revelatory preaching that often locates spiritual insights in ordinary material existence. Something of this is expressed in the hymn 'Loved with Everlasting love' by George W. Robinson (1838–77).

> Heav'n above is softer blue,
> Earth around is sweeter green!
> Something lives in every hue
> Christless eyes have never seen.[5]

Functions of the imagination

Many scholars have explored the different aspects of imagination and how it functions. This section looks at the work of Kate Bruce and the four functions of imagination. Although these functions are presented separately, in practice they interact. The four functions are:

- Sensory.
- Intuitive.
- Affective.
- Intellectual.

The sensory function

This function of the imagination is involved in the way we see the world; it enables us to form mental images from what we perceive through our senses. The imagination also organizes information. This type of imagination has two modes: reproductive and productive. Imagination in its reproductive mode reproduces what we cannot directly see. We don't see every side of a cube, but our imagination supplies (reproduces) what we can't see. We may only be able to see three legs of the table but our imagination enables us to envisage all the legs. Seeing is partial, we don't see things hidden from sight but reproductive imagination fills the gaps. Imagination in its productive mode goes further, it takes material gathered from the senses and experiments with different combinations to explore possibilities.[6]

Questions

Look around the space you are in now. How is your reproductive imagination working? How is it providing you with a full picture when you can only see part of something?

The sensory imagination is active in creating a living text. Sensed experiences from the text can be brought together with ideas in unusual ways. The imagination can draw out some of the sensations involved in the imprisonment of John the Baptist: the small space, the inactivity, the light and shadow, the sense of an untamed person in a cage.

Imagine John,
still in his animal skins,
gripping the bars;
God's untamed prophet,
caged.
Imagine him pacing his cell:
so many steps long,
so many steps wide.
No books,
no TV,
just John and his thoughts.

John was an outdoor man,
he liked open spaces,
he was used to the desert's broad horizon.
Now his world could be measured in feet.
He could pace it in under a minute.
John's world had shrunk.
What light there was, struck prison bars
and played out their pattern on the floor,
a chessboard of light and shade.
Was he just a pawn in Herod's power game?
Was he part of some plan bigger than Herod?[7]

The intuitive function

This is the ability to make connections, rearrange and detect patterns that are 'outside the box', not the obvious connections. These patterns usually take time to form, though occasionally they come in a moment of insight after a period of incubation. This aspect of the imagination is involved in locating and developing an insight. This is the function of imagination that forms metaphors and other types of figurative language. Imagination in this mode can innovate, bringing together ideas that are not traditional partners, breaking new ground. It may bring both surprise and recognition as it may be a variation rather than something completely new. The intuitive function contributes to ways of understanding life that differ from the norm. It can create metaphors that challenge the way people see themselves, others and the world.[8] If we see the world as a cake it can result in a competitive mode of thinking and living. 'If you have more there will be less for me.' Seeing the world as a garden that we share and have responsibility for creates a very different mode of thinking and living (Gen. 2.15). The intuitive imagination sees one thing as another. The passing of Jesus between Pilate and Herod can be seen in terms of a children's game, bringing its own insights.

The powers that be play pass-the-parcel with Jesus,
no one wants to be holding him when the music stops.[9]

In this mode imagination does not go in straight lines towards an insight – it can go from A to E without having to go through BCD to get there.[10] An insight could be seeing the story of Esther as one of loss; Esther loses her name, her home, her family, her community and any control she had over her life. She nearly loses her life.

Question

Look through sermons you have preached. Where have you used this function of the imagination?

The affective function

Affective imagination comes into play in sermon preparation when we imagine ourselves into the situation in a biblical narrative. The affective imagination also helps to enter the situation of the congregation and how they may respond to a sermon. People experience this aspect of imagination in both sympathy and empathy. Sympathy is emotionally standing with someone; empathy is imaginatively attempting to view the world from their perspective. Empathy is an imaginative view from within. This aspect of imagination is powerful and comes with attendant dangers and limitations. Emotion and reason need to be balanced; the process of entering a situation empathetically should not emotionally overwhelm people, taking away their ability to decide their response or reflect at depth. Affective imagination enables preachers to enter a text using Ignatian techniques.[11] Ignatian techniques involve the reader imagining biblical scenes, the experience of characters and placing themselves within the scene.[12] Not all narratives are suitable for this technique for pastoral reasons, as discussed in Chapter 6. This form of imagination is used when people identify with characters in a narrative or when we try to understand those different from ourselves. Such engagement has the potential to generate compassion, understanding and new insights. Stanley Spencer used the affective function of the imagination when he painted the Centurion's servant as himself. Language can do the same.

> The boy tossing on his bed in sickness has the face of the artist.
> It could be your face.
> It could be mine.
> The boy is not praying.
> Sometimes, when we are in distress, we rely on others holding us in prayer.[13]

There are limits to the affective function; the degree to which people can enter another's situation varies, and there are some characters preachers would not want their congregation to empathize with. Some narratives are unsuitable for this use of the imagination as their content is violent, sexually explicit or pastorally unsuitable in some way. Revelatory preaching uses this form of imagination in communicating biblical characters and situations in a way that enables people to identify with them as appropriate. It can help people cross barriers of time, culture and gender. Nevertheless, there are no guarantees of understanding or changed attitudes.

Exercise

Locate two biblical narratives, one suitable for the use of affective imagination and one unsuitable. What renders them suitable or unsuitable?

Intellectual imagination

This aspect of imagination brings together reason and imagination; it allows 'if this ... then that' thinking to happen. Some sermons rely heavily on imagination's intellectual function, employing reason, argument and the imaginative 'if this ... then that' format:

If Christ rose, then ...
If Christ is for us, then ...

This allows people to follow an argument or situation before being committed to its truth. Intellectual imagination's 'if ... then ...' pattern is how people explore possibilities. It allows them to imaginatively try something and see where it leads. Intellectual imagination organizes information and recognizes patterns. Hypotheses are exercises of the intellectual imagination. Reason and imagination work together in noticing anomalies and creating new theories that form a paradigm shift, a transformation, in thinking. In the Christian world conversion is a paradigm shift, a new way of thinking and living, a new way of understanding God, self and others.[14]

Question

Which biblical story do you think would suit the 'if ... then ...' presentation?

God's imagination, human imagination

The doctrine of the creator God is important for understanding the imagination, for God's imagination is displayed in creation (Ps. 19.1). In the Early Church, God was sometimes described as an artist.[15] Human imagination is a pale reflection of God's imagination but it is a gift from God. God fills Bezalel with his Spirit for creative purposes (Ex. 31.1–6). The biblical writers engaged their imaginations, and this is reflected in the imaginative texts of different genres in the Bible. Prophets and poets, letter writers and Gospel writers exercise God's gift of imagination. David could have just said, 'God looks after me'; instead he wrote Psalm 23.

Imagination and creative freedom

How far can imagination go? Imagination is associated with creative freedom; Scripture, Christian tradition and doctrine – the stuff of sermons – have connotations of conformity but this does not have to be so. The Bible, doctrine and tradition create a platform on which preachers stand and from which they exercise creative imagination under the guidance of the Spirit. That does not mean that the elements that make up the platform cannot be challenged. Attitudes to slavery are an example of challenge. Christians reread the Bible and reinterpreted the tradition. The emphasis moved from the acceptance of slavery, a fact of life in biblical times, to the biblical ideal of freedom centred on all made in the image of God, being children of God and equal before God (Gen. 1.27–28; Gal. 3.28; 1 John 3.1). Theological boundaries do not have to be perceived negatively; they can channel imaginative thinking. Creativity needs constraint as it forces thinking beyond the obvious and can bring depth. Warren Wiersbe uses the analogy of a river; without boundaries a river becomes a swamp.[16]

Hesitations

Some people feel uneasy about using the imagination in preaching. This feeling tends to be in areas listed below:

- A view of imagination as an optional extra.
- A view of imagination as an ability that some people have and others don't.
- A muddling of imagination and fantasy.
- A restricted view of what the Bible says concerning imagination.

This section examines these areas with a view to freeing preachers to use their imaginations while remaining faithful to Scripture.

An optional extra?

Imagination is not an optional extra for any preacher, it is integral to every style of preaching. Imagination is involved in all stages of preaching, from engaging with Scripture to when the congregation's imagination engages with the sermon. Imagination is crucial in a revelatory approach when the biblical narrative is reimagined as a living text. Imagination is involved in the use of creative language and in shaping material to show a narrative. It takes imagination to see the spiritual in the material world and to see this world as a place where God can be met. Imagination is used when creating details that the text does not provide and when the congregation fills in gaps and works through possibilities. Drawing on art engages the visual imagination of both preacher and congregation and both need imagination to connect the biblical world with the contemporary one.

An ability a person may not have

I was once told by a friend that he didn't 'do' imagination. This reflects a view that imagination is something you are born with, you either have it or you don't. Some people may have a more highly developed imagination than others, but Amy Kind and Peter Kung stress that imagination is an ability we all have and we use it daily to navigate the world. We use it as we anticipate what might happen; we use it when we think about how people may respond in a situation and what people might be thinking or feeling.[17] Education and upbringing may not have cultivated this ability in some people, but it is never too late to nurture a God-given ability.

Question

Think about your own imaginative ability. On a scale of 1–10 (with 10 as high) how would you grade your own use of imagination?

Muddling imagination and fantasy

The reluctance of some preachers to use their imagination in preaching is sometimes a result of the confusion of imagination with fantasy. Imagination works from what *is* to what *could be*. Fantasy is different, Garrett Green describes it as the illusionary aspect of imagination. The distinguishing between imagination and fantasy is not always easy but we can usually differentiate scientific predictions from the expression of fantasy in science fiction.[18] The star ship *Enterprise* (*Star Trek*) is fantasy, the International Space Station is the result of scientific imagination. Fantasy can still present truth. Tolkien's *Lord of the Rings* is fantasy but it can tell the truth about the human condition.[19]

A restricted view of what the Bible says

Some preachers are reluctant to use their imagination because they assume the Bible has a negative view of it. A close look at the Bible reveals a complex understanding of what we call imagination. In the Old Testament there are references to evil imagination and these are often the verses that come to mind when people are wary of exercising their imaginations in preaching. In Genesis God says, 'the imagination of man's heart is evil from his youth' (Gen. 8.21 AV). The word translated 'imagination' in this verse is translated as 'inclination' in many modern versions. The Bible does not have a single word to cover the modern concept of imagination; both Old and New Testaments use a range of words to cover what we understand as imagination and these words can be positive or negative. However, it is to the biblical words for 'heart' that scholars such as Paul Scott Wilson, Kate Bruce and Garrett Green turn in order to understand the Bible's attitude to what we call imagination.[20]

- *Leb* is the most common Hebrew word that covers many aspects of the modern understandings of imagination. It is the word for heart, will, mind, understanding and the inner person. It can be positive or negative. In Genesis 8.21 *leb* appears twice, once used of God and once of humanity. In relation to God, it refers to inward deliberation, in reference to humanity the heart is named as evil in this verse, but that is not the overall verdict of the Bible: the heart can be wicked (Jer. 17.9) or pure (Matt. 5.8).
- *Kardia* is the Greek word for heart used in the New Testament and it is used for different aspects of imagination. It can have both good and evil intentions. Mark 7.21 talks of evil proceeding from the heart, but

Luke 10.27 reiterates the Old Testament injunction to love God with all your heart.

The words *kardia* and *leb* are key terms in identifying the Bible's under-standings of imagination and attitudes towards it. The heart is the seat of thought, will and worship; it is the centre of emotion, belief and decision making. The heart guides behaviour, it is involved in a relationship with God and it has a part to play in reasoning. It is the place where God's word dwells (Deut. 30.14), where God's new law is written (Jer. 31.31–34) and where the light of God shines (2 Cor. 4.6). The heart is also the place from which people deny God (Ps. 14.1) and devise evil plans (Gen. 6.5). It is the heart that God changes from stone to flesh (Ezek. 36.26). The biblical concept of heart is not the same as the modern concept of imagination but they significantly overlap.[21]

The biblical warrant for using the imagination goes further than the understanding of certain words in the Bible; throughout the Bible there are models of imagination in parables and other types of figurative lan-guage. Death is imagined as the snapping of the silver cord (Eccles. 12.6), God is imaged as an eagle (Deut. 32.11–12) and a mother (Isa. 66.13), while the devil is like a roaring lion (1 Pet. 5.8). The prophets engaged in imaginative dramatic acts, performing words from God: Isaiah walked naked (Isa. 20.3) and Ezekiel enacted a mini-siege (Ezek. 4.1–3). Jesus embraces imaginative language in all its forms, speaking of the Kingdom of God in terms of a treasure, a pearl and a net (Matt. 13.44–50) and the end coming like a thief in the night (Matt. 24.42–43). Each of these forms of imaginative communication is earthed in something concrete and specific: an animal (lion, eagle), an action (walking, besieging), an object (silver cord, pearl, treasure, net), a person (mother, thief). Imagin-ation retains its anchor in the world even if it has a length of chain to give it freedom.

Question

Look through the areas of thinking that cause some people to feel uneasy about the use of imagination in preaching. Do any of them express your own thinking? Which, if any, do you think expresses the thinking of the congregation of the church you attend?

Imagination in Christian history

Biblical language may license the wise use of imagination but the verdict of Christian history also matters if preachers are going to feel comfortable using their imaginations in sermons. Once again there are no simple answers, at times imagination was encouraged and it flourished, at other time a series of concerns were expressed. The concerns revolved around the following:

- The second Commandment.
- A fear of dependency.
- Misuse.
- Distraction.
- Unreliability.
- An inability to communicate truth.
- Unreality.

What follows is a whirlwind tour of how the imagination has been viewed over time, drawing particularly on the work of Garrett Green and William Dyrness. I have included attitudes to images as expressions of visual imagination as well as verbal imagination.

The second Commandment

The first area of concern is the Bible's injunction to make no graven image, an expression of visual imagination. This ban is expressed in very broad terms.

> You shall not make for yourself an idol, whether in the form of anything that is in heaven above, or that is on the earth beneath, or that is in the water under the earth. You shall not bow down to them or worship them. (Ex. 20.4–5)

Although the ban is broad, it does not prohibit the use of imagination to create word-images. It is forbidden to draw God's hands but speaking of them imaginatively is allowed. 'I have inscribed you on the palms of my hands' (Isa. 49.16). As already noted, the ban on expressions of visual imagination does not seem to be total as God instructs craftsmen to decorate the temple, including making cherubim (Ex. 25.18–20). The ban does not seem to have been universally enforced: images of biblical scenes have been found in synagogues at Huqoq and Dura-Europos.[22]

The Early Church

The witness of the Early Church is indecisive. John Chrysostom, the fifth-century preacher, earned his title 'golden mouth' based on his imaginative preaching. Pope Gregory thought images helped people understand God; they were the visual Scriptures of the illiterate.[23] As time progressed, imagination expressed in art came to play an increasing role in the Christian faith. Nevertheless, suspicion of visual imagination led to controversies concerning icons. This was an issue not settled until the ninth century, largely through an appeal to the incarnation. Jesus was the image of the invisible God and depicting his 'likeness' was an affirmation of the incarnation.

The Middle Ages

In the Middle Ages imagination was voiced in preaching, particularly in the popular preaching of Franciscan friars. Biblical narratives were expressed imaginatively in mystery plays, and Christians were urged to engage imaginatively with the Bible through devotional exercises, imagining themselves in biblical scenes. Margaret Miles points out that there was a belief that images could inspire devotion, focus attention, stimulate thinking and affect the will.[24] Thomas Aquinas defended imagination as crucial for understanding.[25] In the Middle Ages there was a concern about external visual images and people being dependent on them, but this existed side by side with an encouragement of the imagination.

The Reformation

The Reformation response to visual imagination tended to be negative. William Dyrness describes the Protestant attitude as 'suspicious' of the imagination, particularly imagination expressed in artwork. However, Luther believed God could speak through all creation and was open to the use of images in worship.[26] The reformed tradition, represented by Calvin and Zwingli, had more restrictive views. Zwingli excluded images from worship on the grounds of idolatry and distraction.[27] Calvin valued painting and sculpture as gifts from God and they could be used 'purely and lawfully' but not in churches.[28]

Generally, visual imagination tended to give way to imagination expressed in words as preaching came to the fore in Protestant churches; there was a distrust of the eye that did not extend to the ear. Although some Puritans were suspicious of imaginative language, labelling it as 'shallow', they used it in preaching. This created a tension that we see in

John Bunyan. When he wrote *The Pilgrim's Progress* Bunyan felt he had to defend his use of the imagination by referencing the Bible's imaginative language.[29] The reformed tradition, for all its suspicion of imagination, produced poets such as John Milton, John Bunyan, Anne Bradstreet and the remarkable flowering of art known as the Dutch Golden Age in the Calvinist Netherlands. It was the tradition that gave us Rembrandt.

Counter-Reformation

The Catholic Church underwent a 'Counter-Reformation' in response to the rise of Protestantism. There was an increasing emphasis on preaching and the Council of Trent (1563) reaffirmed the value of images in Catholic worship.[30] The development of a dramatic form of art, called Baroque, was an expression of Catholic visual imagination. However, the style spread to Protestant countries and became an expression of faith for both Catholic and Protestant. This expression of artistic religious imagination is seen most clearly in Rembrandt (Protestant) and Rubens (Catholic).

The Enlightenment

With the Enlightenment of the seventeenth and eighteenth centuries, reason came to the forefront. For the French philosopher René Descartes, imagination was not something that could be depended on as a source of secure knowledge, and imagination did not have a role in thinking.[31] Immanuel Kant was more sympathetic, acknowledging that imagination could bring ideas and sense experience together.[32]

The Romantic Movement and the nineteenth century

The Romantic Movement of the late eighteenth and early nineteenth centuries viewed imagination as humanity's greatest ability; imagination was the point of contact between the human and divine in terms of creativity.[33] In contrast, philosophers such as Ludwig Feuerbach had a low view of imagination; religion was little more than wish fulfilment and God was just a figment of the imagination.[34] The rise of views of science that limited knowledge to what could be known by deduction from observation and experimentation also tended to exclude imagination. Despite such scepticism religious imagination was alive and well in the nineteenth century. It was expressed in hymns, novels, poems, fairy stories, preaching and religious art. Although Charles Haddon Spurgeon decried imagination from the pulpit, calling it 'building on sand', many Victorian preachers saw its potential and used it.[35]

The twentieth and twenty-first centuries

The twentieth and twenty-first centuries saw imagination labelled as unreliable by some because religious statements used creative forms of language which were deemed less capable of conveying truth than literal language that delivered facts.[36] Despite this, imagination was expressed by novelists and poets such as Graham Greene, Flannery O'Connor, Elizabeth Alexander, James Wheldon Johnson, W. H. Auden and T. S. Eliot. J. R. R. Tolkien and C. S. Lewis both created other worlds that showed how imaginative forms could help people think through different ways of looking at life. There were also alternative voices in science: Albert Einstein valued imagination; Einstein declared he valued imagination more than knowledge.[37] Imagination is currently enjoying a comeback and John Piper from the reformed tradition regards using imagination as a Christian duty and he describes speaking, writing, singing or painting boringly as 'probably a sin'.[38]

This whirlwind historical tour shows that imagination has had a chequered career, from being regarded as evil to being perceived as a reflection of the divine. The use of imagination in preaching is not endorsed without taking account of some of the warnings and encouragements of history. Neither the almost God-like status of imagination expressed by the Romantics nor the early Reformers' rejection is appropriate for preachers today. In whatever way the Fall is understood, neither imagination nor reason is exempt from its effects; both are God-given faculties. Imagination needs to be renewed and transformed, no more and no less than the mind (Rom. 12.2).

Conclusion

This chapter has reviewed various attitudes to imagination, its biblical roots, historical perspectives and different ways of understanding how imagination works. Imagination is involved in preaching at every stage, whatever form of preaching is practised. It is particularly crucial to revelatory preaching with its re-imagining of an original situation, seeing the spiritual in material life and re-presenting a slice of narrative life.

Notes

1 Garrett Green,1989, *Imagining God*, Grand Rapids: Eerdmans, pp. 94–5.

2 Walter Brueggemann, 2012, *The Practice of Prophetic Imagination*, Minneapolis: Fortress Press, p. 25.

3 Green, *Imagining*, pp. 62–5.

4 Kate Bruce, 2015, *Igniting the Heart*, London: SCM Press, pp. 85–6.

5 George W. Robinson, 'Loved with Everlasting Love', *Hymnal Net*, https://www.hymnal.net/en/hymn/h/284, accessed 14.11.2021.

6 Bruce, *Igniting*, pp. 3–8.

7 Margaret Cooling, 'John the Baptist in Prison', *Preaching that Shows*, https://preachingthatshows.com/2018/10/10/john-the-baptist-in-prison-the-duck-test/, accessed 14.11.2021.

8 Bruce, *Igniting*, pp. 8–12.

9 Margaret Cooling, 'The Trials and Mocking of Jesus', *Preaching that Shows*, https://preachingthatshows.com/2018/10/12/the-trials-and-mocking-of-jesus/, accessed 14.11.2021.

10 Michael Austin, 2014, *Explorations in Art, Theology and Imagination*, Abingdon: Routledge, p. 3.

11 Bruce, *Igniting*, pp. 13–17.

12 Kevin O'Brien SJ, 'Ignatian Contemplation: Imaginative Prayer', *Ignatian Spirituality*, https://www.ignatianspirituality.com/ignatian-prayer/the-spiritual-exercises/ignatian-contemplation-imaginative-prayer/, accessed 14.11.2021.

13 Margaret Cooling, 'The Centurion's Servant', *Preaching that Shows*, https://preachingthatshows.com/2018/10/10/the-centurions-servant-real-life/, accessed 14.11.2021.

14 Bruce, *Igniting*, pp. 17–26.

15 Ambrose, 1961, *Fathers of the Church*, New York: Fathers of the Church, pp. 21, 23, 94, 259–60.

16 Warren Wiersbe, 1996, *Preaching & Teaching with Imagination*, Grand Rapids: Baker Books, pp. 202–3.

17 Amy Kind and Peter Kung, 2016, 'Introduction', in Amy Kind and Peter Kung (eds), *Knowledge Through Imagination*, Oxford: Oxford University Press, pp. 1–37 (pp. 17–19).

18 Green, *Imagining*, pp. 63–4.

19 J. R. R. Tolkien, 'On Fairy Stories', *Andrew Lang Lecture* (1939), https://archive.org/details/on-fairy-stories/page/33/mode/2up?q=epilogue, accessed 14.11.2021, pp. 9, 14–15.

20 Bruce, *Igniting*, p. 30–2. Green, *Imagining*, pp. 109–10. Paul Scott Wilson, 1988, *Imagination of the Heart*, Nashville: Abingdon Press, p. 19.

21 Alison Searle, 2008, *'The Eyes of Your Heart'*, Milton Keynes: Paternoster, pp. 34–9.

22 Jodi Magnes et al., 'Explore the Huqoq Mosaics', *Biblical Archaeological Society* (2019), https://www.biblicalarchaeology.org/%20scholars-study/more-on-the-mosaics/, accessed 14.11.2021. Hagith Sivan, 'Dura-Europos Synagogue Paintings' *The Torah.com* (2019), https://www.thetorah.com/article/retelling-the-story-of-moses-at-dura-europos-synagogue, accessed 14.11.2021.

23 William A. Dyrness, 2004, *Reformed Theology and Visual Culture*, Cambridge: Cambridge University Press, pp. 19, 21.

24 Margaret Miles, 1985, *Image as Insight*, Eugene: Wipf & Stock, pp. 65–9, 98, 144.

25 Thomas Aquinas, 1953, *Super Boethium De Trinitate*, Toronto: n.pub., Question 6. Article 2.

26 Dyrness, *Reformed*, pp. 7–8, 53–4.

27 Huldrych Zwingli, 1984, *Writings*, Allison Park: Pickwick Publications, vol. II, pp. 68–71.

28 Jean Calvin, *The Institutes of the Christian Religion*, tr. Henry Beveridge, Grand Rapids: 2002, http://www.ccel.org/ccel/calvin/institutes.html, accessed 14.11.2021, book 1, pp. 68–78.

29 John Bunyan, 2005, *Pilgrim's Progress*, New York: Barnes and Noble Classics, p. 8.

30 The Council of Trent, *Second Decree on the Invocation, the Veneration, and the Relics, of Saints, and on Sacred Images* (1563), http://www.thecounciloftrent.com/ch25.htm, accessed 14.11.2021.

31 René Descartes, 2008, *Meditations on First Philosophy*, Oxford: Oxford University Press, pp. 20–2.

32 Immanuel Kant, 1998, *Critique of Pure Reason*, tr. and ed. Paul Guyer and Allen W. Wood, Cambridge: Cambridge University Press, pp. 225, 237–41.

33 Green, *Imagining*, p. 18.

34 Ludwig Feuerbach, 1967, *Lectures on the Essence of Religion*, New York: Harper and Row, pp. 15–16, 19, 21, 23.

35 Charles Haddon Spurgeon, 2016, *The Soul-Winner*, Abbotsford: Aneko Press, p. 2.

36 Green, *Imagining*, pp. 25–6.

37 Albert Einstein, 'What Life Means to Einstein', *Saturday Evening Post*, 26 October 1929, http://www.saturdayeveningpost.com/wp-content/uploads/sateve-post/einstein.pdf, accessed 14.10.2021, p. 117.

38 John Piper, 'Obey God with Your Creativity: The Christian Duty of Imagination' (2018), *Desiring God*, https://www.desiringgod.org/articles/obey-god-with-your-creativity, accessed 14.11.2021.

11

Interpretation

This chapter concerns hermeneutics, a term that encompasses the ways in which people interpret texts in order to understand their meaning and significance. Throughout this chapter the framework of prayer, contemplation and the guidance of the Holy Spirit is assumed. It is a fact of life that interpretations differ; two preachers can prayerfully study the same text and preach two different sermons and both may be valid interpretations. The same is true of art: two people can look at the same painting and come away with differing interpretations. This poses a question, 'Are there limits to the interpretations of a text or artwork; are some interpretations invalid?' This chapter explores this question and surrounding issues of interpretation.

Why hermeneutics matters

An example from art interpretation may set the scene for this chapter on textual and visual hermeneutics. A fifteenth-century painting known as *Two Courtesans* by Vittore Carpaccio was interpreted as two bored courtesans waiting for clients, according to art criticism at the beginning of the twentieth century. The subject of the brothel was popular at the time and it may have influenced the interpretation. In the 1960s an art critic noticed that the painting had a stem of a plant with no flower head in the top left-hand corner. He also noticed that there was a painting of similar dimensions called *Hunting on the Lagoon* in another museum that had lilies with incomplete stems in the bottom left-hand corner. When the two paintings were put together, and after robust testing, it was proved that they were a single painting. It became clear that these were two bored noble women waiting for their men to return from the hunt, not two courtesans. The inscription has now been changed to *The Wait: Hunting on the Lagoon and Two Venetian Ladies*.[1] The story of this misinterpretation and the two paintings can be found online.[2]

Meaning and reality

Preachers have to grapple with a number of realities that are basic to interpretation:

The original situation:	The situation that caused the text to be written (where a historical situation is indicated).
The author's reality:	The world the author lives in, the world 'behind' the text.
The textual reality:	The world reflected in the text, the way the original situation is presented in Scripture.
The reality of the reader:	The world of the preacher and the congregation, sometimes called 'the world in front of the text'.

An example of these differing realities can be demonstrated by the story of Stephen in Acts 6—7.

The original situation:	The attempt to suppress the growing numbers of followers of Jesus leading to the death of Stephen.
The author's world:	The world of the early churches' spread across the Roman Empire by Paul and others. Later than the death of Stephen.
The world of the text:	Stephen's death as presented from a Christian perspective, interpreting the original situation in theological terms.
The readers' world:	The modern world.

The original situation

A revelatory approach sees biblical narratives as reflecting people and events – an original historical situation – in some way, where that is signalled by the text. Something happened in the real world to cause the text to be written. Texts, such as the accounts of the crucifixion, claim to refer to a historical event. Christianity is a historical faith and that is expressed in the Creeds. The Apostles' Creed roots faith in historical circumstances, Christ's birth and his crucifixion under Pontius Pilate.[3] The date of Jesus' birth and death may not be known exactly but it is important that Jesus was born, died and rose at specific moments in time. The Bible makes historical claims and its authority depends on the reality of those events. As a result, if narrative texts reflect an underlying reality (original situation) then that reality can potentially exercise some constraint on interpretation. Texts can't mean anything we want them to if the historical foundations of certain texts are taken seriously.

Revelatory preaching works backwards from the text to an original situation – as far as that can be known. In the creation of a living text and honing it for a sermon there is a re-presenting of the original situation that may communicate some of its original impact. Sidney Greidanus stresses that the nature of the relationship between text and original situation will depend on genre. A historical foundation is primary for books that claim historical reference and secondary for others. Biblical books with historical reference, such as Kings, the Gospels and Acts, will have more of a relationship with historical events than Psalms, Proverbs and apocalyptic literature. It needs to be borne in mind that biblical history books are not written to modern historical criteria as their primary purpose is theological. However, this does not make them unreliable; Luke emphasizes his concern for accurate recording (Luke 1.1–3). Preachers seek to understand a text in its own time and place, trying to hear a text as it might have been heard originally but without claiming to have access to events *exactly* as they happened.[4]

Exercise

Locate two biblical books that you would classify as primary in terms of their historical foundation, and two biblical books that you would classify as secondary in terms of their historical foundation.

The author's reality

The author's reality is the world he/she lives in, this includes the way they view the world and ways of thinking, believing and living as well as their physical circumstances. The author's world and their aim and intention in writing the text was the deciding factor in interpretation for much of Christian history. What mattered was understanding the mind of the author and how the author intended us to understand the text. The emphasis was on getting behind the text. However, the author's world could be very different from the world reflected in the text. Authors often write about times that are different to the ones they live in; understanding the world of the author is different to understanding the world of the text. In the 1940s this focus on the author's intent came under criticism.

William Wimsatt and Monroe Beardsley cast doubt on the reader's ability to know what was going on in the author's mind and whether this was even desirable.[5]

If the author's world and intention is all that matters, the text becomes just a container of meaning and the reader becomes like an archaeologist who just discovers what was intended but has no other role to play. Past reality (the author's intention and world) dominates and it can be difficult to engage with the present. Anthony Thiselton notes that what the author intended is seldom fully known, and the author may have unconsciously included much that was not intended. Some passages contain depths of meaning that were not necessarily intended by the author. The way the Suffering Servant passages in Isaiah are understood by Christians as referring to Christ may not have been intended by the author but that does not mean that they cannot be legitimately interpreted in this way. Thiselton uses the term 'author direction' rather than author intent; the author gives signals in the text concerning how it is to be read.[6] In revelatory preaching the primary focus is on the world reflected in the text rather than the author's world, but preachers engage with the author's guidance when unfolding a narrative to create a living text.

Exercise

Read Luke 9.51. How does this piece of author direction affect how we read Luke's Gospel from this point? How would reading Luke's Gospel without this direction change how we read the rest of the Gospel?

The textual reality

In the twentieth century the focus of interpretation moved to the text and its role in interpretation. The way the text is written as well as the world reflected in the text all contribute to meaning. The text presents the original situation but it is not just a mirror of everything that happened: style, selection and arrangement come into play. Interpretation and theological significance affect how the original situation is presented in the text. Nevertheless, the relationship to the reality of the original situation is preserved. The account of the raising of Jairus' daughter is not identical in Matthew, Mark and Luke (Matt. 9.18–26; Mark 5.21–43; Luke 8.40–56). Although the basic storyline is the same, the presentation is different.

Texts can relate to real events in various ways. Christopher Wright likens the relationship of texts and reality to maps. Each type of map relates to the real world in a way that is relevant to its purpose. There are geographical maps, political maps and walking maps. Maps can differ: a map of the London underground is different from a map of the geography of London, but each is accurate for its purpose.[7]

Another analogy may help here. Beethoven's fifth symphony can be performed in different ways but the score exercises control over how the music is played. The score allows flexibility but limits the amount of variation. The same is true of texts: the reality underlying the text limits the number of credible interpretations. Interpretations can vary within a range without implying relativism.

Question

Look at the three accounts of Jairus' daughter. What is the effect of the different presentations?

The reader/hearer's reality

From the 1960s onwards the focus turned to the role of the readers and their role in interpretation. The radical branch of this movement gave the reader control of meaning and the radical form of reader-response meant that the reader could find what they want in a text without any constraints by the author, text or original situation.[8] Recognizing a role for readers/hearers does not have to take this radical approach. A revelatory approach recognizes a role for readers/hearers in filling in gaps and exploring possibilities. Characters and situations are detailed and delivered in a style and at a pace that enables hearers to play their part in working out meaning. The experience of readers/hearers can be a positive contribution to interpretation but the reader has a responsibility to the text.

The idea that people bring something to the text was often viewed in a negative light. Hans-Georg Gadamer took the opposite view, maintaining that no one enters interpretation from a neutral stance: we all come with preconceptions – things we assume – and these are a natural part of interpretation.[9] No one comes to a biblical text as a blank slate. We cannot empty our heads, ignore our experience, or deny that the world we live in will influence us. We can, however, seek guidance in acknowledging our assumptions and strive for openness, allowing the Bible to challenge us. Sermons can acknowledge common preconceptions and challenge or affirm as appropriate. Jesus' parable of the labourers in the vineyard (Matt. 20.1–16) challenges assumptions about justice as justice is overtaken by grace. The values of the Kingdom expounded in the Beatitudes are revolutionary (Matt. 5.3–12) and unlikely to affirm modern assumptions about life.

Cooperation

The author, text and reader do not have to be in competition concerning interpretation, they can work together. Scripture as primary witness involves all three: the author offers direction concerning how to read the text; the text guides the trajectory of the interpretation as the reader develops meaning and significance under the guidance of the Holy Spirit. This is a cooperative process. The fact that texts can have more than one interpretation does not have to imply an inability to choose between them or relativism. Questions can be asked:

Does the interpretation lead to a deeper understanding?
Does it fit with the overall message of Scripture, particularly with the gospel message as taught and lived by Jesus?
Is it credible considering the situation presented in the text?

New interpretations remind us that our understanding of Scripture is neither complete nor final. Few Christians today would agree with past interpretations of certain texts that upheld class structures or slavery. The Puritan John Robinson declared, 'For I am very confident the Lord hath more truth and light yet to break forth out of His holy Word.'[10]

Attitudes and virtues

Revelatory preaching presents the realities of biblical people and situations. This can enable voices from another culture and time to speak to us. God can be heard speaking with and through people of the past. This has implications concerning attitudes that are needed to enable us to hear. Richard Briggs and Kevin Vanhoozer describe virtues that are needed for interpretation. Patience and receptivity are needed in paying attention to a text. This means following where the text leads even if it seems a bit weird. Judgement needs to be held in check long enough to consider the challenge that may be there. Richard Briggs calls this 'holding one's nerve' before a text.[11] Paying attention to a text means seeing what is there. This sounds obvious, but sometimes we do not notice how strange some texts are because we unconsciously filter out the difficult parts. We have grown used to the Bible and no longer register how alien it sounds outside Christian circles. One way of noticing the strangeness of some texts and coming to terms with what a text is saying is to imagine a non-believing friend sitting next to you. How would they hear the text?

Openness, honesty, attentiveness, responsibility, respect, conviction, wisdom and obedience are all interpretive virtues, but the primary virtue is humility. These virtues are the frame of mind a reader brings to a text but this does not mean coming to the text without any beliefs; it is about how those beliefs are held. Is the reader open to challenge? Interpretive virtue is being willing to sit under a text rather than over it. This is not abandoning thinking; it is deciding the attitude with which we think. Humility leads to a desire to do justice to the text; it is an attitude of patient attention and appropriate trust and wisdom that has enough confidence to allow questioning to be voiced. Critical scholarship is not rejected. These virtues are exercised within a framework of loving God and neighbour.[12]

Question

When have you had to hold your nerve before a text because it felt weird?

Visual hermeneutics

Visual hermeneutics has undergone a development similar to textual hermeneutics and the role of the artist, artwork and viewer parallels that of the author, text and reader. Interpreting artworks can be a cooperative venture where the artist, viewer and artwork each have a role to play in the quest for understanding and meaning. Interpretation in art is not just what a person feels about an artwork; art can contribute to understanding but ideas are expressed concretely in colour and texture, in gestures and expressions. Just a glance by one person is not enough to interpret an artwork: artworks are understood by spending time in prayer, study, contemplation and engagement with others.

The artist

Art can show how a text has been interpreted by artists down the centuries, giving the preacher insights from other ages and perspectives. Artists express their interpretation through the elements of art (shape, texture, form, space, colour, tone) and use these to guide viewers. Duccio, in his *Maestà* for Siena Cathedral, placed *The Healing of the Man Born Blind* next to *The Transfiguration* so that the blind man – newly healed – gazes out of his painting and appears to be seeing the transfigured Christ. By this placement Duccio expresses his understanding of sight and insight.[13] Artists may represent a scene from an unusual perspective. Andrea Mantegna's *Lamentation over the Dead Christ* approaches the subject feet first. Christ's full humanity is shown in his dead body. There are no halos, no angels, no spiritual glow.[14] Artistic interpretations may vary but do not have to conflict. Sandro Botticelli and Andrea Mantegna both painted the *Adoration of the Magi* but the two paintings are very different. Both are credible understandings of Matthew 2.1–12.

- Botticelli's *Adoration* (1475) places the Christ child in the centre of the painting, above the Magi. The composition directs the viewers' eyes to Mary and Jesus who rest on a rock within a ruined building. The focus is Christ whose reign is founded on solid rock, more enduring than earthly empires such as Rome.[15]
- Mantegna's *Adoration* does the opposite; he removes all background and provides a close-up of the faces of the Magi. It is relational and about worship. The world, represented by the Magi, comes to worship the King.[16]

Paolo Berdini describes artists as active interpreters. Artists are not totally free in how they interpret a text, nor are they completely controlled by it, but they do have a responsibility to the text. Artists go beyond the text in terms of details as they must clothe people, give them expressions and paint a background, none of which the Bible may detail.[17] Artists also develop their interpretation of a text but the trajectory of the text – the direction the text is heading in – guides the interpretation.[18] An example of this is the way artists often interpret the nativity in light of the crucifixion, including indications of Christ's death: the shadow of a cross, a tomb-like manger and a hint of thorn, none of which may have been present in the actual event.

The artwork

A biblical artwork is more than a skilful composition, it refers to something outside itself – a biblical text and the event that triggered the text. The way the scene is painted, the style and composition make it more than just a picture of a biblical scene, there is insight into that scene created by its composition, the use of light and dark, gesture and body language. Gerrit van Honthorst's *Christ Before the High Priest* shows viewers what is going on in terms of power.[19] The artwork does not exist unrelated to the artist or the viewer for without these it becomes something to be admired without engaging with anyone or anything outside itself.

The viewer

A viewer engages with a biblical artwork in the light of the text but the relationship is two-way; the artwork may send the viewer back to the text with new questions to ask. However, there is still a question concerning how free the viewer is to interpret an artwork. The answer is the same as it was for text, if the text reflects an original situation, then that reality exercises some control over interpretation. Giovanni Girolamo Savoldo's *Mary Magdalene* stares out of the painting directly at the viewer and we are left to interpret her mood and expression.[20] The fact that this is Mary Magdalene at the empty tomb reduces the range of appropriate interpretations.

Terry Barrett defines a good interpretation as one that makes sense, relates to the artwork and includes the whole work. An interpretation also considers the world of the artist without that determining the interpretation.[21] Barrett's definition gives interpretation some definite boundaries, however, not all interpretations include the whole work. A sermon may focus on a detail and not necessarily engage in any depth with the whole work. Nevertheless, the interpretation of the detail should be in line with the interpretation of the whole work even if the rest of the work is not discussed.

Exercise

Look at Craigie Aitchison's *Crucifixion 2008* online. How would you interpret this painting bearing in mind the artist, the artwork and your own response? Information can be found online concerning the artist and his style of painting.

Preaching and hermeneutics

The texts on which we preach vary, some are open to a range of under-
standings, other texts are more straightforward by nature. Social justice
texts often state how unacceptable certain behaviours are to God and
demand change. A sermon can reflect that, even a revelatory one. Other
texts are open to a range of interpretations. Jesus' cleansing of the temple
(Matt. 21.12–17) has been interpreted in different ways. Art can be an
integral part of hermeneutics for preachers. It can suggest interpretations,
trigger new perspectives and help preachers earth interpretations in the
material world.

Conclusion

This chapter has considered textual and visual hermeneutics. Interpretation and the quest for meaning begins the moment we start reading
the Bible, it begins for the congregation the moment they hear the Bible
reading. Author, text and reader can work together so that meaning
is understood as part of a cooperative process. The same cooperative
hermeneutic applies to visual narratives. Interpretation relates to the
realities that underlie many biblical texts, exercising some control over
interpretation. Interpretation does not end when meaning is discerned, it
goes on to be practised in the world.

Notes

1 Vittore Carpaccio, *The Wait: Hunting on the Lagoon and Two Venetian
Ladies* (oil and tempera on wood, *c.*1490–95; *Hunting on the Lagoon,* J. Paul Getty
Museum, Los Angeles; *Two Venetian Ladies,* Museo Correr, Venice).

2 Philip McCouat, '*Carpaccio's Double Enigma*', *Art in Society* (2019), http://
www.artinsociety.com/carpacciorsquos-double-enigma-hunting-on-the-lagoon-
and-the-two-venetian-ladies.html, accessed 14.11.2021.

3 'The Apostles' Creed', *The Church of England,* https://www.churchofeng-
land.org/our-faith/what-we-believe/apostles-creed, accessed 14.11.2021.

4 Sidney Greidanus, 1988, *The Modern Preacher and the Ancient Text,* Grand
Rapids: Eerdmans, pp. 80–1, 86–7, 91–3.

5 W. K. Wimsatt Jr. and M. C. Beardsley, 'The Intentional Fallacy', *The
Sewanee Review,* 54/3 (1946), 468–88 (pp. 468, 470). https://www.jstor.org/stable/
27537676?seq=1, accessed 14.11.2021.

6 Anthony C. Thiselton, 2009, *Hermeneutics,* Grand Rapids: Eerdmans, p. 27.

7 Christopher J. H. Wright, 2006, *The Mission of God,* Downers Grove: Inter-
Varsity Press, pp. 68–9.

8 Thiselton, *Hermeneutics,* pp. 30–1.

9 Hans-Georg Gadamer, 1982, *Truth and Method*, New York: Crossroad, pp. 267–74, 278, 282–3.

10 John Robinson, '1620 sermon', *Encyclopaedia Britannica*, https://www.britannica.com/biography/John-Robinson-English-minister, accessed 14.11.2021.

11 Richard S. Briggs, 2010, *The Virtuous Reader*, Grand Rapids: Baker Academic, pp. 187–90.

12 Briggs, *The Virtuous Reader*, pp. 19–21, 46, 63–8, 71–3, 100–2, 104–5, 127, 140–1. Kevin Vanhoozer, 1998, *Is There a Meaning in this Text?*, Leicester: Apollos, pp. 373–7, 383, 386, 395, 462–8.

13 Duccio, *The Healing of the Man Born Blind* and *The Transfiguration* (egg tempera on wood, 1307/8–11; National Gallery, London).

14 Andrea Mantegna, *The Lamentation Over the Dead Christ* (tempera on canvas, *c.*1490; Pinacoteca di Brera, Milan).

15 Botticelli, *Adoration of the Magi* (tempera on panel, 1475; Uffizi, Florence).

16 Andrea Mantegna, *Adoration of the Magi* (distemper on linen, 1495–1505; J. Paul Getty Museum, Los Angeles).

17 Paolo Berdini, 1997, *The Religious Art of Jacopo Bassano*, Cambridge: Cambridge University Press, pp. 1–4, 6–7, 9–14, 34.

18 David Brown, 1999, *Tradition and Imagination*, Oxford: Oxford University Press, pp. 54–5 (p. 306).

19 Gerrit van Honthorst, *Christ Before the High Priest* (oil on canvas, 1617; National Gallery, London).

20 Giovanni Girolamo Savoldo, *Mary Magdalene* (oil on canvas, 1535–40; National Gallery, London).

21 Terry Barrett, 'Principles for Interpreting Art', *Art Education*, 47/5 (1994), 8–13. https://doi.org/10.2307/3193496 (pp. 10–12), accessed 14.11.21.

12

Knowing

This chapter looks at how we gain knowledge; the technical word for this is epistemology – the study of knowing. How we come to know is relevant to all styles of preaching. It is particularly important in revelatory preaching that uses creative language and is concerned with showing, rather than the traditional ways of knowing that focus on information and explanation. This section looks at ways we gain knowledge from biblical narratives and ways in which a revelatory sermon can be a means of knowing for the congregation.

What is knowledge?

Although the answer to this may seem obvious, there are several answers to this question. How we answer this question radically affects how we preach and what we hope our preaching achieves. Below are three responses to that question.

- Knowledge is information: knowing what/that.
- Knowledge is expertise: knowing how.
- Knowledge is a relationship: knowing who.

Although I have listed the different types of knowing separately, they are interconnected and overlap.

Knowing what/that

This is the most common definition of knowledge. It is about facts, definitions and information.

I know what 'blue' is in French.
I know what a black hole is.
I know that Amos was concerned with justice.
I know that King David was the father of Solomon.

Information is important, but knowledge as a collection of facts and an accumulation of information – including biblical information – is limited. Such knowledge can be superficial and may not affect how we live. The Bible is clear that knowledge is to be lived (James 1.22–25). Sermons that just fill people with biblical information are not enough.

'Knowing what/that' needs to lead to understanding. It is possible for people to repeat things they know without understanding. Like most people I can repeat Einstein's equation of special relativity ($e = mc^2$) but I have no idea what it means. At times, our answers may be technically correct, but we cannot be said to know if we do not understand. Even if people have a superficial understanding of something, that may still fail to qualify as knowledge if it is no more than an isolated and undigested piece of data that is not connected to previous knowledge and experience. I can repeat a dictionary definition of Einstein's equation and I understand each of the words separately but still do not understand the whole. Knowledge without a significant depth of understanding does not qualify as knowledge.

Understanding organizes knowledge by making links and finding relevant relationships. A sermon can deepen understanding; the preacher can select and rearrange biblical material so that people can make new connections and think in new ways. Understanding can *reconfigure* previous knowledge. When a narrative is reconfigured the facts of the story remain the same but they are put together in a new way and the level of understanding deepens. The call of Peter, Andrew James and John can be *reconfigured* as a story of Jesus seeing differently, seeing beyond rough fishermen to future leaders. The Early Church *reconfigured* who could be included in the Kingdom of God in the light of Christ's work (Acts 10; 15.1–33). Understanding does not have to be about new information; it can be driving understanding deeper. Many knew that racism was wrong before Martin Luther King, but their knowledge was significantly deepened by his speeches.

Knowing how

This aspect of knowing is about know-how, expertise.

- I know how to ride a bike.
- I know how my computer works.
- I know how to find out information about the Bible.

'Knowing how' is practical, it is experiential and generally has a broad usage. Preaching can build people's know-how in relation to the Bible, faith and living as a Christian. A sermon on David and Bathsheba does not just inform the congregation about David's temptation, it seeks to develop the congregation's know-how in relation to temptation in different situations.

Knowing who

Christianity is a faith centred on a person, Jesus Christ. Truth in the Bible is personal. 'I am the way, and the truth, and the life,' said Jesus (John 14.6). At the heart of the Christian faith is relationship, the relationship within the Trinity and the relationship of the believer with God. The crux of the Christian faith is confessing Jesus as Lord and Saviour (Acts 16.29–31; Rom. 10.9–13), not intellectual assent to a list of doctrines. It is belief in a person. Doctrines are important, they describe the relationship but they are context not core. Knowing about Christ is not the same as knowing Christ. Biblical knowing is knowledge that transforms and is ongoing; we will never be able to tick the box labelled 'knowing God'. Biblical knowing takes place within the big story of God's relationship with the world from creation through to recreation. All knowing is framed by this narrative and understood within it. The separate stories are known in their relationship to the wider biblical narrative.

Question

Sermons need all three types of knowledge. Which do you consider is the most difficult to include in preaching?

Three positions

To understand how we know things we need to look at three positions concerning knowing: the naive realist, the radical relativist and the critical realist. What follows is what each of these may say in relation to the Bible.

The naive realist

The naive realist says, 'What I read in the Bible and how I understand it is what it says.' Knowledge is objective and clear. This position shows an attitude of certainty and rather a lot of confidence in our understanding.

The reality is that we are imperfect human beings who read from a particular time and place that may influence our reading, plus there is always the possible distortion caused by sin.

The radical relativist

The radical relativist says, 'What I read in the Bible is true for me.' The radical relativist does not try to judge between different truth claims. Everyone has their own truth and there is no absolute truth. This is a popular position when it comes to religion where we hear truth claims dismissed as 'it's just your opinion'. This form of relativism is about radical uncertainty. Radical relativism can leave people unable to decide between interpretations.

The critical realist

The critical realist says, 'What I read in the Bible and how I understand it is reliable but I am aware that my culture and personality may influence what I read.' The critical realist accepts human frailty, the incompleteness of our knowledge and the influence of our time and culture. This approach considers our own understanding with a degree of humility. We can be open to having our thinking challenged by the Bible, by other Christians, by being open to perspectives from different times and cultures. Human understanding of what the Bible says can always progress and come closer to the truth. Absolute truths exist but we do not understand them absolutely.

Question

Think of a theological book you have read recently, which of these three positions did they adopt?

This book takes a critical realist position. It is a position that applies to life in general not just the Bible. Most scientists are critical realists, for what we know of the world is reliable but is not always *exactly* what is there; if it were, there would be no progress in science. Our knowledge of the world grows and comes closer to the truth. The physics of Isaac Newton gave way to the physics of Albert Einstein, for Einstein's physics was a better explanation of what scientists observed about the world.

Different aspects of knowing

All knowing is not the same, some knowing comes in the form of statements of facts or belief, other types of knowing are more personal. Knowing can be explicit or implicit, we are not always aware of all that we know. The process of coming to know something can be a logical, linear procedure or it can advance intuitively by leaps. Knowing can be a step-by-step process or the recognition of patterns. The following sections explore these different ways of coming to know.

Propositions

Propositions are basic statements of meaning: grass is green; God is love; ice is cold. Propositions can also be expressed as belief or doubt.

> John believes that it will not snow on Friday.
> Mary doubts that she will be able to come on the picnic.
> Karen believes in God.

This is the way many doctrines are written. Over time a congregation may come to know basic Christian doctrines. Some people will be able to give a dictionary definition of those doctrines, but can this really be counted as knowledge? The statement from the Nicene Creed, 'Incarnate from the Holy Spirit and the Virgin Mary', may be recited and people may be able to say that God became flesh in Jesus, but is this knowing? Narrative preaching communicates doctrine by layering a deeper understanding with each story by showing doctrine in action in specific situations. Each story builds a bit more of the doctrine; doctrine can be expressed narratively.

Personal knowing

The philosopher-scientist Michael Polanyi described knowing as an activity of fully engaged people, not detached observers. Coming to know involves personal struggle and determination and it is an act of trust and commitment by a person. When we seek knowledge, we rely on the work of other people and when something is discovered there is a personal responsibility to obey it.[1] Esther Meek describes the relationship between the knower (the one who seeks to know) and what is known as two-way. When an insight occurs, there can be a sense of gift, a sense of a text opening to us. In this way knowledge can be understood as relational and covenantal; it is knowing within a bond of commitment.[2] Narratives are a form of personal knowledge; they are about people and they invite people to respond. That response can be a sense of discovery, excitement and challenge. When an insight emerges there is a personal responsibility to change thinking and behaviour in a way that aligns with the insight. Narratives, particularly revelatory narratives, are about doctrine embodied in people and their situations, it is personal knowledge through encounter with lived doctrine.

To learn from a sermon there needs to be a relationship of trust between congregation and preacher, knowing happens within this personal setting. When preparing, preachers rely on the work of scholars as they explore biblical texts and images; it is an activity that involves trust. Searching for meaning within a text involves personal commitment, risk and sometimes daring.

Dru Johnson describes biblical knowing as ongoing, a journey into knowledge. In the Exodus and wilderness narratives Israel's journey is both literal and spiritual as the people begin a journey of discovery concerning their relationship with God. God often leads people through a process of knowing that is personal. In Genesis we see God leading Adam through a process of coming to know his 'proper mate' through failure to find a helper and partner among the animals (Gen. 2.20). We also see the moment of discovery when he encounters Eve as 'bone of my bones' (Gen. 2.23).[3]

Non-linear knowing

Polanyi maintained that insights are not achieved by straightforward moves from one fact to the next until knowledge is reached; the experience is more of an encounter and perceiving something as a whole. It is a pattern recognition exercise. The process involves looking at separate pieces of data/information (the particulars) and finding a significant pattern. People may sit before an array of information (the particulars), puzzled at their seemingly random nature, but by immersing themselves in them a pattern begins to emerge, insights are revealed. Polanyi described this process as indwelling, which is followed by breaking out into a new understanding.[4]

A similar process is reflected in a revelatory approach. The preacher returns the text to its particulars: the people, settings, objects and sensed details that make up the narrative. These particulars are the data/information with which the preacher works. This is how creating a living text begins. The existing pattern of the narrative is dissolved to look at the particulars differently. In the example below I have listed the particulars of the nativity randomly, though it may help to list them under headings:

people, places, objects, emotions, sounds, sights etc. Allow the text to decide the categories. The nativity according to Luke could be reduced to:

Mary	**night**	cry	great company	worship
Joseph	**light**	census	Peace on Earth	poor
Jesus	**song**	pregnancy/birth	Saviour	heat/cold
manger	**praise**	**scream**	Christ	**fear**
sheep	**ponder**	homeless	finding	David
Nazareth	Bethlehem	swaddling clothes	hurry	Galilee
angels	fields	**glory/glorified**	**treasured**	Judea
shepherds	travel	joy	time	straw
animal	**sounds**	no room	smells	blood

A preacher might begin to see a pattern such as contrasts. I have marked in bold the particulars that indicate a pattern of contrasts and made rough notes concerning this pattern.

> Light and dark, sounds and silence. The quiet of the night for the shepherds with just the sounds of animals. The breaking of the silence by God, by the great company of angels, the song. The darkness of night split by light. Fear in the night, met with assurance. The everyday pattern of working disrupted by God. The everyday can be punctuated with glory. The quiet of the night split by the cries of Mary as she struggles to give birth. The mewling cry of the baby, a tiny sound but loud enough to threaten the darkness of this world. The night of the world penetrated by the Light of the World. The sound of praise by the angel host, the quiet pondering of Mary who treasures what happened in her heart.

These rough notes may begin to suggest a sermon. It may help to imagine these particulars as dots. Once a text is returned to its particulars the preacher begins to join the dots, to find new patterns. A new pattern needs to join a significant number of dots and the dots joined need to be significant. We indwell the particulars of a narrative, immerse ourselves in the details to identify a significant pattern. Once a pattern is discovered there is often a breaking out into a new understanding. When something is discovered, there is often the excitement of the new alongside a sense of recognition, an exclamation, 'Of course! It makes sense.' There can even be a feeling that it is obvious. George Whalley describes this sense of recognition as the end result of coming to know through the arts, rather than knowledge ending in conclusions.[5] Eugene Lowry described knowing through narrative as more of an encounter than linear thinking. He describes insight coming through moments of illumination.[6]

Polanyi stressed how hard it is for people to break out of habitual ways of thinking; it requires an effort to pierce the 'film of familiarity' and go beyond superficial thinking.[7] Unless there is intervention, thought – like water – takes the path of least resistance and sermons can become predictable. Like a pond-strider insect, a sermon can skate across the surface of a narrative, never reaching its depths. Polanyi's 'joining the dots' way of thinking helps preachers break out of habitual ways of thinking when they are not what is needed.

Exercise

Reduce the story of the visit of the Magi (Matt. 2.1–12) to its particulars. What patterns can you see?

Implicit and intuitive knowing

When people begin a search for knowledge there can be a sense of being on the right track; patterns begin to emerge. This is a form of intuitive foreknowledge that Polanyi calls 'tacit knowing'. Tacit knowledge guides our searching before we fully know. Polanyi claimed that we hold a large amount of knowledge that we are not aware of; we know more than we can tell. Tacit knowledge is not infallible, verification is needed by communities and authorities such as the Bible and trusted interpreters. The moment of insight, when particulars come together to produce insight, often involves what Polanyi calls a 'leap' over a gap that can't be bridged by logic. This leap is enabled by intuition, skill and creativity.[8] The leap may come first and the evidence later.

In revelatory preaching, when looking for patterns of meaning the preacher is guided by tacit knowledge built by experience. The preacher may have an intuitive sense of 'being on to something' and this is explored until an insight is reached. Preachers may recognize this process where an intuitive insight is followed by a checking process, using the Bible, scholars and the community of faith.

Question

How far does this description of implicit and intuitive knowing reflect your own experience?

Knowing and emotion

The emotional realities of a text are integral to a revelatory approach and coming to know. It is passion that drives the knower to know. Sermons devoid of emotion are dull, for it is emotion that tags significant knowledge and makes it memorable, what Sanford and Emmott call 'hot cognition'.[9] To try and grasp something like love by a detached, objective form of knowing misses the very essence of love. Life cannot be studied at a distance. Narrative works are, however, about more than emotion; they can show what something is like, combining both content and feeling. Exploring the emotions within a biblical narrative can help a congregation identify with characters, for feelings are one way in which links are made with the congregation's experience and relevance is signalled. The emotions evoked need to be appropriate to the nature of the text, but that does not mean they are the same as those in the text, which may be inappropriate. Psalm 137 ends with a desire for horrifying revenge, which no sermon would want to evoke, although it should be made clear that rage can be expressed before God, who can handle extreme emotions without implying that he agrees with them.

Emotion has a role to play in preaching without descending to sentimentality. Sentimentality is difficult to define, though it is often recognized when experienced. Brian Wilkie describes sentimentality as part of a spectrum, with sentimental at one end and dispassionate at the other. Emotion appropriate in preaching probably ranges between these two poles without inhabiting the extremes.[10] Used appropriately, emotion can highlight important points in a sermon, turning a narrative from monochrome to colour but the sermon should not emotionally overwhelm people. Doctrine presented narratively does not have to lack emotion for it is seen in characters' lives. How can congregations care about biblical characters if they are not shown expressing realistic emotions?

Narratives and cognition

Narratives cannot argue a case or prove a point in traditional terms, but that does not mean they cannot present a case in a different way. The change that takes place in Paul after his conversion, makes the case for belief in Jesus and the difference it makes. The miracles of Jesus present a case for his divinity (John 10.38). In narratives, love, betrayal, sin and loyalty become embodied in people and situations, which is a narrative way of presenting a case.

Doctrinal truth does not have to be learned in abstract ways; the sermon can show doctrine worked out in the lives of biblical people in a way that validates the way many people learn.

Generalizing knowing: the problem of specificity

Narratives are specific, they are not about abstract principles that can be applied in different situations. Does this cast doubt on the ability of narratives to generalize so that their truth can relate to many different situations? Contrary to expectation, the more specific a narrative is, the easier it is to identify with the people and situations and recognize similar situations in different contexts. Being specific can assist generalization *because* it is specific. It is hard to relate to generalities such as 'sinners' but much easier to relate to an individual such as Peter. The same thinking applies to art, Michelangelo's *Unfinished Slaves* do not just speak of literal slavery, these statues can speak of the struggle to escape many types of slavery across generations: physical, emotional, social and spiritual slavery. Michelangelo achieves this by a very specific portrayal of slaves struggling to escape their prisons of stone.[11] Through a narrative we may gain insight into spiritual reality, a truth about life and faith, which applies beyond the context of the narrative. The story of Peter may give us an insight into the realities of how faith may fail and that applies beyond the situation of Peter, but we come to that insight by a specific focus on the story of Peter. This subject is followed up in detail in Chapter 13.

Anachronism in narratives also helps people to generalize knowledge. Anachronism refers to things out of their proper time. In preaching, anachronism is deliberately adding touches of modern life in a biblical scene. People can 'toggle' between the biblical and contemporary as a form of generalization, helping people to relate the text to modern life. Small touches of anachronism can be added, what Paul Scott Wilson calls 'blending', which should not distract from the biblical text or overwhelm it.[12] This extract uses modern touches in a sermon on the parable of the ten virgins/bridesmaids.

A shout startles them awake.
Five top up their lamps,
which burn brightly.
Five look in despair at their dying flames,
their oil is running out.
'Give us some of your oil,' they say.
The five with lamps burning look at each other,

they've heard it all before:
'Can I borrow your phone?'
'Lend me twenty.'
'Give us a lift.'
It had been hard to say no.
Often, they had reached for the purse,
and passed the phone, rolling their eyes.
But today is different.
This is a day that matters,
a Day of Days.
They will not give their oil,
and run out themselves.
Today is a day for the firm 'No!'
Creased they may be,
but they are ready,
and when the bridegroom arrives
they follow to the feast.[13]

Exercise

Read the story of Jesus turning water into wine. What small touches of anachronism could be used in a sermon on this text?

Language issues

The analytical and explanatory language of traditional knowing is not the language of narrative but imaginative and creative language is not without precision in terms of knowledge. Creative language can address the nuances of situations by a poetic form of precision. George Whalley describes poetic precision as being about relationships between things, between people. It is personal, embodied and specific; it brings knowledge through synthesis, through bringing things together.[14] Gerard Manley Hopkins brings together the mind, cliffs and mountains to bring a knowledge of depression and despair.

O the mind, mind has mountains; cliffs of fall
Frightful, sheer, no-man-fathomed.[15]

Creative, imaginative language employs a metaphorical way of knowing, it helps people to think, reconfigure, consider and communicate truths.

To call the spreading of false rumours 'poison' brings with it a depth of understanding that just saying spreading such rumours is hurtful does not communicate. The word 'poison' brings with it other associations from the world of poisons: its lethal nature, the way it spreads through the body and there is not always an antidote. Creative language can deepen knowledge in this way. Artists use visual metaphors to communicate knowledge: in his *Supper at Emmaus* Caravaggio painted a basket of autumn fruit containing a rotting apple. The basket teeters on the edge.[16] Caravaggio was saying more than the world is rotten and teetering on the edge; the fruit harks back to Eden and autumn fruit has connotations of harvest and judgement.

In revelatory preaching there is a focusing of attention on sensory details in a way that can lead to a degree of re-experiencing an event through creative language. Experience in this sense deepens knowledge, it takes it beyond explanation, it is the difference between being able to define a sunset and experiencing one. The use of artistic language also helps to highlight aspects of a text that may be overlooked. An example of this is the word 'sinner' in the story of Jesus' anointing. Christians are used to the word 'sinner' being attached to the woman in the story of Jesus' anointing (Luke 7.36–50). The course of the conversation during the meal makes it clear Jesus thought differently.

> Simon invited Jesus to a meal
> but as far as Jesus was concerned
> he had just eaten one more meal with sinners –
> and the woman wasn't eating.[17]

Attitudes

Billy Collins lamented the way people treat poems, it is as if a poem is tied to a chair and the meaning beaten out of it.[18] Preachers can become so desperate as Sunday approaches that the text suffers the same fate. Preparation is not about forcing a text to give up its meaning; in preparation there is a sense of letting go before a text. We do not master the text, it masters us. The attitudes with which we approach knowing a text matters. For personal and creative forms of knowing, Martha Nussbaum suggests that humility and openness are needed, we need to be 'active yet porous'.[19] Respect, responsibility and patience alongside commitment and trust are appropriate attitudes at this stage alongside a willingness to take risks and question established patterns. Once an insight is gained, the more traditional knowledge skills come into play: preachers step back, reflect, look at the big picture, analyse, explain and clarify. The attitude appropriate to this type of knowing is a certain distance, an openness to questioning, a willingness to re-think. This stage has more of a sense of control not appropriate to the initial stages.

Conclusion

This chapter has considered different ways of knowing; personal, intuitive, non-linear, implicit and creative, without jettisoning traditional skills. A revelatory approach can deepen knowledge through understanding, it can thicken knowledge by making connections and it holds out the possibility of new knowledge by synthesis and reconfiguration. These routes to knowledge relate to ways of knowing reflected in the Bible where knowledge is personal, lived, and tested in the fires of experience.

Notes

1 Michael Polanyi, 1958, *Personal Knowledge*, London: Routledge & Kegan Paul, pp. 15, 18, 27–8, 59–63, 130, 137, 194, 255–6, 266, 300.

2 Esther Lightcap Meek, 2011, *Loving to Know*, Eugene: Cascade Books, pp. 14–15, 37, 41–3, 49–51, 97.

3 Dru Johnson, 2013, *Biblical Knowing*, Eugene: Cascade Books, pp. 14, 25–30, 32, 67, 70–80, 103, 127.

4 Polanyi, *Personal*, pp. 56–8, 92, 99, 117, 195–202.

5 George Whalley, 1967, *Poetic Process*, Cleveland: Meridian Books, p. xxviii.

6 Eugene L. Lowry, 1985, *Doing Time in the Pulpit*, Nashville: Abingdon Press, pp. 81–5.

7 Polanyi, *Personal*, p. 199.

8 Polanyi, *Personal*, pp. 53, 88, 123–30, 126–9, 143, 164, 207–9, 312.

9 Anthony J. Sanford and Catherine Emmott, 2012, *Mind, Brain and Narrative*, Cambridge: Cambridge University Press, pp. 191–3, 201.

10 Brian Wilkie, 'What is Sentimentality?', *College English*, 28/8 (1967), 564–75 (p. 571). https://doi.org/10.2307/374718.

11 Michelangelo, *Unfinished Slaves* (marble statues, 1520–1534; Accademia, Florence).

12 Paul Scott Wilson, 2004, *Broken Words*, Nashville: Abingdon Press, pp. 64–5.

13 Margaret Cooling, 'The Wise and Foolish Bridesmaids', *Preaching that Shows*, https://preachingthatshows.com/2018/10/12/the-wise-and-foolish-brides-maids-bothered/, accessed 14.11.2021.

14 Whalley, *Poetic*, pp. 119–34.

15 Gerard Manley Hopkins, 'No Worst, There Is None', *Poetry Foundation*, https://www.poetryfoundation.org/poems/44398/no-worst-there-is-none-pitched-past-pitch-of-grief, accessed 14.11.2021.

16 Caravaggio, *The Supper at Emmaus* (oil on canvas, 1601; National Gallery, London).

17 Margaret Cooling, 'Jesus is Anointed', *Preaching that Shows*, https://preachingthatshows.com/2018/10/10/jesus-is-anointed-known/, accessed 14.11.2021.

18 Billy Collins, 1988, 'Introduction to Poetry', in *The Apple that Astonished Paris*, Fayetteville: University of Arkansas Press.

19 Martha C. Nussbaum, 1990, *Love's Knowledge*, New York: Oxford University Press, p. 282.

13

Where is the Application?

Biblical texts are intended to have effects and change the way people interact with God, others and their environment. The Good Samaritan (Luke 10.25–37) may be the only text that says 'Go and do likewise' but such injunctions, implied or explicit, are found throughout the Bible. Preachers pray that God may use the words of their sermons to have effects in people's lives and explicit applications are often included to this end. The word 'application' has featured little in this book and there is a reason for that. The approach this book takes encompasses what many people understand by application but it works on a different model and uses different terms. Nevertheless, much of the same ground is covered. The term 'application' is used in this chapter as it is the one most people are familiar with. This section draws together the material in this book that many would class as application and looks at how it can function in different ways.

Relevance and application

Relevance and application overlap but there is a differing emphasis. Relevance is about relatedness and connection; it is the belief that a text has something to say to today. Application is working out ways in which a text's relevance is expressed. Application tends to be more specific, it answers the question 'So what?' It is putting the sermon into practice; it is what we do with Sunday's sermon on Monday morning. For many preachers this is the most difficult aspect of preaching. Some of this difficulty may be the result of a narrow view of application. Application is not restricted to what we do; it includes actions, but it also extends to our daily habits and practices; it is faith expressed in Christian living (James 2.14–23). Application includes our feelings and desires, what we value and love, for these ultimately affect what we do (Matt. 6.24). It involves our minds, what and how we think and what we believe. How we think and what we think about affects how we live out our faith (Phil. 4.8). Thinking is not enough; belief goes beyond thinking to include trust; it is staking our lives on what we believe (2 Tim. 1.12). Application encompasses our being, our identity, and relationship with God, others and the world. Although these aspects of application are listed separately, they often overlap. Narrowing application to what we do misses much of the relevance of the Bible.

Exercise

Look at the following sermon extracts, what are they doing? Are they concerned with what we do, what we think and believe, what we desire, love and value, or what we are and our relationships? Sometimes more than one application may be indicated in the same sermon.

1 I call you to dance, to quilt, to cook;
   to paint, to write, to build
   to film make, to play, to run
   to caress the ball into the back of the net ...
   And to do it all for me.
   To point to me in being you, wholly you, fully you
   Joyously and outrageously you,
   Energetically and courageously you
   Wholeheartedly and freely you
   All you can be,
   In me.
   My apprentices ...
   Come to me.
   Your master Craftsman ...
   And let's make together ...
   The place of encounter.[1]

2 God is the constant one.
   The only way to nurture our constancy
   Is to abide in him, with him.
   To regularly hang around with God,
   To seek him out, alone and in the quiet places;
   To turn over our inner world to him
   'Search my heart O God';
   'weigh me in the scales';
   Know me ... help me ... heal me.

Tell him your hopes and fears;
Struggles and distorted desires.
And let's submit to his will.[2]

3 'Show me your treasure!' demanded the Stranger.
The rich man pointed to the heaps of grain,
not looking so impressive now.
The Stranger shook his head.
'Not on my list.'
The rich man indicated the gold,
not looking so shiny now.
The Stranger shook his head.
'Not on my list.'
The rich man nodded towards his possessions, piled to the roof,
not looking so imposing now.
The Stranger shook his head,
'Not on my list.'
'Have you any of the following:
hungry and thirsty people cared for,
needy people clothed and given hospitality,
sick people nursed,
prisoners visited?'
The rich man stood in silence,
knowing, too late, that he had invested in the wrong treasure;
knowing, too late, that riches do not consist in the abundance of
possessions;
knowing, too late, he was a fool.[3]

4 There are many things that we may be able to say at the end of life,
but none that matters more than saying we have loved:
loved God,
loved others,
loved family,
loved friends,
loved strangers who have crossed our paths,
maybe even loved our enemies.
We'll probably be able to show the scars
but at least we'll know that we didn't miss the point of it all.[4]

> 5 We don't need a god so heavenly to be no earthly help – as we
> struggle with loneliness, or stress, or overcrowded houses.
> We don't need a god so earthly as to be unable to raise us up, as we
> are bowed by fear or sickness or sadness.
> We need the one who is both profoundly human and utterly divine.
> Jesus. 'Listen to him.'[5]

In general terms, application needs to reflect what the words of the text
do. Do they encourage, correct or teach? Do they warn, praise or lament?
A text that encourages needs an application that does the same. A text
that praises does not need an application that corrects.

Two models of application

There are two popular models of application, the bridge and the wardrobe. The bridge style of application tends to be used with expository
preaching; the 'wardrobe' is a term that I use to describe a form of
application that relates to narrative preaching, particularly a revelatory
approach. Both approaches have their advantages and disadvantages.

The bridge

John Stott put forward the idea of preaching as bridge-building. He saw
preaching as bridging the gap between the biblical world and the contemporary world, with the sermon firmly anchored on both sides of the
chasm.[6] This is in line with his call for 'double listening', listening to the
Word and listening to the world. This includes questions the text poses to
modern life and questions the world may ask of the text.[7]

This model of application is often used in preaching that works
through a text, often verse by verse, expounding its meaning and applying it. This process is sometimes described as what the text meant for
the original listeners followed by what it means now. What modern and
biblical believers share is recognized as well as their differences.[8] The gulf
between biblical cultures and modern cultures is taken seriously; it is
made up of several elements.

Ancient	Modern
Premodern worldview	Modern or Postmodern worldview
Largely rural cultures	Largely urban cultures
Middle East/various empires	Modern political, economic and geographical groupings

A bridge is needed to span the gap and this often consists of illustrations and examples that relate to modern culture but parallel or relate to the biblical text.[9] The opening and ending of an expository sermon that uses a bridge follows. This sermon is based on Habakkuk 3.16–19, which relates to a particular historical situation around the seventh century BC when Judah faced imminent invasion.

> I hear, and I tremble within;
>   my lips quiver at the sound.
> Rottenness enters into my bones,
>   and my steps tremble beneath me.
> I wait quietly for the day of calamity
>   to come upon the people who attack us.
>
> Though the fig tree does not blossom,
>   and no fruit is on the vines;
> though the produce of the olive fails
>   and the fields yield no food;
> though the flock is cut off from the fold
>   and there is no herd in the stalls,
> yet I will rejoice in the LORD;
>   I will exult in the God of my salvation.
> GOD, the Lord, is my strength;
>   he makes my feet like the feet of a deer,
>   and makes me tread upon the heights.

An expository sermon on this text might use the experience of night-time fears to build a bridge to Habakkuk's situation at the beginning and end of the sermon, as illustrated below, but bridges can be built at various points.

Opening
Strange creatures come out at night, particularly when we can't sleep and pace the floor wrapped in a dressing gown, cold feet in slippers, hands warming around a mug of tea. The strangest of these night creatures are the 'What ifs …' 'What if I lose my job?' 'What if I fail my

exams?' 'What if that nagging pain in my back is something serious?' 'What if my relationship fails?'

Today's reading is about the prophet Habakkuk who faced the 'What ifs'. No doubt he paced the floor at night thinking through the worst-case scenarios: 'What if the enemy invades?' 'What if God does not intervene?' In chapter 3 we see Habakkuk moving from 'what if' to 'when'. Verse 16 makes it clear that invasion is coming and God is not going to intervene to stop it. Moving from 'What if' to 'when' was no easy move for Habakkuk and it came after a long struggle. Chapters one and two showed us how he pleaded with God and complained to God, but by chapter 3 we see him accepting that invasion will happen. Disaster is faced with an incredible statement of trust in God, which we see in verses 17–19.

Habakkuk states that he will trust God through all the trouble that is coming, even though everything that sustains life fails. That does not mean Habakkuk is not afraid. Look at verse 16, he is showing all the signs of deep-seated fear, for himself and his people. He shakes, his heart is pounding, his legs can barely support him. He is frightened to his core, his world is falling apart, yet he declares his faith in God. This text is about how we remain faithful through desperate times, when our 'What ifs' become 'when'. First, we will look at just how desperate those times were for Habakkuk ...

Ending

So what do we do when the 'What ifs' strike or when the worst-case scenarios happen? What do we do when the 'if' becomes 'when': when the job is lost, when we don't get the grades we need, when the condition is serious, and when the relationship fails? There are principles we can apply from this text: honesty, rehearsing God's faithfulness, resting and rejoicing.

Our first reaction should be honesty concerning how we think and feel. Habakkuk complained to God (Hab. 1.13) and we are free to do the same, it is not unspiritual. The prophets and the psalmists were great complainers. Jeremiah called God a deceiver (Jer. 20.7 AV) and the psalmist complained that the wicked prosper and God remains silent (Psalm 73, Psalm 13.1). We can express our deepest fears and anger before God.

Second, we look back on God's faithfulness, as we saw at the beginning of this chapter. We name God's faithfulness in the past and trust him for the future. This is literally repeating the times when God has been faithful and giving thanks. Habakkuk takes his eyes off the problem and looks at God, he changes his focus. He has fully faced the danger, he is not being naive, the problem has not gone away. Habakkuk's trust in God's faithfulness holds him in this desperate situation.

Next, when the worst happens, having done all that we can, we rest in God. Habakkuk speaks in verse 16 of waiting patiently, resting in God. This is not resignation; it is an attitude of trusting to God's character. The situation has not changed, but Habakkuk has. Resting in God is not an attitude we just adopt and it happens, it is one we learn in the situation. It is one we learn through failure. 1 Peter 5.7 tells us to 'Cast all your anxiety on him, because he cares for you.' Dutifully we hand our worries to God and attempt to rest in him, only to find that we have taken the worries back ten minutes later and are no longer resting. Handing our worries to God and resting in him is a process, something we do repeatedly; it is not a one-off action. Casting our cares on him is the work of a lifetime. Some people are anxious either by personality or some other reason. Others may have the type of personality that means they are very laid-back. We need to avoid dubbing a laid-back person as spiritual and the worrier as not resting in God. The laid-back person may not be resting in God, they may just not have felt the worry in the first place. The worrier may have already given an enormous amount of their worry to God but may still be left with some anxiety. We need to avoid superficial judgements that can be hurtful.

Lastly, we make a choice to rejoice as Habakkuk does. Verse 18, 'I will rejoice in God my saviour.' Rejoicing is not happiness. I don't think anyone would accuse Habakkuk of being happy in the face of disaster. Rejoicing is sometimes a decision we make despite what we feel. It is a decision Paul and Silas made when they sang in prison (Acts 16.25). It comes from knowing that God is bigger than our troubles, it is rejoicing in a relationship that will survive even when we are stripped of everything else. It is knowing deep down that God loves us and has a future for us, even when the future looks bleak. When the 'what ifs' become 'when' we cling to God all the harder as in Peter's words in John 6.68, 'Lord, to whom can we go? You have the words of eternal life.'

Advantages

The bridge can be used at any point and in different styles of preaching. It is often employed in the latter part of a sermon when a three-stage process of explanation, illustration and application is used, particularly in expository preaching. The meaning of the text is discerned, it is illustrated and a bridge is used to apply it to modern contexts. The meaning of some texts can be carried across to modern life when shared experience is present; other texts are more obscure and the principle behind them needs to be abstracted from its context in order to apply it in different situations. Haddon Robinson calls this the 'ladder of abstraction'.[10] The congregation are made aware of the move to application and 'action points' may be enumerated. The gulf between modern and biblical culture is fully recognized and there is a stress on building a bridge. This approach to application does not exclude showing; Keith Willhite includes narrative showing as part of this approach which he twins with telling.[11] The questions posed by modern culture are included and addressed but they do not *determine* the application as society may be asking the wrong question.

Disadvantages

If application comes late in a sermon it can feel like an 'add-on'; this can happen in the explanation/exposition, illustration, application model.[12] People may disengage if the application is kept to the end. Another disadvantage is the abstracting of meaning from its context, which is sometimes discarded once the meaning is discerned. The abstracted meaning is then applied to modern situations. Abstracted meaning can be difficult to apply and may be too abstract for some people unless very well translated into Christian living. Discarding the original context can leave truth disembodied or as abstract principles.

This style of application works well for epistles and similar material but narratives do not fit as easily into this model, Haddon Robinson admits that narratives present 'special difficulties'.[13] The word 'application' can feel as if something is being applied from outside rather than being integral; many preachers prefer the word 'implication' to describe this stage of a sermon. Application could be seen as authoritarian and making the congregation passive if the application slips into giving dogmatic answers with little involvement of the congregation.[14] If arguments are used in a sermon that 'prove' points and this is carried over into application, people may feel funnelled into a particular response. Bryan Chapell recognizes that some applications may be too predetermined for some people, they may wish to work some things out for themselves.[15] John Stott recognized this danger and in his summary of the bridge-building model he speaks of being authoritative in regard to biblical principles but tentative in applying them to complex situations; both conviction and open-mindedness are needed. People need teaching but they also need to make up their own minds.[16] Despite the disadvantages, the bridge method can be effective but the disadvantages need bearing in mind, particularly in relation to narratives, a perceived authoritarian structure and the passivity of the congregation.

Exercise

Imagine you are asked to preach on John 3.1–21, how would you build a bridge between the text and the modern world?

The wardrobe

As this is the model used in this book, and it is a less well-known approach, it will need more explanation. A revelatory approach, and some other narrative approaches, work on a model that is like the wardrobe in C. S. Lewis's *The Lion, the Witch and the Wardrobe*.[17] In Lewis's book the children go through a wardrobe and enter another world – Narnia. The reader of the story enters Narnia with them and experiences a very different world from the one they normally inhabit; it is a world with different values, beliefs and practices. The reader then looks at their own world in light of this experience. In revelatory preaching, and many narrative approaches, the congregation is drawn into the biblical world and the sermon acts as the 'wardrobe' through which they enter the world of the biblical narrative and look at their own world from the perspective of the biblical narrative world.

Instead of abstracting the meaning from a text and then applying it, a revelatory approach does the opposite: the hearer is drawn deeper and deeper into the world of the text. Instead of abstracting, the process becomes more contextual and embodied; meaning is found in the context rather than abstracting from it. Instead of application there can be identification, recognition and implication. The congregation may identify with a biblical person or their situation enabling them to perceive their relevance or they may relate to a situation and recognize its implications for living as a Christian. The focus on the biblical situation and characters acts like a fabric sample, which is still recognizable even if it is made into different garments. Getting to know the biblical situation and characters well can enable a congregation to recognize modern situations that share qualities with the biblical situation.

The experience of the biblical world provokes questions about our world and the questions are formulated from within the text. Questions our culture asks are borne in mind as we take them with us as we enter the biblical world; however, the immersion in Scripture may change those questions. Implications can be drawn out, but this happens from a position within the biblical situation. The implications may be drawn together at some point, making the implicit explicit, but not always. The congregation does not have to wait until the end to see how a biblical narrative relates to life, it is implicit all the way through. References to modern life can be included but they are woven into the narrative. The extract that follows is on the same text from Habakkuk as the previous example. I have chosen a sermon that was preached at a mid-week service that has a tradition of short sermons. The implications come at the end to parallel the bridge example. Only the opening and the ending are included in this extract. The sermon majored on one key theme – how we arrive at a faith like Habakkuk's.

Opening
It is unsafe to go out at night. It's not particularly safe during the day. Violence stalks the streets. Law and order have broken down and people are afraid to leave their homes. Crime is rampant. Parents cannot protect their families and when the worst happens and you or those you love are hurt, there is no one to turn to. Justice is a joke; it goes to the highest bidder, to those who can pay the biggest bribes. The vicious are free to do what they like and there is nothing ordinary folks can do about it. Money is scarce and taxes are high, leaving people with little to support their families. The rich line their pockets and build their luxurious homes while the people go hungry. Across the country people are abandoning God.

This is no modern inner city, no failed state, this is Habakkuk's world, Judah in the seventh century BC – or thereabouts. It is into this situation that Habakkuk is called to prophesy and his message is a hard one. God does not say, 'Don't worry everything will be all right.' Instead, Habakkuk is to prepare the people for invasion. Habakkuk must face his, and his nations', worse fears ...

Ending
Habakkuk is able to look disaster in the face and commit himself to God, no matter what, and say:

Though the fig tree does not blossom,
    and no fruit is on the vines;
though the produce of the olive fails
    and the fields yield no food;

though the flock is cut off from the fold
   and there is no herd in the stalls,
      yet I will rejoice in the LORD;
I will exult in the God of my salvation.
   GOD, the Lord, is my strength;
he makes my feet like the feet of a deer,
   and makes me tread upon the heights.

These words of trust and commitment are spoken in cold blood.
They are spoken in full knowledge of what they mean.
He will keep faith even though all the things that sustain life fail.
Even though the basic foods of fruit, olives and meat fail.
When the supermarket shelves are empty
Habakkuk will keep faith with God.
These are not the rash words of a naive faith that assumes all will
   be well.
These are the sombre words of a mature faith,
they are the words of one who knows all will be well, one day.
In the meantime, all is very far from well.
There is much to be faced, much to be feared.
Habakkuk confronts his worst-case scenario with trust.
It does not make the worst case better,
but he will face it with God.
Habakkuk commits himself to God's care,
he commits to hanging on to God, whatever happens.
How did he do it?
How did Habakkuk move from complaint to commitment and trust?

I suspect the answer is that he did it the way we all reach trust and
   commitment.
The way of water.
Water carries soil and sand and deposits them on the ocean floor.
Year after year the deposits grow:
sand and soil,
soil and sand,
layer upon layer.
Under pressure these layers become rock
and we can see the layers in the coloured stripes in cliffs.

Commitment and trust build like this.
We commit to God.
We commit to being with a friend through illness.

We commit to another in marriage.
We commit to a child as a parent.

The first time we say:
'I will follow you,' to God;
'I'll be there for you,' to a sick friend;
'I love you,' to a partner;
'I'll care for you,' to a baby;
we mean it with every ounce of our being.
Then life knocks us about a bit
and we face the reality of our commitment.
The challenge of being a Christian:
the assurance, the failures, the love,
the day to day living by a faith that the world derides.
We face the emotional roller-coaster of standing by a sick friend,
sharing the joys and the disappointments, the hopes and fears.
We face the reality of marriage: living with someone 24/7,
the excitement, the rows, the regrets, the fun.
We face the realities of babies:
the sleepless nights, the exhaustion,
the wonder and delight in seeing them grow.
We restate our commitment.
We say the words again:
'I will follow you,'
'I'll be there for you,'
'I love you,'
'I'll care for you.'

Now the words carry more weight;
reality has added a layer of experience to the words.
Over the years we restate our commitment again and again.
Time over time,
for commitment is not a one-off action
but a way of living.
There is no short-cut to a faith like Habakkuk's,
no instant trust.
Each time we commit the words are the same
but each time the words gain weight, layers of experience,
until we say,
'I will follow you,'
as we look back on how God has been there through life's heartbreaks
    and joys,

knowing we will continue with God till the end, facing whatever life
  brings with him.
Until we say,
'I'm still here,' as we sit with a friend in health or in their final hours.
Until we say,
'I love you,' after fifty years of marriage.
Until we say,
'I'll care for you,' as we look at those babies, grown men and women
  now.
The words are impossibly heavy,
under the pressure of experience they have turned to solid rock.[18]

Advantages

Implication, identification, resonance and recognition tend to be used in
this model rather than application. The wardrobe model uses an immersive scriptural approach; people are drawn into the world of the biblical
narrative and they experience the text rather than having it explained. It
is holistic, engaging the mind, body, heart and will. Doctrine is shown in
action rather than being abstract and this may help people to see doctrine
as something to be lived. Doctrine is built up in layers, with each sermon
adding another layer. The very specific nature of the revelatory approach
aims to build skills in the congregation, so that people can recognize
some of the qualities of biblical people and situations in modern contexts. Presenting the reality of biblical situations and characters enables
Christians to learn from them either as warnings or examples.

Relevance is built in from the beginning and is integrated, there is not
always a separate section showing how the text relates to life, though the
implicit may be made explicit and implications may be drawn out at some
point. This reduces the risk of disengaging. The presenting of embodied
insights means that doctrines are presented on a human scale, in their
earthly context and at a pace that enables reflection; doctrines gain flesh
and blood. It is easier to understand doctrines presented at this scale for
this is the scale at which we live and the scale at which doctrine needs to
be lived. It is an invitational approach: the congregation is invited to fill
in gaps and work through possibilities, they are not passive. This means
the approach can be authoritative without being authoritarian.

Disadvantages

How the text relates to life is not always clearly identified, the congregation may be waiting for some introductory line such as, 'How do we apply this to life?' The form may be too open-ended for those who like to be told answers. The revelatory approach requires participation on the part of the congregation, to fill in gaps, to work through possibilities, to identify and recognize. This makes demands of a congregation; would all be willing? Are all able to do this? One solution suggested by David Day is to draw out implications in a prayer or reflection that follows the sermon.[19] This option is seen in chapter 15 in the sermon *The Pedigree of a Nobody*. Although deeply biblical, this approach does not trace a doctrine or a theme across the Bible, it tends to work with single narratives. There are exceptions to this, the sermon *Moses Speaks to the People* in chapter 15 carries a theme across three narratives. These disadvantages need bearing in mind and this style may need introducing to a congregation over a period of time. The wardrobe model works well with narratives but may not work as well with epistles and similar texts.

Exercise

Imagine you are asked to preach on John 3.1–21. Create an opening for this narrative that acts as a wardrobe, drawing people in.

Question

How would you describe the differences between the two approaches?

To be or not to be specific

Being specific in the preaching context is about being precise and detailed; it is the opposite of being vague, general and woolly. This has been discussed in relation to embodiment (Chapter 3) and in relation to knowing (Chapter 12). This section draws those references together in terms of application. Specific presentation provides the opportunity for people to recognize and identify with the biblical characters and their situation, a way of 'applying' what they hear to their lives. People stand alongside the person/situation and 'read' it across into their own life experience and knowledge of the world. The following description of Jeremiah's despair is specific, drawing on the books of Jeremiah and Lamentations, but it is one many people can relate to because it is specific.

> In the past God had sometimes felt absent. God had been like a well that had run dry. Prayers had been like letters posted to an empty house; they lay neglected on the mat. There had been a terrible sense of absence then, the felt absence in a room where a loved one should have been. The presence of God's absence had been almost palpable. But in those times Jeremiah had clung to his memories of God, the echoes of his love from distant days, the mercy and faithfulness that never failed. In remembrance he found hope.[20]

Just saying 'Jeremiah despaired' is too vague to be helpful. Becoming specific is like a train stopping to pick up passengers, it slows the pace and enables people to get on board. The congregation is not *told* to remember God's past faithfulness as a principle concerning what to do when God feels absent, it is something they are shown in Jeremiah's life and can adopt for themselves. Being specific in presentation gives people freedom to participate. In Chapter 3 I stressed the need to be specific in terms of the implications of a text for Christian living, rather than vague exhortations such as 'love more'. Such exhortations are too general and can leave people with a sense of guilt if they are not given some specific help. However, there is a tension between being specific in implication and a need to encourage people to work out the implications of a text for their lives with appropriate guidance from the preacher.

This tension between being specific in application and respecting people's freedom is part of life for a preacher, it cannot be resolved, there is no neat rule that applies in all circumstances. How specific the preacher is concerning implications for living will depend on the text and context. When it is right for implications to be drawn out specifically, they need to be achievable with the help of the Holy Spirit and the support of the Christian community. Setting impossible goals can lead to failure and guilt. John Stott's warnings also need bearing in mind. Many modern situations are complex and guidance in these cases needs to acknowledge their complexity rather than giving simplistic answers. There are times, also governed by the text and context, when guidance needs to be less specific or when the implications are presented as examples and the congregation is encouraged to carry on that process and draw out some of the implications for themselves.

Reorienting congregations

Some sermons end with an orientation towards the future and hope but without detailing specific implications. As already mentioned, the film *Castaway* ends with possibilities. At the end of the film there is a brief conversation between the lead character and a woman he meets on the road. There is one final shot of his face and we know there are possibilities for a new relationship. It is almost as if the script writer is adding 'the beginning' rather than 'the end'. The possibilities are not named but the character is turned from the disappointments of the past to the possibility of a new relationship. He is reorientated towards the future and hope. Sermons can do the same, for at the heart of preaching there is the good news of the gospel that informs every sermon. They can end by orientating the congregation towards the future with hope, hinting at possibilities without naming them as in the examples that follow.

Example 1: Rebekah
We do not know what happened to Rebekah to change her from a woman of faith to a woman prepared to deceive her blind husband. Maybe she changed again after this incident. A wrong turn does not have to set the pattern for life, we can turn again with God, it is never too late. Life is not over until it is over.[21]

Example 2: Jeremiah
Jeremiah rolled himself in his blanket. There was no warm feeling that everything would be all right, no cheery optimism about the future, just an acknowledgement that he would go on with God because God was faithful. He gave that feeling to God. Somehow, he understood that was enough. Jeremiah slept.[22]

Example 3: The Magi
They had met Him
and everything changed.
The world was a different place,
they were different.
They were strangers now in the world,
they did not fit its ways as they had before.
Slowly, as they travelled, they adjusted to their new vision
and they knew that life would be constantly adjusting
to a new way of seeing the world and the people in it:
learning to love it as God did,
learning to hate the injustice and cruelty of it.

They had seen God's Son.
God had come to earth.
If this was true,
then nothing could ever be the same again.
They went home by another way
and continued going home by another way for the rest of their lives
as we do,
as all who meet Jesus do.[23]

This type of ending is not evasion or laziness and it is not for every sermon. Sometimes it is enough to end with a future orientation if identification, relevance and implication are woven throughout the sermon. Every sermon does not have to end with specific applications.

Conclusion

Application is a complex subject and it is not limited to what people do: it covers mind, heart and will as well as action. This chapter has explored some of those complexities and shown how two different models work: the bridge and the wardrobe. Preachers need a broad approach to this subject if application is to relate to the broad nature of human experience.

Notes

1 Kate Bruce, *Creativity*, unpublished sermon.

2 Kate Bruce, *Be More David?*, unpublished sermon.

3 Margaret Cooling, 'The Rich Fool', *Preaching that Shows*, https://preach ingthatshows.com/2018/10/10/the-rich-fool-what-kind-of-fool/, accessed 14.11. 2021.

4 Margaret Cooling, 'Jesus Washes the Disciples' Feet', *Preaching that Shows*, https://preachingthatshows.com/2018/10/12/jesus-washes-the-disciples-feet-the-question/, accessed 14.11.2021.

5 Kate Bruce, *Transfiguration*, unpublished sermon.

6 John Stott, 1982, *Between Two Worlds*, Grand Rapids: Eerdmans, pp. 137–9, 145, 178.

7 John Stott, 1992, *The Contemporary Christian*, Leicester: IVP, pp. 25–9.

8 Haddon Robinson, 2014, *Biblical Preaching*, Grand Rapids: Baker Academic, pp. 58–66.

9 Stott, *Between*, p. 11.

10 Robinson, *Biblical*, pp. 107–8, 201–2.

11 Keith Willhite, 2001, *Preaching with Relevance*, Grand Rapids: Kregel, pp. 95–102.

12 Bryan Chapell, 2005, *Christ-Centred Preaching*, Grand Rapids: Baker Academic, pp. 90–1, 209–14.

13 Robinson, *Biblical*, p. 61.

14 David C. Norrington, 1996, *To Preach or Not to Preach*, London: Paternoster, pp. 79–80.

15 Chapell, *Christ-Centred*, pp. 231–3.

16 Stott, *Between*, p. 178.

17 C. S. Lewis, 2009, *The Lion, the Witch and the Wardrobe*, London: Harper-Collins.

18 Margaret Cooling, 'Habakkuk', *Preaching that Shows*, https://preachingthat shows.com/2018/12/02/habakkuk-from-complaint-to-trust/, accessed 14.11.2021.

19 David Day, 2005, *Embodying the Word*, London: SPCK, p. 54.

20 Margaret Cooling, 'Jeremiah', *Preaching that Shows*, https://preachingthat shows.com/2018/10/11/jeremiah/, accessed 14.11.2021.

21 Margaret Cooling, 'Rebekah', *Preaching that Shows*, https://preachingthat shows.com/2018/11/25/rebekah-its-not-over-until-its-over/, accessed 14.11.2021.

22 Margaret Cooling, 'Jeremiah', *Preaching that Shows*, https://preachingthat shows.com/2018/10/11/jeremiah/, accessed 14.11.2021.

23 Margaret Cooling, 'Wisemen', *Preaching that Shows*, https://preachingthat shows.com/2018/10/10/wise-men-alternative-route/, accessed 14.11.2021.

14

Theological Foundations

This chapter explores the theological foundations of a revelatory approach. A revelatory approach to preaching focuses on the people and the situations reflected in texts, in the belief that God can speak through people and situations. Is this justified when the biblical narrative reveals humanity as fallen? Four areas of theology are relevant to exploring this issue: Creation, the image of God, incarnation, and revelation.

Creation and physical life

A revelatory approach looks for spiritual insights within ordinary life, within the world, not just in supernatural events. Can life in the flesh be a means of knowing God? Can a fallen world reflect God in any way? What does the Bible say about bodily life and the world?

Creation

The early chapters of Genesis present this world as God's creation, affirmed not only as good (Gen. 1.10, 12, 18, 21, 25) but very good (Gen. 1.31). The world is also fallen and not as God intended. The world and its people are good but distorted by sin (Rom. 5.12) and in need of redemption and reconciliation (Eph. 1.7; Col. 1.19–20). Despite this the Bible has a positive view of God's interaction with people and the material world after the Fall. God does not withdraw. God is constantly involved in maintaining the world and interacting with humanity, an active force in history. Both Testaments show the world as a place for God to act and for people to encounter God. This is vital for the revelatory approach that recognizes the role of place, the body and the material world in understanding the spiritual import of a text.

Physical life in the Old Testament

The revelatory approach seeks spiritual insights from embodied existence reflected in texts, but Christian attitudes to the body and physical existence have often been ambivalent. Does the Bible endorse human and earthly physicality? The Bible describes the human body as created and given life by God (Gen. 2.7) and man becomes a 'living being'. The Hebrew word *nephesh* underlies this phrase and is often translated 'soul'. Paula Gooder describes it as the life-force that creates an integrated person, not a body with a detachable soul.[1] Even after the Fall, people are shown in relationship with God and they are commanded to worship God with heart, soul and strength (Deut. 6.5). Problems in relating to God are not defined in terms of a conflict between the physical nature of humanity and the spiritual nature of God; the problem is sin.

Such a positive start endorses an embodied approach and the spiritual significance of human life and action. However, the Bible's attitude towards physical life has not always been interpreted positively. The Bible's own – sometimes confusing – use of language and the influence of Greek philosophy led to attitudes towards the body and the material world that at best undervalued it, or at worst saw it as negative.

Greek philosophy

The world of the early Christians was dominated by Greek philosophy, which had many positive aspects but there tended to be a negative attitude towards the physical world and the body, with the soul valued as superior to the body and able to exist apart from the body after death. The body was perceived as a limiting factor and the senses were a distraction.[2] Another influence on Christianity was Gnosticism, a belief system that emerged as Christianity began. Gnostics believed that ignorance was humanity's problem, not sin. People had a divine spark imprisoned within the body, so escaping the material world and the body was the way to achieve union with God. The world of the spirit and the world of matter were opposed. Gnostic spirituality was timeless, disembodied and cut loose from history.

Physical life in the New Testament

In the New Testament positive attitudes to the body come from Christ's incarnation – a body was good enough for God. The Gospels show Jesus caring for people as whole beings, not split between body and soul. He cared about people's spiritual condition: he forgave sins, taught people about God and blessed children (Mark 2.1–12; 10.16; Luke 6.46–49). He also cared about people's physical circumstances: he healed the sick (Mark 1.29–31), brought sight to the blind (John 9.6) and raised the dead (Luke 7.11–17). Jesus cared about people's emotional state; he comforted the grieving and calmed the anxious (John 11.17–33; Matt. 6.27–34). Tom Wright emphasizes that salvation in the Gospels is both physical and spiritual. Jesus' healing miracles were salvation present as well as hope for the future. Salvation includes the whole of creation, not just humanity (Rom. 8.19–23; Col. 1.20–22). There is both a break and continuity between the present world and what it will be when redeemed and recreated. What is done in this world can have lasting value.[3]

The apostle Paul developed his thinking through his engagement with the young churches. Unlike Greek philosophy and Gnosticism, Paul saw bodies as something precious that could be described as God's temple. The body could be presented to God as a living sacrifice (1 Cor. 6.19; Rom. 12.1) and the actions of the body, such as eating and drinking, can be done to the glory of God (1 Cor. 10.31). It is integrated human beings that are redeemed and sanctified (1 Thess. 5.23). Humans have eternal destinies and that includes a body (1 Cor. 15.42–44). Some of the problems concerning Paul's attitude to the body are bound up with some rather confusing language so this section looks at three words and their original Greek form:

Soul (*psyche*).
Flesh (*sarx*).
World (*kosmos*).

Soul (*psyche*). Paul does not separate body and soul. When Paul uses the word 'soul', he often uses it to mean the complete person, in the sense of who we are, and this includes the body. In Colossians 3.23, the word *psyche* is rendered 'yourselves', meaning the whole person.[4]

Flesh (*sarx*). If the word *sarx* only means flesh, then Christianity does appear to take a negative stance towards the body (Rom. 8.1–8; Gal. 5.16–21). However, Paul's use of *sarx* is flexible: sometimes he uses it to mean flesh (Phil. 3.4–5) but often it means the human tendency to sin. Increasingly, translators distinguish the different meanings of *sarx*, by using phrases such as 'sinful nature', 'selfishness' and 'natural human desires' to communicate its meaning.[5]

World (*kosmos*). Paul's use of the word *kosmos* is also flexible. Robert Bratcher notes that the Greek word *kosmos* can have positive, neutral or negative meanings. Neutrally, *kosmos* can just mean 'world', the planet (Matt. 26.13). Positively, *kosmos* can mean all of God's creation (Acts

17.24). Negatively, *kosmos* can mean the world in need of salvation (Eph. 2.2). The world is not condemned for being physical.[6]

Greek influence on Christianity

Many of the Early Church Fathers (early Christian thinkers) were influenced by Greek philosophy, seeing God as good but this world and physical life in a less positive light. The things of this world were often viewed as transitory; at best they pointed to a spiritual world rather than having value in themselves.

Medieval theologians experienced tensions between Christianity and Greek philosophy but medieval Christianity as practised was deeply embodied: mystery plays, pilgrimages, feasting and fasting were all part of faith. Christianity continued to be influenced by Greek thinking about the body and material life but that was held in tension with a recognition that all life is God's. The Renaissance witnessed a renewed interest in the human body with artists such as Michelangelo and Leonardo da Vinci making detailed anatomical studies. In art more attention was paid to the human nature of Christ and the setting of his ministry. Pieter Bruegel the Elder painted the Holy Family as an ordinary family, without halos, within village scenes. In the Netherlands, both Catholic and Protestant artists developed landscape and still life as subjects in recognition that the everyday world was a gift of God.

The Enlightenment of the seventeenth and eighteenth centuries focused on reason and the mind was valued above the body, which led to abstract thought being valued above the life of the body and senses. Despite occasional positive developments, this valuing of the soul and the mind above the body continued to influence Christianity and western thinking; it can be seen in Emily Brontë's 1846 poem 'The Prisoner':

> Oh dreadful is the check – intense the agony –
> When the ear begins to hear, and the eye begins to see;
> When the pulse begins to throb, the brain to think again;
> The soul to feel the flesh, and the flesh to feel the chain.[7]

This conflicted attitude towards the body continues. Many images of Jesus' crucifixion show Jesus with no body hair. Is there still a lingering doubt about the status of the body? Although a wide range of beliefs continues to exist, there is a trend towards a more integrated view of humanity, with body and soul seen as a unity. There is also a growing emphasis on the environment and physical life as an expression of faith, and this world as the place where God is encountered. Revelatory preaching takes seriously Teilhard de Chardin's statement that Christians have a duty to throw themselves into the things of this world.[8] In showing the spiritual significance of bodily life the revelatory approach could play a part in counteracting these splits between body and mind, body and soul, spirit and matter. The Bible affirms the body and the material world, despite the Fall. There is no inherent theological reason why the material world and the human body cannot mediate the spiritual in some form. The Fall did not mute God; he still speaks through people and his world.

The image of God

The character focus of a revelatory approach makes the doctrine of humanity made in the image of God particularly important. Can we learn something of God from other human beings made in God's image? Can their creative works and their scientific discoveries speak of God even if they are not believers? Can God speak through art and music, architecture and drama made by flawed human beings, or was the image destroyed by the Fall? Genesis 1.26–27 talks of humanity made in God's image and likeness and the image survives, for people are perceived as still carrying that image after the Fall (Gen. 5.1–2; 9.6; James 3.9). The Fall affects the image but does not cancel it. If humanity still possesses something of the image of God, then learning something of God from other human beings is a possibility.

What is the image?

In one sense, what constitutes the image of God does not matter as long as people retain something of that image. Scripture is unclear about the constitution of the image and scholars differ. There are three basic views:

- The image of God is a characteristic or quality humans possess. Reason, the ability to make moral choices and human creativity have been put forward for this role at different times.
- The image of God is about a relationship. This could be the ability to have a relationship with God or the relationship as a gift from God with the potential for it to develop.
- The image of God is something people do, a function. The stewardship of the earth, creativity, learning, science and work have all been suggested as functions.

Whatever the image of God in humanity is, it seems to be integral to being human, and is universal. It confers dignity on all human beings. This means that preachers can draw on the work of artists, thinkers and others who do not necessarily identify as believers but express something of the image of God. Nevertheless, wisdom is needed concerning the people we draw on and the guide for this is Jesus in whom we see the image of God undamaged by sin (2 Cor. 4.4; Col. 1.15).

Incarnation

The incarnation, God revealed in flesh, applies to the whole of Jesus' life, death, resurrection and ascension. The incarnation affirms the body and material life; it shows this world as a place where we can meet God and the body as a way that revealed God in Jesus. Revelatory preaching is fundamentally incarnational: it dwells on the physical realities of Jesus' life. A sermon does not cease to be spiritual if it mentions Jesus' dirty feet, wet hair and stained clothes. Such preaching emphasizes the incarnation. The early years of Christianity were marked by a struggle to develop the implications of the incarnation. It was the early Christian councils that defined the doctrine of Jesus as God incarnate, fully God and fully man. The Bible is explicit in its reference to Jesus' body and the material setting of his life, from his birth in Bethlehem to his death on a cross (Luke 2.1–20; John 19.28). It was a scarred resurrected body that Thomas was invited to touch (John 20.24–29).

Birth and ministry

Jesus' birth is set in a particular place and a particular time. Luke uses two references to locate Jesus in history (Luke 2.1–2) and two locations: Nazareth and Bethlehem. The manger and swaddling clothes further emphasize Jesus' humanity (Luke 2.7). In art on the nativity Christ's divinity is often indicated in light, whereas the humanity of Jesus is frequently indicated by a naked or breastfeeding baby. This is in contrast to Christmas carols such as 'Away in a Manger' – 'no crying he makes' represents Jesus as unlike any other baby.

Jesus' ministry was earthed in Palestine, in specific places: Galilee, Jerusalem, Bethany. Jesus' divinity is held in tension with his humanity in the Gospels. His power over nature (Mark 4.35–41), disease (Matt. 8.1–3) and death (Luke 7.11–16) indicate divinity, but he also knew hunger (Matt. 4.2), human emotion (Matt. 26.37, John 15.11) and temptation

(Matt. 4.1–11). The incarnate God was vulnerable from the threat of Herod's soldiers to the cross.

Death, resurrection and ascension

Jesus' death is presented in all its physicality. The Gospel writers do not detail the execution (Mark 15.24) but they do record Jesus' thirst (John 19.28) and the blood and water from the spear wound (John 19.34). Images of the crucifixion vary, some artists show the physical torture in detail, emphasizing his humanity. Other artists concentrate on the meaning of the event and Christ's divinity, showing an almost serene Christ. Nevertheless, even artists who focus on the divinity of Christ include blood and nails. Jesus in his resurrected state could be seen, heard and touched; he could both eat and cook (Luke 24.36–43; John 21.9–13).

Although there was continuity with his earthly body, Jesus' resurrected body had different capabilities; it could appear and disappear. Jesus establishes his identity and physicality using what Luke describes as 'many convincing proofs' (Acts 1.3). Preaching can present the resurrected Jesus in an embodied form still bearing the scars of the crucifixion. The resurrected body is for a new creation (Col. 1.15–20). Bodies and the material world are transformed, not discarded.[9] Images of the Resurrection often show Christ holding a victory flag standing on a broken tomb or the shattered gates of hell. Jesus ascends to the Father without abandoning his resurrected body (Acts 1.9; Luke 24.50–51). Karl Barth describes Christ's humanity as clothes he does not take off.[10]

Images of the ascension are often rather crude, with Jesus' feet sticking out from a cloud, or ethereal. There still seems to be a problem accepting Jesus' full and ongoing humanity. The incarnation has consequences for preaching; the material situation reflected in texts; the physical being of characters is not something to be left behind when the meaning has been discerned.

Revelation

The nature of revelatory preaching raises the issue of whether creation, people, human experience and culture can be revelatory. Does God speak through people, their creativity, circumstances and creation or does revelation only come directly from God and through Scripture? In theological terms this is the difference between indirect general revelation and direct special revelation.

Special revelation

Special revelation centres primarily on the revelation of God through Jesus Christ, witnessed in Scripture and mediated by the Spirit. Hebrews opens with a statement on revelation (Heb. 1.1–2). 'Long ago God spoke to our ancestors in many and various ways by the prophets, but in these last days he has spoken to us by a Son.' John 1.18 also expresses the revelation through Jesus: 'No one has ever seen God. It is God the only Son, who is close to the Father's heart, who has made him known.' However, the Bible is more than just a record of past revelation; God still speaks through the words of Scripture, and God can be experienced by direct encounter and through the work of the Holy Spirit. The Holy Spirit can speak through a person's words, actions and their character, though Christians are advised to 'test the spirits' (1 John 4.1). This is important for a revelatory approach that focuses on characters and their material situations as presented in the Bible.

General revelation

General revelation is God's revealing of himself outside Scripture and direct encounters. There are various types of general or indirect revelation:

- God is revealed by his actions in nature and history.
- God is revealed by people's innate sense of God or an inborn moral sense.
- Creation can reveal its creator.

God is revealed by his actions in nature and history

In the Bible God is shown as actively using nature. God is shown in control of the climate (Isa. 5.6; James 5.17–18) and droughts and floods are named as God's intervention and reveal his power. This understanding of revelation is evidenced throughout history, but such events may lead to diametrically opposed interpretations. The wind that aided the defeat of the Spanish Armada in 1588 was celebrated with a medal engraved with the words, 'He [God] blew and they were scattered'.[11] Would the Spanish have attributed the wind to God? There is a tension between a biblical witness to God's control of nature but our limited human ability to discern this. The same problem applies to God's working through history. In the Bible God reveals his power over human events through the rise and fall of nations (Amos 1—2; Isa. 40.15–17). God still acts through historical events but these events are open to a range of interpretations and our vision is probably not wide enough to make definitive statements.

God is revealed in people's innate sense

Belief in God in some form is widespread, both across the world and throughout history. However, this can be just a basic sense of a spiritual aspect of life. Paul describes the law as written on the human heart (Rom. 2.13–16). This could be an inborn moral sense, even though it is expressed in different moral systems.

God is revealed in Creation

The nature Psalms (Ps. 8; Ps.19) glory in the silent witness of creation that reveals its creator. Creation should bear the mark of its creator but it is not easy to define what this would be, both beauty and order are possibilities. Creation also bears witness to the Fall, there is ugliness and cruelty in creation, as well as beauty. Colin Gunton notes another facet of this form of general revelation. Nature reveals itself in ways that the human mind can understand. This means that the work of scientists and those who work in the arts can reveal something of the way the world is designed.[12] The compatibility of the human mind and the way the universe works is something that we take for granted but one person who did not take it for granted was Albert Einstein, who thought that the fact that the world is comprehensible to human minds was a miracle.[13]

Both/and

Indirect revelation and special revelation are not in competition. Special revelation acts as a framework for understanding general revelation. Paul Helm warns that without special revelation people may only come to a very basic understanding of God.[14] Creation does not automatically reveal God; if it did, every naturalist would be a believer. Colin Gunton describes the Bible as acting as a pair of glasses that enables people to recognize creation as God's handiwork.[15]

David Brown emphasizes the generosity of God (Luke 6.38; 1 Tim. 6.17) and links it to general revelation. If God is generous, we can expect to find him at work in the world in a way that people can respond to. David Brown describes this as the 'enchantment' of the world. The world was once 'read' as God's second book and many aspects of life were relevant to faith, but that belief has diminished in our more secular age.[16] A return to a broader understanding of revelation means preachers can draw on the art of those who pay faithful attention to the world *as it is*, for it is God's world.

Revelation as propositional and personal

Revelation can take two forms: knowledge of a person (personal revelation) and statements of truth and meaning (propositional revelation). Personal revelation is about a relationship (Jesus is my Lord and Saviour) but it can include propositions about that relationship. Propositional statements can include statements about a person (God is Holy). The two forms of revelation work together. The Bible centres on relationships between God and Israel and between individuals and God. In the Old Testament this is expressed in national covenants (Josh. 24.1–28) and in individual relationships. Abraham walks before God (Gen. 17.1), Moses speaks to God face to face, as to a friend (Ex. 33.11), and Jeremiah and Ezekiel speak of a new relationship based on the heart (Jer. 31.31–34; Ezek. 36.26). In the New Testament it is accepting Jesus as Lord that is the focus (Rom. 10.9–13).

Revelation can be primarily personal with propositions describing the relationship rather than revelation being primarily propositional. How people think about revelation matters for a person's understanding of revelation can affect how faith is understood. *Undue* concentration on propositions can lead to faith being a list of beliefs to assent to. *Undue* concentration on personal revelation without propositions could lead to misunderstandings about the nature of the relationship. The Bible is clear, revelation comes in various ways, it centres on the work of God in Christ as witnessed in Scripture, but God can also make himself known through creation, people, science and culture.

Conclusion

Creation, being made in the image of God, incarnation and revelation are four doctrines that, to different degrees, affirm an approach to preaching that looks for spiritual insight through the things of this world as well as through the Bible and direct encounters with God. This approach sees large areas of human life as revelatory in potential but interpreted through the primary revelation of God through Christ. These doctrines affirm the role of the body, the material world and human culture in revealing God. Revelatory preaching stands on this broad view of revelation that licenses learning from the world and its people, a world that still bears the mark of its creator.

Notes

1 Paula Gooder, 2016, *Body*, London: SPCK, pp. 33–6.

2 Plato, *Phaedo*, 1955, tr. R. S. Bluck, New York: Liberal Arts Press, pp. 8–12, 28, 31.

3 Tom Wright, 2011, *Surprised by Hope*, London: SPCK, pp. 37–8, 204–5.

4 Gooder, *Body*, pp. 33, 39–41.

5 Gooder, *Body*, pp. 64–6.

6 Robert G. Bratcher, 'The Meaning of Kosmos, "World", in the New Testament', *Bible Translator*, 31 (1980), 430–4. https://doi.org/10.1177%2F026009438003100406.

7 Emily Bronte, 1846, 'The Prisoner', *English Verse*, https://englishverse.com/poems/the_prisoner, accessed 14.11.2021.

8 Pierre Teilhard de Chardin, 1960, *The Divine Milieu*, New York: Harper, pp. 37–9.

9 David A. Wilkinson, 2010, *Christian Eschatology and the Physical Universe*, London: T&T Clark International, pp. 89–91, 98–9, 156–7.

10 Karl Barth, 2008, *Church Dogmatics* IV.2, Edinburgh: T&T Clark, p. 102.

11 Gerard van Bylaer, *The Defeat of the Spanish Armada* (silver medal, 1588; Royal Museums Greenwich, London).

12 Colin E. Gunton, 1995, *A Brief Theology of Revelation*, Edinburgh: T&T Clark, pp. 26–30, 56–62.

13 Albert Einstein, 'Physics and Reality', *Journal of the Franklin Institute*, 221/3 (1936), 349–82 (p. 351). doi.org/10.1016/S0016-0032(36)91047-5.

14 Paul Helm, 1982, *Divine Revelation*, Vancouver: Regent College Publishing, pp. 27–31, 35.

15 Gunton, *Brief Theology*, p. 61.

16 David Brown, 2004, *God and Enchantment of Place*, Oxford: Oxford University Press, pp. 6–10, 33.

15

Sermons and Commentary

This chapter contains four sermons with brief commentaries. The sermons show how some of the issues and techniques discussed in this book are worked through in a sermon. Not every technique or issue is followed up in every sermon; the nature of the sermon was decided by the text and the context within which it was preached. The sermons demonstrate different structures: prologue, epilogue, twice-told and theme.

SERMON 1: ANNA

Reference: Luke 2.22–24, 36–38

This sermon is included as an example of a sermon with a prologue. I have deliberately ended it abruptly; it needs an epilogue and you are invited to add one. This sermon was preached during Advent, and meditations that accompanied the sermon have been included. Anna fasts and prays, a normal part of the Jewish faith; however, Anna's degree of prayer and fasting was unusual – it was a witness to the nation's need of God. It was a protest, a demonstration that all was not well if such prayer was needed. Her hope for her people rested on the promise of the Coming One, the Messiah. Anna highlights the people's need while knowing that the Messiah would answer that need. The story of Anna is the story of an elderly woman, a group often overlooked. Alongside the insight, this story helps us to appreciate those who faithfully exercise ministries that do not attract attention but without whom we could not function.

Insight

Anna is presented as insignificant in terms of birth and position but she is named as a prophet and she has spiritual insight. Her insight enables her to know her people's need of God and she has hope in the Messiah to meet that need. Anna faithfully witnesses to that need and hope.

Embodiment

Anna's quiet faithfulness and waiting in hope is embodied in her physical presence in the temple and her continued prayer and fasting. This long-term faithful witness is sensed in the physical signs of ageing and the events that took place around her. Her insight is embodied in her perception of the nations' need of God expressed in prayer and fasting beyond what was required, and in her recognition of Jesus. Her insignificance is embodied in the details of her pedigree.

Notice the following:

Structure

The meditations are an example of some of the implications being made explicit after the sermon. A transition sentence is used to move from prologue to main sermon text. There is also a move from the general nature of the prologue to the specific opening of the main text; from the baby who will save the world, to Anna's pedigree.

Anachronism

There are touches of anachronism: wedding photos, placards, headlines, John and Jane Smith. These are a way of signalling that this story has relevance today.

Developing details

The sermon makes explicit implied details based on the common pattern of life for women at the time. Life followed a predictable pattern: marrying young, raising a family and working together to provide. The text only tells us Anna's age, I have developed the physical implications based on the human experience of ageing, a process that does not change. The Bible describes her constant presence at the temple over many years. From this statement details can be developed using the trajectory of the text; people would have been used to seeing her when they came for festivals and ceremonies. The construction of Herod's temple, which was begun in 20 BC, would have continued during her lifetime. If Jesus was born around 6 BC and Anna was eighty-four when she encountered Jesus, that means she would have experienced many historic events.

Physicality

The sermon stays with the physical realities: Anna's ageing body, Mary's healing body after childbirth, Mary and Joseph's changed way of life, the temple setting. Jesus' name is not just described as 'ordinary', a domestic scene is imagined where Mary calls Jesus and other boys with the same name respond.

Language

There are examples of figurative language: 'her face a calendar of years', 'compassion sculpts a beauty that is not obvious'. Touches of description are employed, focusing on Anna's changing hair; the language is specific, the hair turns from grey to white: these signal this is a real person. The tense moves between present and past, and there is rhythm in the language, but a consistent rhythm is not maintained. There is some repetition but it is broken after two or three lines.

Relevance

The relevance of Anna's life is portrayed rather than applied. The congregation is not told to copy Anna in waiting in hope and in faithful ministries but it is implicit in the sermon and the meditations. The relevance of modern ministries like Anna's is indicated in the meditations.

Sermon

Prologue

Our reading opens forty days after Jesus' birth. Mary's body is healing but remains for ever changed. It is linked to her baby's body now, responding to every cry. Mary and Joseph are learning a new way of life, a life that includes feeding, changing and disturbed nights. Jesus is only forty days old but for Mary and Joseph that night in Bethlehem and the visit of the shepherds probably feels long ago. They have not forgotten those events, Mary has kept the memories and hidden them in her heart. Those memories are there to be drawn out and contemplated whenever this child, this Jesus, looks so normal that seeds of doubt are sown. He is a baby, like any other baby. Would God's son really be so ordinary? They have named him 'Jesus' as the angel said. It is a very ordinary name. Mary knows that when she calls his name in future, other boys called

Jesus will look up. But this is their Jesus, God's Jesus, the one who has come to save.

They arrive at the temple; it is massive and it is crowded. They come to offer a sacrifice as part of their worship and they choose the option of the poor – two pigeons. Jesus will grow up without the advantages of wealth, without the safety net that money provides. Amid the crowd one elderly lady, called Anna, spots Joseph, Mary and Jesus. The temple is swarming with people – lots of parents have brought their children, but Anna has been waiting for this moment all her life. She has been praying for this moment for over sixty years, and that has sharpened her spiritual sight; she knows this baby is the one she has been waiting for. Mary and Joseph just see an elderly lady until she begins to speak; then they realize that this elderly lady has a rather direct line to God. She is a prophet. Anna's words reassure Mary and Joseph, their baby is the one the world is waiting for. The one who will save.

That is more or less the story of Anna, but if we look closer at the Bible reading, those three verses reveal much more.

Pause.

Who is Anna?
Our reading gave us some information.
Anna, daughter of Phenuel of the tribe of Asher –
and we are none the wiser.
Anna, daughter of a man about whom we know absolutely nothing,
from an obscure tribe in the extreme north of the country.
This is the pedigree of a nobody.
This is Jane Smith, daughter of John Smith,
from an obscure northern town. (Add the name of a town if you wish.)

(My apologies to anyone called Jane or John, and to the North.)

Anna does not have famous parents.
She does not come from anywhere exotic.
Anna does not do much.
She does not go anywhere.
Anna is ordinary.
She is also at least eighty-four.
Anna fasts, prays and waits –
not the sort of ministry that grabs the headlines.
Luke goes to some lengths to tell us how insignificant she is,
then he drops the bombshell;

this apparently insignificant woman is a prophet!
There had been a dearth of prophets for hundreds of years
and the temple officials would not expect this elderly lady to be one.
Never underestimate elderly ladies.

Anna of course had not always been old.
Wedding pictures would have shown a smiling teenage bride,
an ordinary couple.
Anna had all the hopes that came with marriage at that time:
working together to provide,
bringing up a family,
growing together as a couple.

The young smiling bride worked, and she waited.
Month after month she waited,
year after year.
The smile faded
and the children never came.
Death came instead and robbed her of her husband.
By the time she was in her twenties,
Anna had been stripped of her hopes.

Loss was not the end for Anna,
it was a beginning.
Anna rebuilt her life.
She did not remarry;
instead she took to prayer and fasting in the temple.
Her life became marked by a new hope,
not for herself but for her nation.
A hope in God.
Her early life had taught her how to wait,
now she waited once more.
This time she knew her hopes would not be in vain.
She hoped for the One that God would send to save his people.
She waited in hope.

Anna fasted, prayed and waited.
Her fasting and praying was not a strange sight to begin with,
after all, people came to the temple to pray
and fasting was part of the Jewish faith.
But Anna prayed day after day.
She fasted more than was required.

Her fasting was a sign of mourning,
not for the loss of her husband,
but for the plight of her people.
Her fasting was a sign of protest,
it was her placard saying,
'All is not well, we need God.'
She knew God would hear.
She trusted God would come.
She knew how to wait in hope.

People got used to the young widow.
She became a bit of a fixture in the temple.
Year after year she stayed
into her thirties, her forties, her fifties,
Her youthful looks gave way to time,
her face a calendar of years.
When people came for the festivals, Anna was still there,
still praying, still fasting, still waiting.
A trip to the temple would not have been the same without seeing Anna.
There was comfort in it.
There was hope.
There was challenge.
Anna's fasting and waiting continued to proclaim,
'All is not well, we need God.'

Anna prayed through the nation's ups and downs.
She prayed while the temple was rebuilt around her.
Still her presence proclaimed,
'All is not well, we need God.'

Anna prayed into her sixties and seventies.
Her hair turned grey.
Hope, that time often erodes, lived on in her.
It was in her eighties when her hair was white
that Anna's hope was realized.
Anna must have seen many parents bring their babies to the temple.
Jesus was probably not the first baby she had given thanks for.
She had prayed for many over the years,
but this baby,
this family,
this Jesus,
was different.

Anna's eyes may have dimmed with age
but her spiritual sight was untouched.
This child was the One,
the One she had waited for,
the One she had spent a lifetime praying for,
waiting in hope.
Anna the prophet becomes Anna the evangelist
as she spreads the word to all who are waiting for God.
The waiting is over.

Meditations

The following meditation uses two images:

Old Woman Reading, Probably the Prophetess Anna, Rembrandt van
  Rijn, 1631, oil painting, Rijksmuseum, Amsterdam.
Self-portrait as the Apostle Paul, Rembrandt van Rijn, 1661, oil painting,
  Rijksmuseum, Amsterdam.

Meditation 1

This is a picture of Rembrandt, a famous artist; one of the leading biblical
painters of all time. This is his painting of an old woman reading, sub-
titled *The Prophetess Anna*. It is thought that Rembrandt used his mother
to pose as Anna for this painting. We know little about his mother;
her name was Cornelia, she was a baker's daughter, she had about ten
children, she died in 1640. Rembrandt's mother was not famous but
Rembrandt paints her many times. Rembrandt's parents were ambitious
for him and enrolled him in a university but Rembrandt had other plans:
he wanted to be an artist, so he left university and the young Rembrandt
started his education as an artist. No doubt his mother and father were
disappointed, but they supported him, sending him to renowned painters
for training. Without their encouragement a major artist would have
been lost to the world.

Spend a few moments looking at the painting of Rembrandt's mother.
Share your thoughts with people near you if you wish.

Rembrandt paints his mother's face in the shadow. There is no background and light falls on the Bible. It is a portrait of faith. Maybe
Rembrandt's mother as Anna represents the people in the background;

the prayers, the encouragers, the doers, the people like Anna who faithfully serve year after year. It is the Annas of this world, with their prayer and their service, who keep the world turning. It is the Annas of this world who teach us to wait in hope. Their ministry may not always be noticed, but we would soon notice if they stopped.

In the silence think of people you know who are the 'Annas' today. They can be men or women, young or old. In the silence quietly give thanks for them, for their faithfulness, for their service. Think of a person who has been an Anna for you. *Silence.*

Meditation 2: *Reflection on a eulogy*

Today I listened to a eulogy,
they spoke of his brilliance, his kindness.
Such a shame he did not hear those words in life.
Why wait to speak a eulogy over a coffin
when they cannot mumble, 'Thank you, I never thought you noticed.'
So here it is, a eulogy to the Annas of this world.
They come in both genders,
they are the quiet of the land,
the ordinary people we pass in the supermarket,
the ones we don't notice at the petrol station.
They are the men and women who do not stand out in a crowd
for they are not the sort who try to catch the eye,
and compassion sculpts a beauty that is not obvious.
But they are the beautiful people.
They are the ones, like Anna, who just get on with the job.
No fuss.
No drama.
They are the prayers,
the encouragers,
the doers,
the ones who wait in hope.
The world may not notice the Annas, but God does
and so do myriads of people who feel the effects of their lives.
Theirs is not a splash of a stone tossed into a pool
sending waves to break against the banks.
Theirs is a pebble gently dropped, sending smooth ripples that spread
    ever wider.
So let us praise the quiet of the land, the Annas,
the human glue that holds it all together.
And that is all that needs to be said,

except to echo the words of God,
'Well done, thou good and faithful servant.'

Prayer

For all the Annas we give you thanks, O Lord. For the faithful ones, who teach us how to wait in hope. Bless their ministry, strengthen them in service. Lord, teach us to grieve for the state of the world, the state of our nation, for protest begins in grief; it begins in that moment when we stop pretending that everything is fine. We need you. Our world needs you. Come, Lord Jesus. Amen.

SERMON 2: ABRAM TO ABRAHAM

References: Genesis 17.1–8, 15–17; Micah 6.8; Ephesians 1.13–14

This sermon is twice-told, once in prose, once more lyrically. It focuses on the loss of hope and doubt and yet remaining faithful, and the Almighty God's power to keep his promises. It is sometimes forgotten that Abram laughed at God's promises, it was not just Sarah. Despite the laughter, Abraham and Sarah continue with God. The promises eventually come true but just one son, just one plot of land.

Insight

Our doubt and lack of hope does not negate God's promises. In doubt or in hope our calling is to walk through life with God according to those promises. God is El Shaddai, the Almighty One, the All Sufficient One, the God who can deliver on the promises.

Embodiment

Abram's age and his dried-up appearance (he lived a nomadic lifestyle in a dry, hot climate) embody hope dried-up. The sound of his laughter embodies his doubt. New names embody the promise in sound as a mark in the body (circumcision) embodies the covenant for Abram.

Notice the following:

Structure

There is a transition sentence between the first telling and the second, asking the congregation to think about their own lives in light of Abram's experience of God's promises. The second telling does not have all the detail of the first, it is more creative in style.

Anachronism

Small touches of anachronism are used: antenatal classes, tea, highlighting, 'a walk in the park'.

Developing details

Details implicit in the text are drawn out: Abram's age is given and from that his physical appearance is detailed. The mixture of faith, doubt and despairing that God's promises will come true are present in the text, I have developed these drawing on the book of Ecclesiastes, which has a similar mixture of faith and despair.

Physicality

The physical nature of the narrative is made specific: Abram's face pressed against the dry earth, the smudge of dirt, his size compared with the landscape, the lack of sound and the sound of the new names. Abram is not just described as old; age is communicated through the physical difficulty in getting up.

Language

There are small touches of figurative language: 'a desert of a man', 'a nation of two'. The language is specific, not just 'childless', but 'Always uncle and aunt, never mum and dad'.

Relevance

This sermon is included to show relevance and application threaded throughout:

> We know there are times when just closing our eyes in prayer won't do ...

You do not have to reach old age to despair, to abandon hope, to just give up ...
We have laughed like that.
Abram's doubt does not stop God. Neither does ours.

Sermon

First telling

The stage is bare for this scene in the saga of Abram and Sarai, we are not told where we are, just somewhere in Canaan. Somewhere in the land that Abram and Sarai have wandered for decades. Abram is by himself, an old man dwarfed by the landscape, but he soon discovers he is not as alone as he thought. We are never as alone as we think.

God shows up and introduces himself as El Shaddai, the Mighty One, the All Sufficient One. He will need to be the Mighty One if the things he is about to promise are going to come true. Abram does what you do when you meet God, he falls to the ground, face pressed to the dry earth. We look at Abram and know why he is on the ground. We know there are times when just closing our eyes in prayer won't do, when just bowing our heads is not enough. There are times when we need to get down on the ground before God, in spirit even if we can no longer do it physically. God speaks and repeats a promise he has made before. Abram will have land and children, but this time the promise is increased: lots of land as a permanent possession and a nation full of children. God continues to speak, and the promise is upgraded to an eternal agreement, a covenant, a promise to be Abram's God.

There are lots of 'I's in this speech by God, 'I will this and I will that.' God is binding himself to Abram and to Abram's people. Abram listens for what he will have to do. It is there, a command to walk before God in faithfulness and integrity. Such a simple statement that hides an enormous truth. God has just promised his ongoing presence. Life will now be a walk in the company of the Almighty, though it will never be a 'walk in the park'. Abram is to orientate his life by God, reference each step by him. God is to be the compass of his life, deciding not only its direction but its quality; a life lived with integrity, a life marked by faithfulness.

Most of life has been a test for Abram and Sarai; they were called to leave their home and wander in Canaan. There are still tests to come and this is a test of faith. At his age, can Abram believe God's promise of children and land? No, Abram laughs. Believing in lots of descendants was difficult. As far as Abram is concerned one child would be good, but he does not even have that. God promises him lots of land but at ninety-nine he does not own an inch of it. Those hopes had withered, his future looks bleak, so Abram laughs. Not the joyful laughter that comes with good news, not the chuckle at a joke, but the dry, dismissive laughter of a man who has heard it all before.

Abram is sceptical. He has reached a despairing old age, though you do not have to reach old age to despair, to abandon hope, to just give up. It can happen in the midst of life and for some it even happens in youth, a sense of hopelessness, disappointment, the loss of a future. When we hear Abram's hollow laugh some of us may recognize the sound, we have laughed like that. Later, Sarai will laugh when she hears the promise. At their age a child was unthinkable. It's one thing being an elderly mother at the antenatal classes, but Sarai was older than most grandmothers.

In the face of Abram's doubt, God carries on confirming the promise. Abram's doubt does not stop God. Neither does ours. The sound ceases. God stops speaking. Abram gets up, his forehead smudged with dirt, but he is not Abram anymore but Abraham, the father of nations. In future, every time Sarai calls him in for tea, he will be reminded that he is to be a father of nations. And Sarai is no longer Sarai but Sarah, the mother of kings.

Once again Abram listens for his side of the covenant and it is there, a physical sign that will forever mark him as God's – circumcision. Every day he will see the sign, every day he will be reminded of what God promised and his commitment in response. We too carry a mark, an invisible one, the seal of God that reminds us that we are his. We are marked with the seal of the Holy Spirit. The sign of the cross made at baptism is still there. The water may have dried but the mark remains. We are his.

We rise with Abraham as God offers us a future. We scrape ourselves off the ground and we, too, are given a new name: daughter of the King, son of the Father. It takes a while for Abraham and Sarah to get used to their new names, but the names repeat the promise and name the future. That did not mean life became any easier; they were still tested. They only ever had one son, Isaac, whose name meant 'laughter', and it was a bit of a joke having a child at their age. They were tested. But God kept his promise of children, they had a son who went on to have children and those children had more children and the nation of Israel was born. But Abraham and Sarah did not live to see the nation they were promised. They were tested. God's promise of land came true; the nation of Israel under Joshua, hundreds of years later, claimed the land of Canaan as their own. But Abraham and Sarah did not live to see it. The only piece of the Promised Land that Abraham ever owned was the field in which he buried Sarah.

What God promises comes true, because he is El Shaddai, the Mighty One. But God does not deliver his promises according to our timetables and they are often followed by testing. But it is the God of Abraham and Sarah who walks with us through the testing. El Shaddai, the Mighty One, walks with us and he is the one in control of the future, for he is the one who has written the ending. As we reflect on this story, we can think about our own walk with God and God guiding the direction and quality of our lives.

Pause.

Second telling

Abram is old,
dried up,
desiccated by years of wandering in sun and wind.
He and Sarai left home and wandered an alien land
on a promise of land of their own.
It had not happened.
Sarai and Abram trod the land
but owned not one inch of it.
Always guests.
Always strangers.
Always foreigners camping on someone else's soil.

Abram and Sarai roamed Canaan
sustained by a promise of children,
yet they had none.
Always uncle and aunt,
never mum and dad.
Sarai and Abram remained a nation of two.

The Lord appeared.
Abram fell with his face to the ground,
not too difficult at his age,
getting up was more of a problem.
Face in the dirt,
Abram listened as God's words flowed over him.
The promise was repeated.

A promise of fruitfulness to this desert of a man.
Not just land but the whole land.

Not just fruitful but very fruitful.
Not just a nation but nations.
Not just a promise but an everlasting covenant.
A promise repeated in capital letters, underlined and highlighted.
Abram listened intently; not just 'I will make you'
but 'I have made you the father of many.'
The desert was about to bloom.

One day they would hold a baby in their arms.
One day Abraham would own one small patch of the Promised Land.
Big enough to bury Sarah.
Big enough to sustain hope.
But right now, it felt laughable.

The man on the ground laughed,
but despite his doubt
he would keep his side of the covenant.
He would walk before God:
let God decide the direction of his life,
let God decide its quality.
That would be life for him
and for us,
and for all those that follow.
For what does the Lord require of us
but to do justice, love mercy
and walk humbly with our God.

SERMON 3: MOSES SPEAKS TO THE PEOPLE

References: Deuteronomy 30.11–20; Jeremiah 21.8–9;
Matthew 7.13–14

Earlier in this book I noted that a revelatory approach tends not to follow a theme across several texts. A theme that draws together many texts needs a different approach. However, a revelatory approach can be used across a few narrative texts if there is a strong link between them. This tends to mean majoring on one story and linking in less detail to others. This sermon on choices majors on Moses speaking to the people (Deuteronomy 30) but links in less detail to Jeremiah and Jesus. All three are narratives that offer people a choice.

Insight

Throughout the Bible people are asked to make a choice and that choice was between life and death; they are encouraged to choose life and a relationship with God. The choice is about a way of life, not just assent to a belief.

Embodiment

The choices are not abstract, they are embodied in concrete situations in history, both personal and national. The choices are presented fully embodied, the people are described physically, they are not just 'a crowd', these are real people who had to make a choice.

Notice the following:

Structure

The prologue is explanatory, giving dates and events; these moments are linked by the theme of choice. The three situations in the prologue could be abbreviated and projected if you have that facility. There is a transition sentence between the prologue and the main text, which moves the focus from the general to the specific, from the broad historical situation to one man.

Details

Details are added that are not in the text: Moses' physical appearance is based on human experience of ageing. Moses' memories I have based on Deuteronomy 29 where Moses reminds the people of the miracles of Egypt. I have added details of the people listening because 'crowd' is an anonymous word that is difficult to relate to. I have added emotions, drawing on other Scriptures: Jesus wept over the people and Jerusalem (Luke 19.41–44; 23.27–30); Moses prayed for forgiveness for the people and offered his own life (Ex. 30.30–33), Jeremiah wished his eyes were a fountain of tears to weep for his people (Jer. 9.1).

Physicality

I have briefly described the physical appearance of Moses and some of the crowd: 'The set of a jaw, the slant of an eye, the curve of a cheek.' The passing of time is documented in the death of different generations, not just 'later'.

Language

I have put the words spoken by Moses, Jeremiah and Jesus in speech marks, but they are paraphrased and draw on a wider context of Scripture. The main text is in the present tense to give the feeling of immediacy. There are touches of figurative language such as: 'Children of rock and sand'; 'Death casts its shadow backwards from the grave'. The language of the main text is lyrical and has rhythm and repetition, but the rhythm changes and the repetition ceases after a few lines.

Relevance

Relevance is woven throughout implicitly and it is made explicit at the end. There may be identification concerning the call to choose and the sermon also switches to 'we' to include the congregation and the preacher.

Sermon

Prologue

On many occasions in the Bible, people are given a choice; here are three of them.

The thirteenth century BC (or thereabouts).
Now is the moment of choice for the people of Israel as they come to the end of their desert wanderings and they stand expectantly before Moses. Their parents had been slaves in Egypt and they had followed Moses to freedom as they crossed the wilderness to reach the Promised Land. That first generation of freed slaves had disobeyed God and had died in the wilderness. It is their children who will enter the Promised Land. It is this second generation who now stand before Moses. Moses is old, he knows he will die soon and he gives them a choice.

587 BC
Now is the moment of choice for the people of Jerusalem in the Kingdom of Judah. They are besieged by the Babylonians who have killed and burned their way across the land, but Jerusalem has not yet fallen. The state of Judah teeters on the edge of extinction. The prophet Jeremiah pleads with the people and he gives them a choice that may save lives.

Around AD 28
Now is the moment of choice for the people of Palestine. Jesus stands before them and calls them to make their most important choice, between a way of life and a way of death.

We start with that initial choice as the people stand before Moses as they wait to enter the Promised Land. *Pause.*

Moses was an old, old man:
No longer a prince of Egypt,
No longer a tough desert shepherd,
No longer the courageous opponent of Pharaoh,
No longer young.
His sinewy frame tells of a strength not yet gone.
But death is closer than his shadow.

What do you say when you know you are about to die?
What gift of words can you give?

Moses stands facing the Israelites and the crowd sinks into silence.
He is the only leader they have ever known,
this desert generation.
They had been born in the wilderness,
children of rock and sand;
a nation of free people who had never known slavery.
Moses looks at their youthful faces.
These are the children of the slaves he led out of Egypt.
Their parents died in the desert where they had wandered for forty
years.
For Moses, the memories of those early days,
when God led them out of Egypt,
increasingly fill his mind.
He would catch himself reminiscing with people:
'Do you remember when the Nile turned to blood?'
'Do you remember when the Angel of Death passed over?'
'Do you remember when we walked dry-shod across the sea that
parted?'
'Do you remember ...?'
Then would stop himself.
Of course, they didn't remember,
they weren't even born then.
Those who did remember were buried in the desert.
Moses scans the crowd again.
He can see those slaves he led across the desert in the faces of their
children:
the set of a jaw,
the slant of an eye,
the curve of a cheek.
These children of freedom reflect the faces of those who had walked
with him
out of Egypt,
out of slavery
and into the wilderness.
That generation had died there.
But this is a new generation,
straining towards the future,
towards the Promised Land,
not back to the past,
his past,
Egypt.

Their parents had been condemned to die in the desert for their
faithlessness, but Moses could not forget them; they had been through
too much together. He would keep faith with that faithless generation,
for they had not always been so. They had taken the risk and trusted
him as their leader when they were Pharaoh's slaves. They had stuck
with him and trusted God in those early days, even though the road to
freedom had been a hard one.
He would remember the best in them and give a gift to their children.

But what do you say to a generation that will found a nation?
What does a man who is about to die bequeath?
What words are weighty enough
to carry what he and their parents learned over forty years of wandering
in the desert?
What he said was simple.
He would give them a choice.
Despite his age his voice is strong,
and the clear desert air carries his words;
the words of God in the mouth of Moses:
'I put before you today life and death.
Love the Lord your God,
walk in his ways, live in his blessing.
Choose life.
For if you give your lives to what is worthless,
forsaking God and his ways,
you will live lives that are a curse to you and others;
lives that destroy what is good in and around you.
Choose God's way. Choose God's blessing. Choose life!'

Time passes, generations are born and buried.
That young generation that exploded from the desert into the Promised
Land
is dead,
long dead.
Centuries have gone by.
Now their children's children face disaster.
The enemy is at the gate,
an enemy who will not spare the sword.
The prophet Jeremiah stands with a message for the people.
He has served this nation for forty years,
watched them make wrong choices time and time again.
He had watched as idolatry, injustice and greed corrupted society.

He had pleaded with them, but they had not listened.
Now death is close, its shadow falls across the whole nation.
What do you say to a nation that is about to die?
Jeremiah closes his eyes and calls to mind the people and their leaders.
The message is for them.
Once again, the words ring out,
the words of God in the mouth of Jeremiah:
'I put before you today
a way of life
and a way of death.
Choose life, it is not too late.
It is never too late.'
But they choose death and are taken into exile.
Judah as a nation ceases to exist.

Time passes, generations are born and buried
The children of the children that Moses addressed
are dead.
The children of the children that Jeremiah pleaded with
are dead.
Centuries have passed.
Now a new generation stands on a hillside before Jesus of Nazareth,
and they are listening.
Jesus surveys the crowd.
He knows these people, they are his people.
In the hush of the crowd he waits and scans their faces.
He sees generations that have gone before.
But this is a new generation.
They are not tied by the choices of the past.
Jesus knows his death is not far away;
its shadow fell across the manger.
What do you say to people
when you know your death will not be long in coming?
What gift can you give?
Once again, they hear the words of God,
spoken by the Son of God.
Jesus offers them a choice:
'I put before you today a way of life and a way of death.
One way is narrow and hard but leads to life.
One way is broad and easy but leads to death.
Choose life!
Choose me, the Way, the Truth and the Life.'

In sadness he knows many will choose death,
for death is a hard habit to break.
Death is the name of a path we choose to walk;
like many roads, it takes its name from its destination. (Name a local road.)
Death is a series of choices we make
not just an event that happens to us in the future.
It is a pattern of behaviour, a destructive life-style.
Every time we choose hatred, lies, injustice, bitterness,
something dies in and around us.
Death is a negative; it is a 'No' to all that is vibrant, good, beautiful and true.
It is life in all its thinness, a mean, skinny version of life.
Death casts its shadow backwards from the grave in bleak, meagre lifestyles.
Life is a hard habit to acquire.
Life is the name of a path we walk;
like many roads, it takes its name from its destination. (Name a local road.)
Life, resurrection life, is a series of choices we make,
not just an event that happened to Jesus
and will happen for his people in the future.
Life is a pattern of behaviour, a life-affirming lifestyle.
Every time we choose love, faith, forgiveness and hope,
life kindles in and around us.
Every time we choose peace and justice we take the Jesus option
bringing new life in and around us.
Each day we wake and say, 'Today I choose life,' we take the resurrection option.
Resurrection casts its light backwards over our lives.
It is God's 'Yes' to all that is vibrant, good and true.
It's life in all its fullness, a generous, overflowing version of life.
But it's not the easy option.

Jesus stood before the crowd.
His heart went out to these sons and daughters of the past
and he offered them a future:
'Choose life.
Choose me.
Take the resurrection option.'

SERMON 4: RUTH: PROMISES AND PAIN

Reference: Ruth 2

This sermon demonstrates a scenic delivery, it covers the whole story of Ruth but majors on one scene that introduces the idea of Ruth's life being a working out of her promise. It only briefly touches on the other scenes. The hard, physical nature of the work Ruth did and the pain it must have caused stands in sharp contrast to the poetic nature of her promise, but the two are closely connected. Promises might be made in poetry but they are paid in pain, an experience that is true of our religious commitments as well as our everyday commitments. Commitment is embodied in the way we live.

Insight

Commitments are often made in moments of high emotion, in poetry, but they are often paid in pain and the hard work of everyday life.

Embodiment

Ruth's commitment is paid in the hard work of gleaning and the dangers she faced. It is expressed in her faith and in submitting to Israelite custom and law.

Notice the following:

Structure

This is an unusual structure, having two tellings and a short epilogue. The second telling is more lyrical, has more engagement with the emotions and detail of daily life. The first telling provides the outline of the story and background, it also alerts people to the hidden presence of God in the narrative. The second telling is structured around Ruth's promise and how it had consequences in Ruth's life. (Note: The words of Ruth's promise are rendered freely in this sermon.)

Anachronisms

In this sermon the anachronisms are in language style: 'off limits', 'brushes it off', 'talk of the town', 'a big if'.

Details

The details of Ruth's work are not given in the text but can be deduced from human experience. Sweat, hair sticking to the forehead and backache are things that happen when engaged in heavy physical labour. Ruth's emotions are based on human experience and the nature of life in biblical times, marriages were not first and foremost about romance; security and producing a family was a major factor. There is no mention of homesickness in the text (even if Ruth had little time to indulge it) but the Bible tells of the Israelites' homesickness in exile, and people of other nations must have felt the same about their homes. Ruth had committed to Israel's God so I have her joining in the response to 'The Lord is with you', it is not in the text but likely in the context.

Physicality

This is a narrative that cries out for a very physical presentation that shows the depth of Ruth's commitment. Cracked skin, heat, sitting alone, what she eats, the looks from the men, being able to see Moab.

Language

The language of the first telling is factual and broad. The second telling is more lyrical and specific. The poetry of the promise is repeated and its rhythm described. The pattern of Ruth's promise structures the second telling.

Sermon

First telling

The story of Ruth is not a modern romance. It would not make a romantic film. It is set in a patriarchal society and it is a very earthy story where the heroine is drenched in sweat and has blisters on her hands. This is a story where two women take the initiative in a society where women had little power. It starts with a refugee family: there is a famine around Bethlehem so Elimelech, Naomi and their two sons leave for Moab, a more fertile land but an enemy nation. The boys grow up and marry two Moabite girls, Orpah and Ruth, but tragedy strikes – Elimelech and the boys die. Three widows are left on their own. As Bethlehem now has food, Naomi decides to go home but she begs her daughters-in-law to return to their parents, for they are young enough to remarry. She can offer them only poverty. Orpah reluctantly returns but Ruth refuses and goes on to commit herself to Naomi in one of the most striking poems of the Bible.

Intreat me not to leave you,
or to cease from following after you:
for where you go, I will go;
and where you lodge, I will lodge:
Your people shall be my people,
and your God my God:
Where you die, will I die,
and there will I be buried:
the Lord do so to me, and more also,
if ought but death part you and me.

Ruth and Naomi arrive in Bethlehem at harvest time and Ruth starts work in the fields as a gleaner; it happens to be the field of a near relative, Boaz. She walks behind the reapers picking up dropped grain. Boaz gives her his protection and some extra grain. Naomi now plans to help Ruth, to give her long-term security. There is a law in Israel that if a man dies and there are no children, the nearest relative marries the widow to stop the line dying out. Boaz is a near relative. Naomi tells Ruth to sneak into the barn where the harvest celebrations are happening and creep beneath Boaz' cloak while he sleeps. Hopefully he will recognize this as a sign that Ruth wants him to take responsibility for her. This is a dangerous move. Ruth is a Moabite; did Israelite law apply to her? Would Boaz accept responsibility, or would he react very differently finding a woman lying by him at night? Boaz reacts as Naomi hoped and accepts responsibility for Ruth. But there is another relative who could claim Ruth, so a legal process is involved. Ruth and Boaz eventually marry and have a son, King David's grandfather.

This is a story of incredible faithfulness on the part of Ruth. She makes a commitment and carries it through, though it means back-breaking work and danger. God does not say a word in the story, yet his finger-prints are all over it. Ruth and Naomi arrive in Bethlehem at harvest time when there is a possibility of work and Ruth ends up working in Boaz' field, who happened to be a near relative. These two 'coincidences' mean they have food and protection. The law that stops Naomi and Ruth from starving, giving Ruth the right to glean, is one of God's laws. The laws about caring for widows are God's laws. We also see God in Boaz. Ruth was vulnerable, he could have taken advantage of her but at every point he acts with respect. In both language and action, Boaz' relationship with

God shines through. Today we are looking at Ruth and following how she puts her poetic promise into action. We start with her in a field in Bethlehem on a hot day.

Pause.

Second telling

Ruth stands and arches her back.
She places her hands in the small of her back,
and stretches.
Her back aches from working bent double in the heat.
Strands of hair stick to her forehead,
her clothes are dark with sweat.
She looks at her hands,
the fingers are cracked from the rough stalks of barley.
Her apron is bulky with what she has collected
but she knows that by the time she has threshed it
there will be little to take home.
There will be just enough to make bread for her and Naomi.
It was good they arrived at harvest time,
she is fortunate to have work,
even if she does work apart from the others.
She recalls her promise:
'Where you go, I will go.'
And here she is, in a field in Bethlehem.
She thinks back to a moment on the road between Moab and Bethlehem,
the moment she pledged herself to Naomi,
the moment she decided to leave Moab.
Moab was home, but she hardly thinks of it now.
She is so tired there is little time for homesickness
but on the Sabbath she can walk to the top of the hill
and look across to Moab.
Bethlehem is her home now
and will always be so.
She will live and die here,
for that is what she promised Naomi,
'Where you die I will die.'
Even after Naomi is dead, she will stay,
for she promised that too,
'and there will I be buried.'
Ruth whispers the words of her promise again:

'Intreat me not to leave you,
or to cease from following after you:
for where you go, I will go;
and where you lodge, I will lodge:
your people shall be my people,
and your God my God:
where you die, will I die,
and there will I be buried:
the Lord do so to me, and more also,
if ought but death part you and me.'

Ruth smiles.
She had spoken in the poetry of Naomi's people
with its wave-like rhythm.
Ruth had lived with Naomi's family for many years
and the sounds came naturally to her now,
but when she thinks of what she promised,
she is frightened.
Such things are easy to say in a moment of high emotion
but much harder to live.
For good or ill she has bound herself to Naomi, her people and her God.
Promises might be made in poetry,
but they are paid in pain and sweat and loneliness and hard work.

At midday Ruth sits down to rest.
She eats a little of the flatbread she has brought with her
and drinks water from her jar.
She sits alone.
She is a foreigner.
This is what it means to keep her promise, loneliness.
The men look at her,
she knows she is not safe,
she has no man to protect her.
Will anyone care what happens to a foreigner?

Suddenly there is a commotion and people struggle to their feet.
The owner, Boaz, has arrived.
He greets the people, 'The Lord be with you.'
They respond, 'The Lord bless you.'
Ruth adds her blessing.
This is what she said she would do,
'Your God shall be my God.'
She calls down a blessing from the God of Israel on Boaz.

Boaz talks to the foreman and looks at her,
she quickly lowers her eyes.
She cannot hear all the conversation
but she knows they are talking about her.
She catches the foreman's words as he points to her,
'The Moabite woman from Moab.'
(Where else would a Moabite come from?)
To her distress Boaz walks towards her.
She is fearful.
Will he stop her working on his land?
But he speaks kindly to her,
calls her 'daughter'.
Boaz turns to the men and his tone changes;
he makes it clear that Ruth is off limits,
and he asks them to drop extra grain for her.
From now on she is to work and eat with the other workers,
and drink from the communal water jars.
Ruth no longer works alone.

Ruth is overcome, her thanks are profuse,
she had not expected to find kindness.
Boaz brushes it off, she is the kind one,
her kindness is the talk of the town.
He admires her for the way she left father, mother and homeland.
Like Abraham, she came as a stranger to a strange land,
all for the sake of Naomi.

That night Ruth returns to the small dwelling that is now her home,
there is little furniture,
no luxuries,
just the basics.
But this is what Ruth committed herself to,
'Where you lodge, I will lodge.'
This evening Ruth has news to tell Naomi
as well as grain.
Naomi is excited,
for the Boaz Ruth speaks of is a near relative,
one who has responsibility for them.
Naomi looks at Ruth;
day after day she comes home from the fields exhausted.
Naomi knows it is for her she works,
that is why she tried to send Ruth back to her parents,

to spare her this.
Now Naomi seeks Ruth's good,
her long-term future.
The plan is daring, dangerous.
Ruth listens to Naomi's instructions.
If this goes wrong her reputation will be terminally damaged,
even if she physically escapes unharmed.
And that's a big if.
If Boaz misinterprets her action and thinks she is offering herself
she may be violated.
She may no longer be able to work in his fields,
and to work elsewhere is risky.
Only on Boaz' land is she protected.
Still, she committed herself to Naomi,
she will follow Naomi's instructions.

Washed, dressed and wrapped in her cloak
Ruth makes her way to the barn where the harvest celebrations are held.
She waits in the shadows until Boaz sleeps.
Once she hears his breathing change she lifts the edge of his cloak
and slides underneath.
Boaz wakes and is startled to find a woman there,
but on learning it is Ruth, he accepts his responsibility.
Ruth stays till it is almost dawn,
then leaves before she can be seen by others.

The legal process to marry Ruth is complex,
for there is another relative with the right and responsibility to marry her.
Ruth waits to know her fate.
Would she have had more freedom in Moab?
Probably not.
She submits to Israelite custom, to Hebrew law.
This is what she signed up to,
'Your people will be my people.'

Epilogue

The story ends with a wedding and a baby.
It is a story of commitment
played out in hard work and danger.
The story of a promise made in poetry
but paid in pain.
It is Ruth's story,
it could be ours.
We make our promises:
Those promises may be unspoken
but they bind us.
The emotion carries us to begin with,
but ultimately promises are paid in hard work,
pain, boredom, sleepless nights.
Our promises to God are likewise paid in day-to-day living,
in a willingness to work them out in the mundane,
for that is where we continue to meet God.

Conclusion

This chapter has sought to illustrate some of the principles detailed in this book in complete sermons. No sermon illustrates all the practices, each draws on the well of ideas as appropriate for the text and context. Overall, the result should be a sermon that engages the congregation and re-presents the biblical narrative in a way that does justice to the characters, their situation and the message inherent in the text, leaving the congregation with possibilities for the future and hope.

Concluding Thoughts

This book has aimed to demonstrate ways in which preachers can 'show' biblical narratives in a sermon using the language of this world to communicate the spiritual insights integral to the text. The focus is on the characters and situations within narratives, putting the spiritual insights into their human and material context. The emphasis is on encountering God within ordinary Christian living alongside the more direct encounters with God.

Embodiment has been a key theme for we are embodied people, and we live out our faith in the physical world. The message of a text is not preached abstractly, devoid of its material context; insight is embodied in people and things that can be sensed. Art is integral to this book, it is offered as a way of preparing, as a model and as part of the sermon. Art offers the preacher ways of engaging with the text and insights into how a text has been interpreted over time. This book has also sought to remove anxieties about using art and imagination in preaching and ignite in preachers a desire to faithfully use their creativity within the sermon context.

The showing style of language is embedded within a new approach to preaching structured by the revelatory plot. The revelatory plot gives preachers a way of exposing the realities within a text so that the congregation can 'see' a situation. The indwelling of a narrative, and the focus on character, context and insight, holds out the possibility of the congregation identifying with people and situations within a biblical narrative; in this way, relevance is woven into sermons from the beginning. I have developed one way of using the revelatory plot to structure sermon preparation, others could be developed. What matters is doing justice to biblical narratives, honouring the genre and the way people learn and live out their faith.

Index of Bible References

Old Testament

Genesis

1.10, 12, 18, 21, 25	196
1.26–27, 28	143, 200
1.31	196
2.7	197
2.15	140
2.20	169
2.23	169
5.1–2	200
6.5	146
8.21	145
9.6	200
12.10–20	43
16	43
17.1	205
17.1–8, 15–17	215
18.1–15	57
18.12	17
20	43
23	15
24; 25.22–23	71
37; 39—50	121
42.24	17
50.19–20	121

Exodus

1.22—2.1–10	79
2.1–10	95
2.2	80
6.8	25
6.20	79
14.1—15.20	100
15.8, 10	100
16	21
20.4–5	73, 147
25.18–20	147
25—29	74
30.30–33	222
31.1–11	74
32.1–6	120, 143
33.11	205

Deuteronomy

6.5	197
12.1–32	45
14.1–21	45
16.1–16	45
22.13–30	45
23.12–14	45
29	222
30.	7, 94, 221
30.11–20	221
30.14	146
32.11–12	146
34.7–8	94

Joshua

3	85
5.6	129
24.1–28	205

Judges

4.21	100
4—5	100
5.27	100
11.1–2	96

Ruth

1.3–5, 20–1	95
1.16–17	23
2	34, 228

1 Samuel

1.7	19
9—10	34
16.12	129
17	12, 14
24	19

2 Samuel

12.16	95

1 Kings

6	74

New Testament

INDEX OF BIBLE REFERENCES

Luke		*John*		20.7–12	110
1.1–3	155	1.1–18	97	28.16, 30–1	15,
1.39–56	113	1.18	203		166
2.1–2	201	3.1	143		
2.1–20	201	3.1–21	186,	*Romans*	
2.22–4	207		191	2.13–16	204
2.7	201	3.16	34	5.12	196
3.1–22	82,	4	12	8.1–8	198
	88, 92	5.1–15	19	8.19–23	198
3.3	93	6.68	184	10.9–13	166,
3.7–8	93	8.1–11	54,		205
3.7–14	93		85, 88	12.1	198
6.38	204	9.6	198	12.2	150
6.46–49	198	10.38	172		
7.11–16	201	11.17–33	198	*1 Corinthians*	
7.11–17	198	13.1–17	34	6.19	198
7.36–50	93,	13–17	14	10.31	198
	175	14.6	166	13.4–8	37
8.40–56	156	15.1	201	13.12	10
9.51	38,	19.28	201	15.42–4	198
	156	19.34	202	15.45–8	72
10.25–37	178	19.28	201,		
10.27	146		202	*2 Corinthians*	
10.38–42	131	20.24–9	201	4.4	201
12.16–21	34	21	102	4.6	146
15.2	93	21.9–13	202		
15.8–32	17			*Galatians*	
16.1–13	2	*Acts*		3.28	143
18.9–14	42	1.1–8	25	5.16–21	198
19	24	1.3	202		
19.1–10	12, 20	1.6–11	12	*Ephesians*	
19.28–40	127	6—7	154	1.7	196
19. 41–4	222	1.9	202	1.13–14	215
22.14–23	51	9.1–19	44	2.2	37,
23.27–30	222	10	112,		199
23.44–9	12		165		
23.56	28	15.1–33	165	*Philippians*	
24	12	16.29–31	166	3.4–5	198
24.13–24	102	16.16–19	133	4.2–3	128
24.36–43	202	16.25	184	4.8	178
24.50–1	202	17.24	198		

Index of Names and Subjects